Here's a differen, closer look

The Reagan Revulsion

by

Steven Bové

THE REAGAN REVULSION

The 30-Year Unwinding of Democracy and the American Dream

STEVEN BOVÉ

ISBN: 978-0-578-81044-7 (print)

Contents

Introduction

How did we get here—to the day when time stood still? Somehow, the hours linking November 8 and 9, 2016 were more than just the passage of time; they were a presage of a world many of us thought wasn't possible. In the span of 24 hours, hope gave way to fear. America stopped being the shining city on a hill and turned into a dystopian wasteland overtaken by crime, carnage, and immigrants. As the rhetorician turned his fantasy into reality, was there ever any doubt who would light the match?

Today, as gestapo armies are being sent into American cities and unmarked vans kidnap our citizens, it is clear that democracy and society at large are on life support. While the malfeasance of Donald Trump is undeniably responsible for this catastrophe, the disease that is Trump is a by-product of a sickness that has afflicted America for decades. After all, who is truly to blame: Frankenstein's monster or the man who created him? Just as heart disease takes root long before the heart attack kills you, the disease killing America started long before 2016. It began with the election of our first reality-star president.

The differences between 1980 and 2016 are not as stark as they appear. Both represented a time when there seemed to be an existential threat to our democracy. In 1980, Americans were exhausted and looking for a savior. The failure in Vietnam was still a fresh wound in the minds of many Americans. After nearly 20 years, the Vietnam War ended on April 30, 1975—not with an American victory parade, but with helicopters evacuating Americans from the fallen city of Saigon. As Saigon fell, it took the myth of American invincibility with it. This loss of self sent Americans reeling and longing for a mythical past—one where America was great and invincible. A past that our previously most corrupt president would distance us from even further. America couldn't be great as long as it was busy dealing with self-inflicted wounds.

Watergate and the ensuing cover-up had toppled a presidency, further eroding our collective faith in the institutions that made our country great. We were left looking for answers; instead, there were only more questions. President Nixon resigned in disgrace. Rather than answer for his crimes, Nixon was summarily pardoned by his Republican vice president, Gerald Ford, for any and all crimes he committed. No trial, no justice, and no repercussions. The criminal was set free, but the crime lingered. Seeking a moral bath, the country turned to a devout evangelical born-again

Christian. We elected Jimmy Carter the 39th President of the United States in 1976.

The Christian salve was illusory, however. The realities of Washington coupled with Carter's naiveté proved no match for the cold, calculated realities of the world. Carter followed his moral compass provided by his Christian faith. Irrespective of political calculus, he sought the higher ground. Meanwhile, the rest of the country sought the ends regardless of the means needed to achieve them. Outcomes trumped morality. It was the beginning of our moral decay and a harbinger of the "greed is good" ethos that was on the horizon.

Carter's presidency was marred by recession, inflation, and an energy crisis. By 1979, the country was suffering through long gas lines and the Iranian hostage crisis. With the failure of the Vietnam War still fresh in our subconscious, Carter attempted unsuccessfully to rescue the American hostages in Iran. The failure to do so further undermined Carter's leadership and most likely cost him reelection. Americans were sick of losing. Americans wanted to win. America wanted to be great again.

America found what it was looking for. Fresh out of central casting rode our savior: Ronald Reagan. The swashbuckling, all-American, B-list actor was just what America wanted. The actor who got second billing to Bonzo the chimp told us what we wanted to hear instead of telling us what we needed to hear. Brandishing his "Let's make America great again" button, Ronald Reagan made us feel great without *making* us great. There was no need for shared sacrifice—or any sacrifice, for that matter. The age of excess was dawning, and there was no better exemplar of this than Ronald Reagan. He was our own personal Gordon Gekko. Giddy with excitement and anticipation, we stopped thinking and started feeling. Reagan told us we could have it all for no reason other than because we were Americans.

Except that we couldn't. Rather than make America great, Ronald Reagan made America weak. One of the most egregious things he did to our country was to weaken us fiscally—in the process, setting the stage for decades of GOP fiscal depravity. By running up massive deficits and slashing taxes for the wealthy, our country is now saddled with crippling debt. Under Reagan, the Grand Old Party (GOP) began its grand transformation from the party of ideas to the party of an idea. By transferring wealth to the wealthy, it would magically trickle down to the rest of us. It didn't, but what it did do was change the definition of what it meant to be a conservative.

No longer did being a conservative have anything to do with conserving anything. Rather than conserve the environment, conservatives feel our natural resources are there to exploit instead of protect. The Reagan Administration was so opposed to protecting our environment, his head of the EPA was forced to resign. This was a huge philosophical departure from the party who created the Environmental Protection Agency—ironically enough, under the Nixon Administration.

Protecting the environment is not the only duty Republicans have shirked. In lieu of protecting consumers, Republicans choose to protect corporate profits at all costs. Their deregulatory zeal is just a ruse—one used to pass on private expenses to public taxpayers. Worst of all, Republicans no longer view being fiscally conservative as having anything to do with matching spending to revenue. Cutting taxes is their lone mantra. Rather than save for a rainy day, as the rest of us do, Republicans would rather lower tax revenue and allow deficits to skyrocket as long as it lines the pockets of the well-to-do.

There is also nothing conservative about their ultimate objective: to slay the great white whale. Ronald Reagan tipped his hand back in 1961 when he railed against the sins of socialism. Trying to prevent Medicare from ever happening, he made an album entitled *Ronald Reagan Speaks Out Against Socialized Medicine*. Republicans have been attacking anything the government did well and labeling it "socialist" ever since. The intent is to play on our fears so when their objective is within striking distance, it will be too late.

By pushing us ever closer to the fiscal breaking point, Republicans hope to realize their ultimate goal of dismantling Social Security and Medicare. Anything else that remains of the safety net will be in tatters. There is nothing grand about this—nor is there much grand about the Grand Old Party these days. Any grandeur left the GOP long ago. What's left is a morally, intellectually, and fiscally bankrupt coalition of politicians that more closely resembles a cult than a party. Not that there's anything fun about the GOP. It's the kind of party you would rather not be invited to. Rather than an invitation, it requires an indoctrination.

Today's members of the Republican Party are all disciples of Ronald Reagan's orthodoxy. His teachings drive the party to this day.

The orthodoxy revolves around a disdain for the public good and a veneration of corporations. At its essence, this doctrine boils down to a belief that government should be used to benefit the few, not the many. It is antithetical to the will of the people and to the mission to do the greatest good for the greatest number. Portraying the government as an enemy has allowed the GOP to chip away at individual liberties while bestowing them on corporations. It's how corporations became people.

It was Mitt Romney who said, "Corporations are people, my friend." This was at the Iowa State Fair on August 11, 2011. For the uninitiated, it may sound like a ridiculous statement. But for the indoctrinated right, it makes complete sense. Corporations became people after the Republican Supreme Court removed spending restrictions on corporations in *Citizens United*, essentially giving them rights under the First Amendment. In doing so, the Republican activists on the Supreme Court overturned a century-old precedent allowing the government to regulate such spending. They also ignored the framers' intent for individuals, *not corporations*, to enjoy constitutional protection. It was just another step in dismantling our Constitution.

Integral to this effort was Republicans hijacking what it means to be an American. Claiming to protect something as you sabotage it is the most effective way to achieve your goals while ignoring what it took to get you there. By waving the Constitution as they dismantle democracy, Republicans have fundamentally changed our country. Wielding the cross and weaponizing religion as they undermine everything Jesus stood for shows that winning by any means necessary is their morality. Wrapping themselves in the flag, Republicans feel free to launch the kind of incendiary rhetoric that tears at the fabric of our country. They have become the party of personal responsibility that never takes responsibility for anything they do, perfectly inoculating themselves against any consequences for their actions and their continued neglect of our republic.

The Grand Old Party has become the party of Greedy Oligarchs and Plutocrats, beholden only to mammon. If our country is on the wrong track, it's because Republicans have pulled us so far to the right, America is no longer a country of the people and for the people. It is of the few and by the few. Their ideology has spread like a virus through statehouses, judiciaries, legislatures, and every facet of our government. Republican orthodoxy is running and ruining America. Their overarching tentacles seek to destroy every part of government they touch, no matter how beloved or needed.

The extremism and anti-Americanism of today's Republican Party has infected every facet of our lives. We need to take our county back from the greedy demagogues, oligarchs, and plutocrats who stole it. It's time to make America...America again. Even though the day that time stood still seemed like it happened overnight, it was over 30 years in the making. Donald Trump didn't happen in a vacuum. He was the logical manifestation of decades of political groundwork. His triumph, as unsettling as it is, wouldn't have been possible without Ronald Reagan and his revolution.

When Republicans launched the Reagan Revolution, it wasn't an accident. Calling Reagan's ascendency "The Reagan Revolution" was intentional—"revolution" being the operative word. Words matter, and Republicans know that better than any marketing agency. A revolution occurs when the population *revolts* against the government. When Ronald Reagan said, "The nine most terrifying words in the English language are: 'I'm from the government and I'm here to help,'" it was the first shot in the Republican war against our country.

The war they started has been raging ever since. Institution after institution has been attacked. With effective government being the enemy, Republicans have made government intentionally ineffectual. Preventing government from doing good enables them to claim that government can't do good. It's a self-fulfilling prophecy. Donald Trump is the logical manifestation of this effort. The only differences between him and Ronald Reagan are superficial. Whereas Ronald Reagan came across as a lovable grandfather, Donald Trump is the crazy uncle the family only lets out of the closet for holidays.

But they are the bookends of the demise of our democracy and middle class—two reality-star presidents from different eras. Where Ronald Reagan operated behind the scenes, Donald Trump operates out in the open. While Ronald Reagan used charm to disarm his critics and soothe America, Donald Trump is blatantly disdainful of our country and anyone who disagrees with him. Stylistic differences aside, Donald Trump is harvesting the seeds sown by Ronald Reagan. While the seeds seemed benign, they were anything but.

Waking up and seeing Donald Trump in the White House is like waking up one morning and finding an oak tree in your backyard. Somehow, without your realizing it, an oak tree has overtaken your yard and is destroying your house. You may be shocked to see it there, but the truth is, it didn't just show up one day. It had been growing for decades. You just weren't paying attention.

Decades of lethargy have led us here. Like the unwanted oak, the predicament we find our country in has been growing for decades. Without realizing it, the seedling turned into a sapling. Ever distracted by life, we never considered that the young tree would flourish. Inadvertently nurturing it through our collective ignorance, we ensured it would grow into an all-consuming menace to society. The question remains: what will we do now?

Is our country at a crossroads, or have we passed the tipping point? Our democracy hangs in the balance, and we have precious little time to save it. Each Republican victory pushes our country further away from having a democracy. Fascism is no longer verboten. It is happening here. Our founding fathers didn't prepare for the threat from within. As voting rights are stripped away and elections rigged, our last vestiges of hope are slipping away. Democracies die in plain sight. Collectively, we must act to save what will soon be lost. If there is one thing that should unite us, it is saving our democracy and our country—before it is too late.

In politics, being deceived is no excuse.
—Leszek Kolakowski

Chapter 1: Day One

Tuesday, January 20, 1981. Inauguration Day for the 40th President of the United States. It was an inauguration that would change the course of history and place America on a path it would cling to for nearly 40 years. Only 39 other men had come before him in the 204 years since our country's founding. The magnitude of that was not lost on the ex-governor of California as he was preparing to become the most powerful man on Earth. Neither was it lost on him how he got here, to the West Front of the United States Capitol in Washington, D.C. It was the first inauguration on that side of the Capitol.

Ronald Reagan knew the circumstances that propelled him to victory in the prior year's election, and he would honor that on this day. The mood of the country was dark—its hues intensified by the crisis in the Middle East. Our dependence on oil-rich nations and our failure to free American hostages from Iran were two of the major forces thrusting him to victory.

On this day, it would be no more. Ronald Reagan would declare America the shining city on the hill. America would become a beacon for other nations to follow. No longer would America place its destiny in the hands of other nations. It would lead but never follow. Ronald Reagan would use his inauguration day speech to chart the course of America's future.

"The storm is upon us. For years, America has navigated through turbulence and uncertainty only to regain its moorings and emerge stronger on the other side. Now is such a time. The forces of evil may shake us, they may stir us, but they will never overtake us. America will not be rocked and rolled into submission. Capitulation is not in our nature. It is not who we are and it is not how our great nation was founded. We were founded and forged in strength, not weakness. It is that strength that steeled our resolve in our Declaration of Independence and enabled us to persevere in our quest for liberation. It is that strength that propelled us to defeat tyranny in not just one, but two World Wars. And it is that strength and resolve which I call upon you now to summon once again.

Like all great nations before us, we have faced trials and tribulations. The mark of a great nation is not the absence of challenges; it is the wherewithal to rise to them and ultimately overcome them. America is in the midst of such a time. Our calling is to meet the challenge head-on, not to shrink from its magnitude. That is why I'm asking each and every American to stand beside me as we conquer the grave threat facing this nation.

America and our very independence are at stake. The threat is one we can surmount if we pool our collective resources and resolve to ensure America is no longer vulnerable or dependent on others for its greatness. I'm calling on America to no longer be held hostage by petro-dictators. I'm calling on America to sever our ties to the instability that is the Middle East and break the stranglehold OPEC has on our citizens. I'm declaring on this day a new Declaration of Independence."

◇   ◇   ◇   ◇   ◇   ◇

Little was known about this new Declaration of Independence at the time, but as it formed, one thing became crystal clear: Ronald Reagan was a true visionary. He began pursuing a policy of energy independence that was ahead of its time. If nothing else, President Reagan believed in America first, and he knew that America would always be vulnerable as long as we relied on fossil fuels from hostile and unstable Middle Eastern countries. That reliance cost Jimmy Carter a second term, and Reagan was determined not to suffer the same fate.

Skeptics would argue it wasn't vision driving Reagan, but self-preservation. While his thirst for politics was certainly an impetus, so was his desire for greatness. What better thing for the history books than to be immortalized as the man who thrust America into true independence all while leaving the Middle East in its wake. The text practically writes itself. Felling our enemies without a shot fired would be truly revolutionary.

And it was made possible because of one of President Reagan's most notorious missteps. Obsessed with securing America, he at first thought militarily, not strategically. This led to the ill-formed Strategic Defense Initiative, which was nicknamed "Star Wars." The goal of the Strategic Defense Initiative was admirable; it was to protect the U.S. from Soviet nuclear warheads. However, the details proved untenable. It called for the creation of a network of ground-based and space-based missile defense systems capable of shielding the country from attack. The space-based portion would have used lasers armed with nuclear warheads to shoot down incoming Soviet missiles. The cost and technology needed to pursue such a grand feat truly made it worthy of a George Lucas film and not part of a legitimate U.S. defense plan.

While roundly ridiculed, without the Strategic Defense Initiative, we never would have had the Energy Freedom Initiative, which was ultimately the moniker given our new energy program. While the technology to spare the U.S. from nuclear attack did not pan out, it led to the development of the technology needed to truly protect America. Often, great failure leads to great achievement. Never was this more evident than with the Strategic Defense Initiative.

When constructing the shields that were to be instrumental in the defense initiative, a scientist discovered something remarkable. The shields had a luminescent coating that was designed to protect them from severe heat and cold. The satellites as well as ground defenses were required to be able to withstand extreme temperatures that could potentially come from being near rocket exhaust. This led to the discovery that the nodes were able to retain heat during testing. Later, it was found out that these conductive properties were able to transfer, not just store the energy they were exposed to.

All it took was one man to see where this could lead. If the heat from exhaust could create sustainable, transferable energy, could other sources as well? This question led to the invention of the photovoltaic cell that became the key component of the Strategic Defense Initiative's greatest legacy: the solar panel.

After the Strategic Defense Initiative was credited with creating the solar panel, the idea that the U.S. would be protected with laser beams became less laughable. The U.S. would be protected by something far better: Mother Nature. Once the military got wind of what was happening, they wasted no time in plowing resources into its funding and development. Within a few years, the Pentagon and every major U.S. military installation were installing solar panels on their facilities.

What the military discovered was they were able to use their newfound energy independence to their strategic benefit. Their obsession with the Middle East crumbled as their freedom from fossil fuels took over. Not only did this change regional deployments, it also altered the military's budget. Funds earmarked for fuel as well as military deployments in and around oil-rich nations altered their budget calculus. This provided the military with the resources they needed to begin developing strategies to combat the war they foresaw: terrorism.

As the Soviet Union fell, our military leaders knew future wars would be fought against insurgents rather than armies. They also knew that making America safe required the constant updating and improving of our infrastructure. A nation is only a strong as its weakest link, and protecting our vital means of communication, water delivery, transportation, and electricity was paramount to securing our borders.

Oil-rich nations were able to anesthetize their citizens as long as oil revenues remained abundant. An unforeseen consequence of President Reagan's Freedom Initiative was the collapse of petro-dictators across the globe. The first to fall were the smaller nations of Bahrain, Comoros, and Djibouti. Once the United States began harnessing the power of "free" energy, other nations followed. This cascade of dominoes eviscerated traditional energy prices, leaving once-prosperous nations searching for revenue and unable to quell the citizen rebellions they faced. This ushered in a wave of democracy across once autocratic nations.

It also completely altered America's energy policy. The Department of Energy became the Department of Renewal Energy. Solar, wind, thermal, and other renewables were all subsets of the D.R.E. They had offices in both of the twin towers located in the World Trade Center in lower Manhattan.

As the stature of these agencies grew, so did that of Ronald Reagan. His foresight transformed the history books before our very eyes. Not only did he propel America into an era of clean, free, abundant energy, he did it while reinvigorating American manufacturing. The Upper Midwest region of the U.S. became known as the renewal belt. As coal died off, more and more states joined Pennsylvania, Michigan, and Ohio in this resurgence of American manufacturing might. Being a leader and innovator put the United States in the enviable position of becoming a global supplier of renewal hardware.

All of these changes led the nation to revere Ronald Reagan—so much so that Congress passed an act so rare it had never been done before. The authorization of the Reagan bust on Mount Rushmore was approved by unanimous consent despite the fact that he was still living. It was to be sculpted on the west-facing cliff so his likeness could watch the sunset over his California home in perpetuity. The symbolism of the sun gracing his image as it set day after day was lost on no one. It was his crowning achievement and made America great and free.

☼ ☼ ☼ ☼ ☼ ☼

If you haven't read this version of history or heard this speech, you're not alone. It's an aspirational version of what could have been—a history that was never written because it was sacrificed at the altar of mammon. Reagan was handed an unprecedented opportunity—to unite our country in a common goal: achieving energy independence. It was a goal that would make us safer and more prosperous. On the heels of the Iranian hostage crisis, it was never more apparent how our reliance on fossil fuels put us in jeopardy.

Rather than seize this historic chance to extricate us from the tyrannical grip of oil, Reagan sacrificed our safety and future for black gold. Instead of his bust on Mount Rushmore, he earned a place on "Mount Gushmore." Ensuring his status as an oil sycophant, Reagan went one step further. He decided to rip off the White House solar panels. Jimmy Carter had them installed because he saw the future and the dangers oil dependency posed. Reagan saw something else: a way to tell the world we would not lead, but rather follow into history.

Prior to Reagan's election in 1980, Republicans cared about the environment. As mentioned previously, the last elected Republican president before Reagan actually created the Environmental Protection Agency (EPA). That same president also signed into law the Endangered Species Act in 1973. It was designed to protect critically imperiled species from extinction as a "consequence of economic growth and development untempered by adequate concern and conservation." This explicitly acknowledged the fact that unfettered business activity had costs. This environmentalist was none other than President "I am not a crook" Richard Nixon, of Watergate fame.

Ronald Reagan was no Richard Nixon, at least when it came to the environment. When Reagan took office in 1981, one of his first initiatives was to undo much of Carter's environmental agenda. He was obsessed with eliminating governmental regulations and with deregulating the EPA. When the EPA wanted Reagan to address the causes of acid rain, he dismissed their proposals as too burdensome to industry. Profits over people.

Reagan's hostility to the environment didn't stop there. In fact, it transferred to his first EPA administrator, Anne Gorsuch (whose son happens to sit on the Supreme Court). She started the Republican doctrine of search and destroy. That which you disdain but cannot kill must be rendered ineffective or neutered—which is what she did. And there is no better way to cripple a governmental agency than by starving it of funds.

Barely nine months into his Presidency, it was clear where the Reagan Administration stood on protecting the environment. By September 30, 1981, it was so draconian, it made the front page of *The Washington Post*. "Budget cuts at the Environmental Protection Agency will strip 3,200 personnel of their jobs by the end of 1983, eliminating 30 percent of the agency's 10,380 employees at a cost of $17.6 million just for severance pay. The cuts are so massive that they could mean a basic retreat on all the environmental programs of the past 10 years."[1]

Which was the point. But stopping progress wasn't enough. Reversing gains and undoing any good the government did was the objective. The fact it would cost $17.6 million didn't matter. It was $17.6 million taxpayers would pay, not corporations. Coupled with the EPA's inability to fine polluters, that would result in an even larger transfer of wealth from taxpayers to corporations. Helping businesses avoid paying for their expenses is one of the ways corporations are able to reap ever-larger profits.

While Anne Gorsuch did her job in one respect, her scorched-earth policies were too extreme for the 1980s. She was a few decades before her time. In 1983, she was forced to resign. But her policies and the direction of the administration didn't change. As stated in *Scientific American*, "By 1986, the Reagan Administration had gutted the research and development budgets for renewable energy at the U.S. Department of Energy (DoE) and eliminated tax breaks for the deployment of wind turbines and solar technologies— recommitting the nation to reliance on cheap but polluting fossil fuels, often from foreign suppliers."[2]

Reagan's Administration also moved rapidly to slash budgets, reduce environmental enforcement, and open public lands for mining, drilling, grazing, and other private uses.[3] Reagan began the long process of Republicans trying to take public resources and transfer them to private companies. It is a pattern of privatizing gains and socializing losses. What should also sound familiar was his approach to many of the environmental problems our country faced then and still does today. He deliberately delayed attacking long-term problems like global warming linked to pollution, acid rain, toxic waste, air pollution, and the contamination of underground water supplies. His mantle was assumed by his successors.

With both Bush presidencies continuing his legacy, Bush Senior proposed opening millions of acres of wetlands to development. Then his Administration wanted to officially lower the risk estimates for dioxin and other long-feared contaminants. Lest we forget, he also tampered with testimony regarding global warming. His son was worse. Within the first 100 days, Bush reneged on a campaign promise to regulate carbon dioxide from coal-burning power plants.[4] These emissions are the biggest contributors to global warming. The Bush White House also pulled America from the Kyoto global climate change treaty. They withdrew so his Administration could be used to cast doubt on global warming, continuing the long assault on reason and science that had been started decades earlier.

Fast-forward to 2017, and the trend continues. One of the first things Republicans did in 2017 was to vote to overturn an Obama-era law to protect Alaskan bears and wolves. The law prohibited hunters from shooting or trapping wolves while in their dens with their cubs. Obama also prevented them from using airplanes to scout for potential grizzly bear targets, trap bears with wire snares, and lure bears with food to get a point-blank kill. By reversing the law, hunters could once again kill wolves and bears from the comfort of a plane or helicopter. It passed 225-193, mostly along party lines.[5]

After it passed the Senate, our polluter-in-chief signed it into law. I believe it's called the "It's now legal to shoot hibernating bears and kill wolf families in their dens or from a plane act," which caused a great deal of consternation amongst the wildlife it threatened. Immediately after passage, it was rumored there was a frantic meeting of the Woodlands Wildlife Committee. Worried about what would happen to their fellow friends of the forest, a brave rabbit tried to quell the hysteria. He pointed out that the Endangered Species Act would save them if the carnage got out of hand. "They can't kill us all, can they?"

Not so fast, my furry friend. They can and they will. Republicans in the White House are trying to weaken the Endangered Species Act as well in the hope of doing away with it. It's being done at the executive level to bypass Congress. Now that Democrats have taken the House of Representatives, there is no chance it could become law. So, it's being done by fiat. Ironically, when looking at both the Endangered Species Act and the Environmental Protection Agency, they share a haunting similarity. The environment needs protecting from the same thing that is endangering species—Republicans.

This should come as no surprise. Ever envious of President Obama, Donald Trump has been working overtime to undo his environmental legacy. Almost immediately after his inauguration, he attacked environmental protection after environmental protection, including our drinking water. He undid the Obama-era Stream Protection Rule, a regulation designed to protect waterways from coal mining waste. Soon, we'll all be longing for the good old days when we just worried about acid rain.

And we have reason to worry. Trump's first head of the EPA was Scott Pruitt. This is the attorney general from Oklahoma who sued the EPA over a dozen times in six years for its efforts to regulate mercury, smog, and other forms of pollution. Heading the organization in charge of keeping our air breathable and our drinking water safe seems to be a cruel joke. While Pruitt had no intention of doing either, he was even worse than anticipated.

By July 2018, Pruitt was under at least 14 separate federal investigations by the Government Accountability Office. Plagued by a string of seemingly never-ending scandals and charges of corruption, he resigned on July 5, 2018. Pruitt's frequent use of taxpayer-financed first-class travel, chartered planes, and military flights as well as his leasing a deeply discounted condo in Washington, D.C. from a lobbyist—whose clients were regulated by the EPA—finally caught up with him. He was replaced by his Deputy Administrator Andrew Wheeler, a former coal industry lobbyist.

While Ronald Reagan sought to overturn environmental protections, Donald Trump is attempting to undo the environmental legacy of President Obama. This is why he nominated Scott Pruitt and Andrew Wheeler to head the EPA in the first place. President Obama not only enacted laws to keep the environment safe, he also used his bully pulpit to educate Americans about the risks of climate change. When he enacted his Clean Power Plan, it became the first ever national limit on carbon pollution from its source.

The Obama Administration also put pollution limits on smokestacks and reduced the air pollution from oil and gas operations. The enhanced fuel efficiency standards for cars and trucks from the Obama EPA will go a long way in reducing greenhouse gases. His Administration invested billions in clean energy technology while helping farmers adapt to climate change. The U.S.-China carbon pact was the first time the world's two largest greenhouse gas emitters have pledged to reduce carbon pollution. President Obama also joined the Paris Climate Accord.

Climate change has the potential to uproot millions of citizens, cause lasting economic damage, and threaten our food and water supplies. This is why every nation has signed on to the Paris Climate Accord—every nation except the United States. Once Syria signed, we ended up being the lone holdout. The Paris Agreement is designed to combat climate change and adapt to its effects. In addition, it supports developing countries in their efforts to do so. It is the first ever global climate effort, and we are alone on the sidelines.

When Ronald Reagan rode into town and extolled gluttony, he ushered in an era of identity politics. He equated being American not just with consumption, but with overconsumption. Real Americans don't wear sweaters when it's cold out; they strip down to their underwear and crank up the heat. Caring about the environment and reducing energy consumption somehow became un-American. President Carter wore a cardigan and urged us to conserve energy for the nation. Ronald Reagan ripped off the solar panels from the White House and gutted the EPA. That's one of the reasons Americans constitute less than 4.5% of the world's population but consume nearly 20% of its resources.[6]

This wasn't lost on his fellow Republicans, and they used it to their political advantage. Overconsuming energy became a way of distinguishing "us against them." Republicans weaponized the environment and began the war against facts, science, and reason. The world implications of this assault on the environment are still being felt today. Republicans' embrace of anti-intellectualism combined with their degradation of science has catapulted us to the brink of environmental Armageddon. The line connecting Reagan and today's Republican Party is fluid. You could almost hear Ronald Reagan whispering in Ari Fleisher's ear when he was asked whether then-President George W. Bush would urge Americans to change their habits regarding their disproportionate consumption of energy. He replied:

"That's a big 'no.' The president believes that it's an American way of life, that it should be the goal of policy-makers to protect the American way of life. The American way of life is a blessed one ... The president considers Americans' heavy use of energy a reflection of the strength of our economy, of the way of life that the American people have come to enjoy."[7]

Like father, like son. A decade earlier, Poppa Bush was laying the groundwork for his son's stance on the environment and our role in destroying it. It was May 8, 1989, and then-Senator Al Gore heard a rumor about the George H.W. Bush Administration. Apparently, the Bush Administration had tampered with testimony on global warming from a leading scientist. This became a key part of the GOP playbook: doing whatever it took so they could make the claim that there was no scientific consensus on global warming even though— and especially because—there was.

For Republicans, consensus equals what the majority of their donors tell them. You see, Republican math is not like regular math. If 97 out of 100 scientists agree that man-made climate change is real, the jury is out—even when the other three work for Exxon and climate-denying think tanks. However, if they can find one economist to draw a tax cut theory on a bar napkin that justifies tax cuts for corporations and the uber-wealthy, it's settled science. In other words, if you want to know the truth, follow the money.

Luckily, that isn't hard to do. Money is being made by the extraction, production, and distribution of fossil fuels. Denying climate change is a profit-maximizing con. Acknowledging climate change would lead energy companies to have to pay their own expenses. Denying climate change allows them to pass these expenses on to the rest of us. Anytime corporations can foist their expenses on someone else, it raises profits—ones we are not sharing in. We pay, they profit.

On the other side of climate science are the scientists. Do scientists have a financial incentive to lie about climate change? Is there a profit motive on both sides? If we follow the money, where does it lead? How many scientists are getting rich from their work regarding climate change? Are they getting wealthy by pointing out man's role in increasing atmospheric temperatures? Are any of them famous enough for you to list the top ten? Top five? Top three? Anyone other than Al Gore?

If you can't name anyone who has become rich or famous by publishing research-intensive studies on global warming and man's impact on making the planet warmer, it refutes one of the Republicans' biggest talking points. According to right-wing politicians and their propaganda and media outlets, scientists are only publishing such material for financial or personal gain. Take out the gain and you take down their argument.

Then ask yourself who *actually* benefits financially from denying climate change. The Koch brothers come to mind. That's why, according to Greenpeace, they've given at least $100,343,292 directly to 84 groups denying climate change science since 1997. If they've spent over $100 million denying climate change, can you imagine how much they've made? What about Exxon, Chevron, BP, Shell, China Petroleum & Chemical Corp, Total, Gazprom, Rosneft, Reliance, Lukoil, PTT PLC, Phillips 66, Valero, Enbridge, Respol, ONGC, Indian Oil, Marathon Petroleum, Surgutneftegas, Gas Natural Fenosa, China Petro, Kinder Morgan, Centrica, Petrobras, and Sempra Energy?

Do you think the largest 25 oil and gas companies in the world profit from climate change denial? What about all the other energy companies? Do coal companies profit from climate change denial as they spew toxins into our atmosphere? As the single biggest air polluter in the United States, don't they have a financial incentive to lie about climate change? Does it matter how many scientists tell them otherwise?

How about the politicians? Does one party have a financial incentive to deny climate change? According to Opensecrets.org, yes. Since the 1990 election cycle, more than two-thirds of oil and gas political contributions have gone to Republicans. As lopsided as those contributions are, they have only gotten worse. As the accompanying chart that follows this chapter illustrates, in 2020, all major oil and gas companies are contributing almost exclusively to Republican politicians.

The flow of petrodollars into Republican pockets proves Upton Sinclair's prescient musings. When he said, "It is difficult to get a man to understand something, when his salary depends on his not understanding it," he could have replaced "a man" with "the Republican Party." In fact, it has become the way Republicans approach governing and running for office. Most of their platform requires them not to understand things.

Over the past 30 years, the party of knowing turned into the party of "no" and "I'd rather not know." Even more importantly, Republicans don't want voters to know. Lack of knowledge turned into a method to market their party. Anti-intellectualism and fact-denying became another way to divide the country. Those who believe in science are "them"; those who don't are "us."

Of course, they need their "us" to keep believing climate change isn't happening. It's the best way to ensure profitability and maximize profits. Overconsumption and climate denial became two necessary bedfellows. You couldn't have one without the other. If climate change was real, then the risk of consuming, let alone *over*consuming fossil fuels would jeopardize the planet. But if it was a hoax, orchestrated by "them," well, that was a different story. And the "thems" are Democrats. Inconceivably, Democrats are attacked as a threat and an enemy of real Americans. Real Americans being those who believe they have a God-given, constitutional right to destroy *our* planet.

And that is exactly what is happening. A new report from the U.N.'s scientific panel on climate change predicts that if greenhouse gas emissions continue at their current rate, the atmosphere would warm by as much as 2.7 degrees Fahrenheit above pre-industrial levels by 2040. That could cause as much as $54 trillion in damage because of effects like worsening food shortages, wildfires, and droughts.[8]

Behind closed doors, it is purported that most Republican politicians believe in climate change. How could you not? Just look out the window. Unfortunately, it has become Republican orthodoxy to deny climate change and man's role in it. Publicly, they use climate change denial to mislead their voters and add to their arsenal of identity politics. Doing so allows Republican politicians to energize their constituents while lining their pockets and the pockets of their donors.

While they are profiting from the destruction of our planet, somehow Republicans managed to equate accepting climate change as being un-American. Is there anything more un-American than sitting by as our planet becomes uninhabitable? Climate denial may be good for Republican politicians, but it's bad for the rest of us. We have a hundred-year storm every six months with no end in sight. Hurricane Harvey marked the third time in three years the Houston area was hit with a 500-year flood.

At this rate, we might as well just move into the ocean and get it over with. The movie *Waterworld* is starting to look more like a documentary. If watching your home flood, get destroyed by a hurricane, get knocked down by a tornado, or become engulfed in flames by a wildfire isn't enough to get you to even *consider* that climate change may be real, there's no way saying it differently is going to change anyone's mind. Overcoming decades of propaganda to believe what you are seeing unfold in front of you might not be possible for many climate change deniers, which puts us all at risk.

Conceptually, the science isn't very complicated to comprehend. When it comes to hurricanes, they get their fuel from warm water. The warmer the water, the stronger they become. One of the main by-products of global warming is the increasing of ocean temperatures. That's why we've had such violent and sustained hurricanes this year. Not only does the warmer water increase the intensity of storms, it increases the duration. Storms that should have died off in the Caribbean make landfall in Florida. So do the floods. Besides deadly winds, hurricanes also produce flooding from storm surges. Global warming causes wet areas to get wetter and dry areas to get drier. There isn't a part of the country that is immune to science.

In fact, we are inextricably altering the planet. Farming, mining, and clear-cutting have transformed more than half of the earth's ice-free landmass as we emit a hundred times more carbon dioxide than volcanoes.[9] Our ecosystem is too fragile to handle much more disruption. Man-made earthquakes are increasing in frequency and intensity. An earthquake in Pawnee, Oklahoma was felt in Des Moines, Iowa.[9] That's a distance of over 500 miles away.

We are irrevocably altering the planet—the only one we have. Lands that flood will not unflood. Neither will their ecosystems. According to Brad Plumer of *The New York Times*, "Humans are transforming Earth's natural landscapes so dramatically that as many as one million plant and animal species are now at risk of extinction, posing a dire threat to ecosystems that people all over the world depend on for their survival, a sweeping new United Nations assessment has concluded."[10] Species that die off will not be reborn. Considering we are one of those species, it is in our best interest to try and reverse the thing that will inevitably lead to our extinction. With an increase in warming from 1.5 degrees to 2 degrees, 150 million people would die from air pollution alone, which is equivalent to 25 Holocausts.[11] If our plan is to react, it will be too late.

When it comes to the environment, one party is pro-environment and one party is anti-environment. Republicans undo environmental protections and Democrats come in to clean up the mess. Democrats conserve, Republicans exploit. This makes you wonder what being a Republican means. If there's no "conserve" in "conservative," what are they for? Republicans will have you believe they are pro-business and pro-military. But if either was the case, they wouldn't be denying climate change; they'd be the environment's biggest cheerleaders.

Consider how the Pentagon views climate change. They take climate change seriously and view it as causing real, imminent harm. One of their jobs is to evaluate all potential threats. Anything that could impact mission readiness, personnel health, and installation resilience is considered. Climate change is one of those threats. From the political and social instability climate change is expected to cause globally to the potential for military bases to be inundated with rising floodwaters, the military considers climate change a threat. They view it as real, inevitable, and upon us.

So does corporate America. More and more companies are factoring climate change costs in future cash flow and profitability projections. Insurance companies are going one step further and factoring them into actuarial assessments that affect premiums. Even Exxon Mobil has gotten into the game of reality acceptance—if for no other reason than survival. While it has been known for years that Exxon has funded climate denial research, the tide may be turning.

Even though the First Amendment protects their right to deceive the public, it doesn't insulate them from lying to shareholders. In a free-market twist that must flummox those on the right, it may be Exxon's undoing. As California sues 37 fossil fuel companies for knowingly emitting dangerous greenhouse gases, they are hoping to go after energy companies in the same manner as tobacco. Just as tobacco companies failed to warn their consumers about the dangers of smoking, oil and gas companies failed to warn us about the dangers from burning fossil fuels.

New York may agree, but they're going about it a little differently. The top New York prosecutor says Exxon misled *investors* on climate change. Attorney General Eric Schneiderman said he had evidence of "potential materially false and misleading statements by Exxon." Accordingly, these false and misleading statements could have led investors astray. Investors may have been led to believe that Exxon had been fully assessing the risks associated with climate change when it had not. You can lie to the public, but you'd better not lie to a stockholder. Putting our health at risk is one thing; jeopardizing stock returns is another.

But it's not for congressional Republicans. Their allegiance is to a select group of shareholders, the ones at the top who know climate change is real and spend billions of dollars keeping their voters from knowing it. Perhaps they view climate change as something that affects "them," the less fortunate—which is true; at least at first. Initially, climate change will punish the most vulnerable of our global citizens. Small island nations will be the first to be displaced. Islands will go under, people will flee. In Puerto Rico, a forgotten part of America, U.S. citizens are being forced to relocate to the mainland. It seems being thrown paper towels after a hurricane wasn't enough to save their homes.

So, we need to get used to a new term: climate change refugees. They won't be the last, and money will insulate no one from climate change's fallout—even if you don't believe. That includes the Republican politicians who have an intractable and self-interested detachment from reality. Winning elections at all costs means they are pushing us closer to an uninhabitable planet. Unless we stop rewarding their recalcitrance with electoral victories, they will continue to be the firewall that prevents us from saving the planet. Until their voters *demand* they take action, they won't.

From Reagan to Trump, the Republican anti-environment identity has only strengthened. At least when Reagan was beguiling us with his B-list actor bona fides, he came across as likeable and trustworthy. Now, we are led by a morally and ideologically bankrupt con man who seems only interested in pleasing his base and satisfying his ego while the rest of us watch as the idiot-in-chief stares at a solar eclipse without sunglasses. He continues a decades-long Republican message. You don't need protection from the environment; you need protection from scientists. "Look at me; I'm staring directly into the eclipse."

Meanwhile, the rest of us gasp in horror at the spectacle of someone intentionally trying to blind himself, much like the rest of the Republican Party. His science-denying followers are right behind him. Without hesitation or an inkling of thought, his devout following look to the sky to see what dear leader sees. Gleefully, the blind king leads them over a cliff. We think *They deserve it* until it dawns on us. They're dragging us down with them.

There's an old saying about there not being any atheists in a foxhole. The same can be said of Republicans in a hurricane. It's easy to believe when you're underwater. The problem is: how many of us have to drown first?

Top Oil & Gas Contributors, 2019-2020*

Top Contributors, 2019-2020

Contributor	Amount
Koch Industries	$6,212,852
Marathon Petroleum	$2,596,328
Chevron Corp	$2,573,715
Midland Energy	$1,802,121
Parman Capital Group	$1,782,054
Energy Transfer Partners	$1,624,805
ConocoPhillips	$1,472,904
Samson Energy	$1,154,552
Walter Oil & Gas	$1,143,235
Energy Transfer Equity	$1,100,000
Hunt Companies	$1,079,137
Exxon Mobil	$983,098
Red Apple Group	$870,686
Valero Services	$785,351
Otis Eastern	$739,980
Valero Energy	$663,391
Occidental Petroleum	$651,295
Berexco Inc	$558,655
Hilcorp Energy	$505,865
CI Machinery Co	$500,000
Petroplex Energy	$500,000

Contributions to:
Democrats ■
Republicans ■
Liberal Groups ■
Conservative Groups ■
Nonpartisan ■

Contributions per party, 1990-2020*

Party Split, 1990-2020

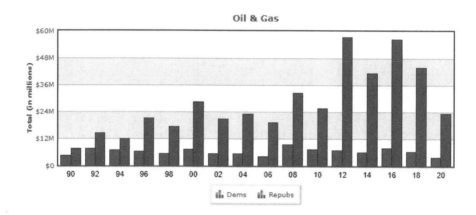

*Source: OpenSecrets.org

Chapter 2: Ask Alec

Once upon a time, there was a scorpion. Like most scorpions, he loved to be in the sun. He loved sunning himself so much that his friends called him Ray Ray. One day, little Ray Ray walked down to the river. When he got there, he noticed the riverbed was dry. He'd never seen the river like that and wondered if it was a mirage. Hesitantly, he reached down with his right pedipalp and touched the dirt. Fearing he'd drown, he quickly turned around and scurried back toward safety. Realizing his pedipalp was dry, he turned back to the empty bed once more.

He stared out at the dry river and noticed a plateau seemingly jutting out of nowhere. *That would be a great place to sun myself,* he thought as he gingerly tested the floor of the river with his body. It was a little mushy, but it supported him, so he moseyed on to his newfound mesa.

As he settled in, he spread out his body. With a gentle breeze and a comforting warmth enveloping him, Ray Ray soon found himself drifting off to sleep. Hours passed as Ray Ray happily napped, basking in the sun. Awakening drearily from his slumber, Ray Ray thought he must be dreaming as he noticed the feeling he was getting rained on. Sleepily, he stretched out, unfurling his tail. That's when he felt it. It was wet.

Unbeknownst to him, Ray Ray hadn't stumbled upon some messianic nirvana where he could worship the sun at will; he was in the middle of the river. The mesa was a death trap. With water surrounding him and the borders of his safe place giving way to the rising river, Ray Ray prepared for the worst.

Just as he was ready to accept his fate, he saw it. Off in the distance was a frog, swimming merrily toward him. "Hello there!" called Ray Ray.

"Hello back!" bellowed the frog.

Ray Ray beckoned the frog to come closer, but the frog hesitated, knowing he was no match for a scorpion's stinger.

"Mr. Frog, I mean you no harm," pleaded Ray Ray. "I fell asleep in the sun and now I'm going to drown. Please help me, for I can't swim."

"But you can sting," answered the frog.

"If I sting you, we'll both surely die," countered Ray Ray. "Why would I do that?"

"When you put it like that, I guess you wouldn't," the frog responded. "By the way, my name is Ribbert."

Just as the river was getting ready to swallow Ray Ray, Ribbert swam toward him and lowered his head so Ray Ray could climb onboard.

"Thank you," said Ray Ray. "I thought today would be my last."

Ribbert just grinned at his new friend as he sailed toward the shore.

Then, just as Ribbert saw land in the distance, he felt a warm sensation throughout his body. He looked back and saw Ray Ray's stinger being thrust into his abdomen. As Ray Ray pumped venom into Ribbert's body, he could only get out one word. "Why?"

"Because it's in my nature," replied Ray Ray as the two began sinking into the river.

Anticipating his burial at sea, Ray Ray noticed his descent had stopped. He was underwater, holding his breath, when he realized his feet were on something solid. He thought for a moment he was on the bottom of the riverbed and must be dead. Then it dawned on him. *I'm moving upward.*

At the exact moment he could hold his breath no longer, he rose from his watery grave. He looked down and saw a rounded shell. Then he looked forward and saw land. Knowing how close he was to salvation, he still couldn't control himself. His stinger started to get warm, then it began to shake. With a mind of its own, Ray Ray's stinger started attempting to pierce the shell beneath him like a runaway jackhammer. There was no thought, just motion.

Exhausted, Ray Ray collapsed and got ready to submerge once again. Breathing deeply, he was prepared to meet his watery end. But to his surprise, his tortoise-colored lifeline kept drifting toward the shore. Just shy of its destination, it seemed to capsize. Without warning, he was thrown off his platform and into the wet sand at the water's edge, where the sand clung to every orifice.

Ray Ray glanced up as he heard a sound. The platform was talking.

"Oh, I didn't know I had company," stuttered the turtle Ray Ray had unwittingly hitched a ride with. "Was that you tapping me on the back?"

"It was," answered Ray Ray. "I was trying to thank you for giving me a ride and saving my life. I was sinking, and out of nowhere, you appeared."

"When I saw the frog cascading toward the bottom of the river, I thought I better have a look-see," explained the turtle. "His misfortune makes this your lucky day."

"Indeed, it does," Ray Ray responded. "By the way, I want to thank you. What's your name?"

The turtle, who was a safe distance from Ray Ray, said, "My name is Mitchell, but my friends call me Mitch. You can call me Mitchell."

With that, Ray Ray nodded toward Mitchell and scuttled away. As the sun began to set, he was too tired to do anything else but look for a rock. All he wanted to do was nestle in for the night and look forward to another day in the sun.

🌲　🌲　🌲　🌲　🌲　🌲　🌲　🌲　🌲　🌲　🌲　🌲

Just like Ray Ray pierced the heart of his friend the frog, Ron Ron drove a dagger through the back of the American middle class. As his second day in office drew to a close, Ronald Reagan managed to plant the seeds not only of the demise of blue-collar America, but the planet itself. You could say it was in his nature.

Like the scorpion, Ronald Reagan hid his true intentions. Prior to the 1980 election, he was trying to shore up as much support as possible. Amazingly, he turned to unions for help. As luck would have it, air traffic controllers were approaching a new contract. They wanted better benefits, hours, and wages. Given the fact that President Carter had not responded adequately to the air traffic controllers' concerns, Reagan sensed an opening. As such, he sent the following letter to the President of the Professional Air Traffic Controllers union (PATCO).

Dear Mr. Poli:

I have been thoroughly briefed by members of my staff as to the deplorable state of our nation's air traffic control system. They have told me that too few people working unreasonable hours with obsolete equipment has placed the nation's air travelers in unwarranted danger. In an area so clearly related to public policy, the Carter administration has failed to act responsibly.

You can rest assured that if I am elected president, I will take whatever steps are necessary to provide our air traffic controllers with the most modern equipment available and to adjust staff levels and work days so that they are commensurate with achieving a maximum degree of public safety.

As in all other areas of the federal government where the President has the power to appoint, I fully intend to appoint highly qualified individuals who can work harmoniously with Congress and the employees of the governmental agencies they oversee.

I pledge to you that my administration will work very closely with you to bring about a spirit of cooperation between the president and the air traffic controllers. Such harmony can and must exist if we are to restore the people's confidence in their government.

Sincerely,

Ronald Reagan[1]

Never trust a scorpion. Ronald Reagan sent that letter on October 20, 1980, just weeks from the election. After receiving it, Robert E. Poli believed Ronald Reagan's promises. By pledging to work with the union and address their concerns, Poli took his word at face value. Ronald Reagan promised to provide updated equipment, more staffing, and a less onerous work schedule. It was in the name of public safety, after all.

But it wasn't in Ronald Reagan's self-interest, and it certainly wasn't in his nature. PATCO was one of only four AFL-CIO-affiliated unions to endorse Reagan over Carter. Reagan got his pre-election endorsement, and the union got a piece of worthless paper and a broken promise. Reagan never intended to cede to the demands of a union; doing so would set a bad precedent. Instead, Reagan's Transportation Secretary, Drew Lewis, responded to

PATCO's demands with a counteroffer of roughly 1/7th of what they were seeking.[1] Seeing no other viable option but to strike, that's what PATCO did. In doing so, they gave Reagan what he wanted all along. He wasn't looking for a harmonious working relationship with the air traffic controllers; he was looking for a reason to crush them.

They struck, and he struck back. Invoking the Taft-Hartley Act, he fired all of the striking air traffic controllers on August 5, 1981. Over 13,000 people joined the walkout, and only 1,300 came back to their jobs after Reagan threatened them. More than 11,000 strikers lost their jobs, and Reagan replaced them with 5,500 scabs. As justification for such a dramatic decrease in the number of people securing our skies, Drew Lewis claimed there had been a "surplus of controllers." I guess that's why the FAA reduced flights by 25% and brought in 370 military controllers to help out.[2] Because if you have too many employees, the only logical thing to do is decrease service and add outside labor.

But this was never about honoring a promise he made in his pre-election gambit—one that paid off handsomely for him. Reagan's true intentions had been on display months earlier. In February of 1981, nearly six months before the strike, the Reagan Department of Justice put together a list, with the help of the FAA, of air traffic controllers who would be arrested and prosecuted should there be a strike. If that's operating in good faith, what does bad faith look like?

Undoubtedly, it looks like what's been happening ever since Reagan broke the back of PATCO. His deception has been playing out in red state after red state. Republicans from Reagan onward have been decimating unions, and with them, what used to be the middle class. It may be the single greatest contributor to the dismantling of the American Dream. The path Reagan forged reached its logical conclusion in 2011. Then-governor Scott Walker (R) of Wisconsin stripped public employees of their collective bargaining rights in a party-line vote.[3]

Portraying unions as bad for America, what Reagan and his counterparts neglect to say is what they really care about. Unions are good for America if you believe in a strong middle class. But strong unions mean fair wages and a decent standard of living—both of which mean lower corporate profits. Or higher government outlays in the case of public sector employees. Neither of these fit into the Republican narrative, and both are antithetical to Republican orthodoxy.

That orthodoxy states that corporations should maximize profits with little regard for anything else—like the well-being of their employees. And at all costs, preventing the government from doing anything good, including providing a living wage. Or even worse, insisting that corporations do so—which is why the demise of unions has mirrored the rise in inequality. Without a counter to the structural power imbalance between employee and employer, wages have stagnated.

This is true despite the fact productivity has soared. With the bulk of productivity gains being funneled to the top, the resulting concentration of wealth has risen to a level last seen in the 1920s. This has led to a massive wealth gap that grows more intractable by the year. Looking into the future, things don't look bright. The war being waged against everyday Americans is being fought by an even more powerful adversary.

One of the reasons Republicans are so emboldened in their quest to undermine workers' rights is that they have a clandestine ally. Their bedfellow is none other than the American Legislative Exchange Council, better known as ALEC, formed in 1973. This fledgling organization might have drifted off into obscurity were it not for Ronald Reagan. Reagan embraced ALEC with open arms. He was their cheerleader and advocate when ALEC pushed efforts to privatize government and advance corporate interests. Privatizing government is another way of transferring public assets into private hands.

Under Reagan's tutelage, ALEC grew into the force it is today. Over 200 corporations and a quarter of state legislators belong to ALEC. State legislators are the focus of ALEC's efforts to write legislation, as it is much easier to work in a clandestine fashion at the state level. These corporations and the nearly exclusive Republican representatives vote as equals on "model" bills. Approved bills are called models because they are then taken to statehouses nearly verbatim across the country with the goal of making them into laws.

As expected, the objective of these bills is to advance corporate interests often at the expense of—and in opposition to— the public. These bills promote everything from environmental deregulation to busting unions to eliminating sick days to the privatization of government responsibilities. One of the more lucrative ALEC endeavors is the promulgation of privatization.

Privatizing public assets is one of the most efficient ways to transfer public money and assets to private corporations.

Prisons in Wisconsin serve as a prime example of this. Prisons and the fate of prisoners are usually not a concern for most citizens. Empathy is an afterthought, if it is a thought at all—which makes the prison system ripe for corruption. What better way to transfer public assets than under the auspice of protecting taxpayers from violent criminals? It's even easier when you don't have to worry about drafting legislation.

This is what Scott Walker did. Working with fellow Republican and ALEC member Governor Tommy Thompson, they devised a prison bill. By "devise," I mean they were handed a model prison bill drafted by ALEC. Then-Representative Walker would claim he was the author of the Truth in Sentencing bill and did not disclose that, in fact, it came from ALEC.[4] So when ALEC's Truth in Sentencing bill became law in 1998, Wisconsin voters were in the dark about its origins and true intent—both of which were geared toward creating a perpetual prison system that minted money for private corporations.

To keep the printing presses rolling, the prisons needed prisoners. The bill eliminated parole and early release. As intended, it resulted in an explosion of prison populations. Increasing the prison population was baked into the legislation. It was prison ALEC-mode. Since crime deterrent or punishment was never the objective, Scott Walker needed to monetize his newly overstuffed prisons. In other words, he needed to privatize them.

After the Truth in Sentencing bill became law, with the ink barely dry, Walker introduced a bill to open the state to private prisons. This was always the endgame. Private prison companies were waiting in the wings, eager to capitalize on the increased prison population and monetizing other people's suffering in the process. Though Walker's bill to privatize prisons failed to become law in Wisconsin, he was still determined to transfer Wisconsin tax dollars to the private prison industrial complex.

Not letting a little nuisance like the law get in the way, Walker sought a workaround. "Throughout the 1990s and early 2000s, with Walker at the helm of Wisconsin's Committee on Corrections and the Courts, Wisconsin shipped close to 5,000 inmates to Oklahoma, Tennessee, and Minnesota. Most of the prisoners, along with almost $45 million in Wisconsin taxpayer money, went to private prisons operated by one company: The Corrections Corporation of America (CCA)."[5]

Because Walker could not pass legislation to privatize Wisconsin prisons, he did the next best thing. He moved Wisconsin's money out of state. Benefitting Wisconsinites was never the objective. Any benefits that would come from additional jobs, infrastructure, etc., were incidental to the goal of transferring public assets into private hands. ALEC's infiltration of Wisconsin's government and their model legislation certainly paid off.

For taxpayers, on the other hand, the payoff hasn't been quite so generous. Wisconsin spends more on prisons than it does on higher education. Even though Wisconsin began rolling back Walker's Truth in Sentencing law after he left the assembly in 2002, a funny thing happened nine years later. In 2011, he was elected governor and pushed to restore ALEC's Truth in Sentencing requirements. Despite calling Wisconsin "broke," he felt the cost of incarcerating more people for more time (approximately $32,000 each year) was worth it.[3] But $32,000 for every inmate you lock up starts to add up—and quickly. This is why Wisconsin spends roughly $1.5 billion annually on corrections at the state and local levels.[6]

If Wisconsin is broke, it's only because Scott Walker made it so. Claiming Wisconsin is "broke" while funneling $1.5 billion into the prison system may make one question what the definition of "broke" is. Paradoxically, "broke" is a term that's relative to whom government is serving. When government is being used for the public good, then there's a problem. That's when Republicans insist fiscal discipline is in order. Conversely, when taxpayer money is being funneled into private hands, government is functioning as it should. When that's not possible, government shouldn't function.

Nowhere is that more emblematic than with the legislature in Florida. Since 1998, Florida's legislature has been controlled by Republicans—or should I say by Republican donors. One in particular when it comes to compromising the public good. If you want to know why Florida is considered a banana republic, look no further than to Marion Hammer. For nearly four decades, she has been the most influential gun lobbyist in the United States.[6] Using Florida as its petri dish, Hammer and the NRA have pushed forth the most lenient gun laws in the country. Like ALEC, her model legislation is then passed on to other states.

Getting pro-gun laws through the Republican legislature is a relatively smooth process. Her clout and the threat of the NRA have created a symbiotic—albeit dysfunctional—relationship between Hammer and congressional Republicans in Florida. She gives orders and they follow them. Doing otherwise risks her wrath as well as getting primaried. If you end up in her crosshairs, you can expect the following to happen: she'll get the NRA to pull its support for you. That support will be given to your Republican opponent. Together, they will then vilify your lack of gun credentials and support from the NRA—in the process, planting the political kiss of death on your forehead. This is the equivalent of a scarlet letter in Florida, quickly ending your political career.

That's why since 1998, Republicans have enacted nearly 30 of her bills.[6] The most notorious of these is the Stand Your Ground Law. As a consequence, Florida has become a gun-owner's paradise. Instead of having to walk away from a deadly confrontation, now, gun owners can almost instigate one. Before Stand Your Ground, you always had the ability to defend yourself if your life was threatened, but only if there was no option to flee. Thanks to Hammer, as long as you "reasonably" feel you could be in harm's way, you can fire away.

Considering how often I "reasonably" feel things, there's a lot of latitude here. So much so, it's possible to feel so threatened that you *feel* you need to shoot someone from behind to *feel* safe. In fact, that's precisely what has happened. After Stand Your Ground passed, two boaters ended up getting into a fight and fell overboard. Thanks to Hammer, when one of the boaters was attempting to climb out of the water, he was shot in the back of the head and used Stand Your Ground as his defense.[6]

Reasonable people can disagree, but the law was designed to remove reason from the equation. Is it threatening to be left alone in the water as your adversary is swimming away? It is in Florida. The jury would acquit. Justifiable aquatic homicide. By land, by sea, by air—homicides in Florida flourished...predictably so. According to a study published in *JAMA Internal Medicine*, justifiable homicides in Florida rose 75 percent in Stand Your Ground's first decade.[6]

The gun lobby obviously felt this number was too low. Being allowed to fire at someone's back as they fled was still too restrictive. The NRA must have been worried shooting someone in the back might lead rational people to question the logic of Stand Your Ground. Especially if it was used to justify murdering someone fleeing for their safety. Luckily, Hammer was there for them. She was worried, too. Imagine if there's another aquamarine brawl, someone gets shot in the back of the head while retreating, and a jury actually convicts? To the NRA, that's terrifying. There's only one way to prevent that: change the law.

As things stood, someone claiming Stand Your Ground bears the burden of proof at a pre-trial hearing. In essence, that means if you shoot someone, you need to prove you felt threatened. Hammer wanted to change that and push the burden of proof onto the state. In Hammer's world, the state would have to prove that Stand Your Ground *didn't apply* at a pre-trial hearing. They would have to prove a negative in order to get a trial. Then the prosecutor would have to prove it again at an actual trial. It's kind of like reverse double jeopardy. Except in this case, the only people in jeopardy are the ones without guns.

Unsurprisingly, Senate Bill 128 Passed. Florida prosecutors will have to prove a defendant cannot claim "Stand Your Ground" rather than making the defendant prove he can. All this will do is make it easier to commit justifiable homicide and make it more expensive for the state to prove otherwise. The vote was 23 yeas, 15 nays, and two abstentions. Twenty-three Republicans voted for the measure with zero Democrats. Fourteen Democrats and one Republican voted against the measure, with one Democrat and one Republican not voting.[7]

If you're wondering how Republicans can be so blinded to the interests of the gun lobby, it's because they suffer from a serious affliction. It's a disease similar to the one that prevents them from understanding anything their donors don't want them to understand. Symptoms of both diseases are the near-unanimous political contributions Republicans receive from energy companies and the near-unanimous support they receive from the gun lobby— one whose products will kill us slowly and the other instantaneously. They put our lives at risk because they are suffering from a rare genetic disorder. It predisposes them to the condition known as Corporate Stockholm Syndrome (CSS).

Similar to regular Stockholm Syndrome, CSS is a disease that causes hostages to develop a psychological alliance with their captors as a survival strategy. This allegiance causes Republicans to be unable to see anything past their corporate donations. The moneyed walls of their prison blind them while the sounds coming from their bill counters deafen them. Unable to see or hear anything beyond their gilded cages, escape is futile. They don't even see the outside world. It explains why Republicans can't see climate change or that Stand Your Ground Laws increase gun violence.

Just ask recovering Florida Republican Charles McBurney. He chaired the Judiciary Committee that Hammer needed to get her revised Stand Your Ground bill passed. As he was entering his last term in office, the haze of his Corporate Stockholm Syndrome was lifting. McBurney was planning his escape to a judgeship. Suddenly, he thought about Hammer's proposed law differently. Not beholden to her or the NRA for campaign financing, he was able to actually start doing his job.

Maybe this wasn't in the best interests of his constituents. Maybe it would make his coveted job as a judge more difficult. Maybe it would make Florida even more lawless. Whatever "maybe" convinced McBurney, he didn't bring Hammer's bill up for a vote. Of course, the one "maybe" he didn't consider was that Hammer would end his chance at a judgeship. She wanted revenge. So, Hammer made sure Republican Governor Rick Scott appointed someone else while still managing to get her bill to become law.[6]

You have to forgive anyone suffering from Corporate Stockholm Syndrome. It's a disease that's easy to catch and difficult to recover from. I should know since I suffered from a derivative form of it recently. All manifestations of the disease emanate from a general sense of corporate worship or delusion. Unlike Republican congressmen, my affliction was not based on corporate donations.

No one imprisoned me in a catacomb of dollars in order to purchase my ability to think on my own. Rather, it was self-imposed.

I ended up suffering from Corporate Delusion Syndrome, or CDS. It started innocently enough—with a purchase. One purchase led to another, and before I knew it, I found myself enthralled with a large consumer electronics company I'll call Three Star. My troubles began when I made one ill-fated decision. I assumed a company that makes great TVs and monitors must be good at everything else, too.

By doing so, I ignored my own experience with other Three Star products. Outside of monitors and TVs, my experience with them had been pretty poor. One watch died after a year and a half. Another had a battery die after six months. Not to mention my Three Star phone, which barely made it through the day. Why exactly did I think they would be any better at making external hard drives?

Because I was suffering from Corporate Delusion Syndrome. I clung to my misplaced faith in a company that had failed me more times than not. When I plugged the Three Star external hard drive into my computer, it didn't work. *It must be the computer,* I thought, so I bought another hard drive. When it didn't work either, it just proved my point. *The PC must be the problem.* I replaced the PC.

After setting up my computer yet again, the first thing I did was plug in the Three Star hard drive. It didn't work. The problem was Three Star. Now the odyssey began. Still under the delusion, I called Three Star for help. Part of the disease is buying into the myth of the infallible corporation. But just like Florida Republican Charles

McBurney, the delusion was lifting. That myth was shattered after one phone call.

When I spoke to a representative, I was told he would send me out new cables. Then I received an email. I wasn't getting replacement cables; Three Star wanted me to send everything back to them. After doing as I was told, the drive was returned to me dead on arrival. Trying to call Three Star, I found myself in a perpetual phone loop. The phone kept ringing. My fever was starting to break. Unable to even get through to someone, I fired off a complaint to the Better Business Bureau.

Complaint received. Montez from Three Star called me early one Tuesday evening and tried to allay my concerns. He was from Corporate Headquarters and kept reassuring me he was a "problem solver." The more he spoke, the more it felt like he was trying to sell me a used car. When I hung up the phone, I checked to see if I still had my wallet. I did, but I couldn't help thinking I had inadvertently signed up for a timeshare. Another odd thing about Montez was he seemed more interested in telling me how great Three Star products were than about fixing mine.

Nevertheless, Montez called the next morning and told me I would be getting a brand-new hard drive. I should expect an email from him with two links. One would be to a phone number I could call for help. The other was to the department that would send me a replacement hard drive. Neither worked. Then it dawned on me: the only problem Montez solved was his own—which I tried unsolving by writing a letter to Three Star's CEO. This resulted in another call from Montez.

Apparently, escalating problems at Three Star gets you one outcome: Montez. When I asked for his supervisor, he told me didn't have one. Any other escalations would end up back at his desk. Staring down an obvious dead end, I asked why I couldn't get the replacement he promised. Montez told me because it wasn't in the manual. How about a refund? Refunds aren't in the manual either, he said. Talking to anyone other than Montez? Not in the manual.

This was worse than dealing with the government. At least if a bureaucrat tells you something's not in the manual, you kind of get it. Of course, it's not—you work for the government. Manuals are for bureaucrats. Aren't corporations supposed to be better than that? Corporations are people, after all. They're free-thinking defenders of the free market. Unlike the government, they *want* my business. They'd never be so intractable as to only be able to do what's in the manual. Don't corporations value us if for no other reason than they want us to keep buying their stuff?

Something wasn't right. Baffled by my experience, I decided I must have fallen into *The Matrix*. I swallowed the wrong pill. Red, blue? I can't remember. All I know was it was the wrong one. Now up was down and down was up. In *The Matrix*, companies were monolithic, lumbering entities that couldn't do anything not in the manual. Government, on the other hand, was nimble, flexible, and full of solutions. Swallowing the wrong pill had me dealing with what must have been the Three Star Administration—a governmental agency under the Department of Hapless and Hopeless. Where's Morpheus when you need him?

Apparently in the New Jersey Attorney General's office. That was the one road that didn't lead to Montez. Knowing there was no resolution coming, I sent a last-ditch complaint to the NJ AG. Within a few weeks, I received a form to fill out requesting arbitration. Turns out companies that do business in New Jersey have to agree to have disputes resolved. Because Three Star is headquartered there, that includes them. Thanks to a consumer-friendly (Democratic) state like NJ, I got my refund...painful as it was.

Getting a check certainly helped me break free from my Corporate Delusion Syndrome. Now, when I go shopping, I'll be free of the haze of corporate veneration. While my options continue to dwindle, as a consumer, I still have *some*. It's not like I was shopping for cable. I can take my business elsewhere, which I have. Republican politicians, on the other hand, are the product. As something bought and paid for, they aren't even aware they are suffering from Corporate Stockholm Syndrome. Getting paid not to know things is not how government is supposed to work.

If you want to know what's wrong with our country, ask ALEC and all the Republican politicians who let them write our legislation. There is no equivalent on the left. The only Alec the Democrats have is a Baldwin. Planned Parenthood and PBS don't write laws for Democratic congressmen and congresswomen. Whereas Alec Baldwin does a great Trump impersonation, he doesn't masquerade as a legislator. Maybe he should. Between ALEC and Alec, he'd be better for the country.

Chapter 3: No One's Laughing

Perhaps no other legacy from the Reagan years has been more devastating to our middle class than trickle-down economics. It embodies all that is wrong with the modern Republican Party and their way of thinking. Birthed on a bar napkin, this theory was not rooted in math or science. Had it been, it would have been dismissed long ago. The same holds for its implementation. Time after time, experience has shown that tax cuts for the wealthy don't trickle anywhere.

Even Reagan had to reverse course when it became clear his tax cuts wouldn't pay for themselves. Yet the myth lives on. Luckily for Reagan, what would become Republican orthodoxy for the next 40 years was already in place when he arrived in Washington. You would think an economic theory of such consequence would emanate from a think tank or a university research facility instead of a bar napkin—but you'd be mistaken. Ronald Reagan was the first in a long line of Republicans whose policies were based on what they wanted to believe rather than what was.

The history of the Economic Doctrine of Bar Napkins predates Reagan's election, taking us back to 1974. It also involves another Republican operative notorious for dubious claims with little regard for consequences: Dick Cheney. It was on December 4, 1974 when Dick Cheney and Arthur Laffer met at the Two Continents Restaurant in the iconic Hotel Washington—the same hotel that had appeared in scenes from *The Godfather II* just months earlier.[1] Their meeting would alter the course of our nation.

The lengths Republicans will go to avoid paying taxes know no bounds. But it wasn't always so. Before Reagan entered the White House, Republican presidents had basic math and accounting skills. In fact, President Gerald Ford wanted to raise taxes in order to increase government revenue. That was when Republicans didn't believe in magic. Raising revenue required raising taxes.

It should come as no surprise that when President Ford's Deputy Chief of Staff, Dick Cheney, heard about his proposal, he was apoplectic. Unlike his boss, Dick Cheney didn't believe government revenues should be increased by raising taxes. He believed in David Copperfield. So, Cheney sought another answer. As the saying goes, "Seek and ye shall find." If you look long and hard enough, eventually you'll find someone to tell you what you want to hear. That someone for Dick Cheney was "economist" Arthur Laffer.

According to Arthur Laffer, by reducing taxes, you would increase tax revenue. Until then, conventional wisdom for raising revenue was based on economics. Raising government revenue required raising taxes. Reducing taxes to get more income would be like your boss giving you a pay cut so you could pay your mortgage. Receiving a lower paycheck so your boss would have more money to spend in the hopes it would trickle down to you and your mortgage company is essentially what Laffer told Cheney and is the nexus behind supply-side economics.

By reducing taxes disproportionately on the wealthy and corporations, all those tax savings will be unleashed in the form of hiring and investment that will turbocharge economic growth and accelerate tax revenue. Laffer even drew up his theory on a cocktail napkin. (Whether it was cloth or paper is still in dispute.)

On the vertical axis is a tax rate going from 100% to 0%. On the horizontal axis is the heading tax revenue with no values. Then he drew a perfectly symmetrical sideways "U" that started at a 100% tax rate and curved outward and back to the tax rate axis at 0%. An arbitrary line was drawn signaling tax rates above a certain level were "prohibitive." That tax rate was never specified. Without data points or a sense of coherence, The Laffer Curve was born.

Source: Gwynn Guilford, "Almost everything Republicans get wrong about the economy started with a cocktail napkin in 1974," *Quartz*, April 29, 2017

The name notwithstanding, real economists didn't find it amusing or credible. (Though it's been said more than one economist suggested that Arthur change his last name to Laugher). Unfortunately, the joke's on us—especially in light of the fact Republicans have been using this discredited idea ever since Reagan adopted it in 1981. Without research, facts, or figures, how could an "economist" could come up with such an outlandish proposal? What was he really trying to accomplish?

Assuming he was a real economist and just wanted to find a way to justify tax avoidance, I wanted to imagine what his pre-meeting must have been like—the one before he met Dick Cheney at the Two Continents Restaurant in Washington, D.C. Arthur must have thought about what he would tell Dick beforehand. Right? He couldn't have come up with something this absurd on the fly. He must have thought it through first.

Given this supposition, I wanted to recreate what that pre-meeting must have been like. To get a better sense of Arthur's thinking, I plan on transporting myself to 1974. For the sake of narration and so I can inject my interpretation of what *may* have happened, I'll play his counterpart. We will both be playing economists. The following is an interpretative staging of the "pre-meeting" that would change economic history as I've envisioned it.

＊　　　＊　　　＊　　　＊　　　＊　　　＊

Art agreed to meet me at a Georgetown bar called The Dungeon. It wasn't a place for the beltway crowd, and he knew it would be the perfect place for us to talk without being spotted. We weren't there for the scenery; The Dungeon looked more like a roadside pub than the types of high-end watering holes we were accustomed to. Lobbyists have expensive tastes, after all.

Nevertheless, we were there to think and drink, not necessarily in that order. And there was no better place for that than The Dungeon. When I walked in, it was almost 10 pm, and Art had already secured a booth. It was dark and secluded—the perfect spot.

"Over here," Art said as he motioned for me to come join him. "So what do you want, a warm beer or a cold scotch?"

"That's funny, Artie. You love your bar jokes, don't you?"

"I do, but not as much as I love my drinks."

And with that, Art reached across the table, hand extended. It looked like Art had a head start and I had some catching up to do.

When the waitress came over, I ordered a warm beer *and* a cold scotch. We told her to keep the drinks coming. We expected it was going to be a long night.

"Let me ask you a question," Art said. "What do you think is the most important thing to Republican donors: tax cuts or deficits?"

"Tax cuts, obviously. As long as it's *their* tax cut."

"Exactly. And what are we here to do?"

"Figure out how to cut their taxes?"

"That's right," Art replied, "and I know how to do it."

"So, you figured this out on your own, all before I got here? I knew you were a few drinks in, but I didn't think it was *that many*."

"Yes and no. While I was sitting here drinking alone, I couldn't shake the feeling that I'd been here before, to this bar."

"Have you? I thought this was your first time."

"It is," he responded. "But it's so familiar. Then it dawned on me. This is the kind of place where we'd go drinking in college. No one had any money, so we would find the darkest, dingiest hole-in-the-wall that served the cheapest drinks. That's this place."

"So, a dive bar is going to help us sell tax cuts for the wealthy? I think the waitress should cut you off."

"First of all, this kind of place only cuts you off if they have to carry you out. Second of all, you're missing the point. It's not this bar that has the answer; it's what this bar reminded me of."

"What's that, tetanus shots?"

"No." Art chuckled. "Pond Scum."

"Okay, I'm not going to spend my night getting drunk just so I can be your sounding board for moronic ramblings."

"Let me finish. When I say this place reminds me of Pond Scum, I'm not talking about real pond scum. I'm talking about the game."

"There's a game called Pond Scum, Art? If this ends up being one of those weird, you-had-to-be-there fraternity stories, I'm out of here."

"It's not; besides, you know I was only a member of academic fraternities. Pond Scum was a drinking game we played in college."

"Well, we didn't play it at my college, and I doubt a beer pong analysis is going to get a massive tax cut through Congress."

"You're missing the point," Art insisted. "Pond Scum is the game of life. When you start out, everyone is the same. But then the game begins. In Pond Scum, everyone is dealt one card. Soon, no one is equal. Just like in the real world. Everything changes. The highest card becomes president and then the next highest card gets to be VP, all the way down to the lowest card. That's the Pond Scum."

"So, what's the point of the game?"

"The point is to become president and stay president, obviously. The president can make any player from the VP down do anything he wants. The VP has authority over everyone except the president and so on. Everyone can boss someone around except Pond Scum. The beauty of the game is that once you become president, you pretty much stay president. And once you end up as Pond Scum, you pretty much stay Pond Scum. There's a little upward and downward mobility throughout the middle, but for the most part, where you start is where you finish."

"Who would want to play a game that was rigged?"

"Everyone, because they don't *think* it's rigged. After everyone gets one card, the society is set. Then Pond Scum deals the deck of cards until they're gone. The president gets Pond Scum's best cards and gives him his worst. Then the president starts the game. He dictates everyone's moves."

"So how is Pond Scum supposed to ever not be Pond Scum?"

"He's not. But he *thinks he can.* Look, people stay in it because they think they can get ahead, even when they're giving up their best cards and taking someone else's worst. There's always hope. Everyone wants to be at the top and thinks they can get there if they play their cards right."

"Funny, especially because the deck is literally stacked against them."

"Exactly, but do you know why they stay in the game?"

"Because they want to get drunk and possibly laid?"

"Yeah, that too," Art concurred, "but more importantly, because they want to be the one in charge. They want to be president. Even as they're giving up their best cards, they still think they can win. And when the person right in front of them, the bootlicker—the only player above Pond Scum—is ordering them around, all Pond Scum can think about is what they're going to do when they become the bootlicker."

"Why do you call them bootlicker, Art; shouldn't they be Vice Pond Scum?

"No, because when the president steps in Pond Scum, he needs a bootlicker, doesn't he?"

"Good point, and nobody thinks of themselves as being something to step in or lick off. Hope and envy. Now I see it. We can pass a massive tax cut that favors corporations and the wealthy because everyone wants to own corporations and be wealthy."

"Exactly. Not everyone can be exceptional, but almost everyone thinks they're exceptional. That law of averages makes that impossible." Art chortled. "Just like most people will never be or do anything exceptional, most people will never be wealthy. But they want to be. As long as they look at a tax cut for the wealthy as a future tax cut for themselves, we'll be fine. Greed is good."

"They'll think, 'Hey, if I were rich, I wouldn't want to pay taxes.'"

"That's right," Art agreed, "as long as they wouldn't want to pay taxes if they were rich and buy into the notion that they can become rich, the tax cuts sell themselves."

"But won't pay for themselves."

"No, they won't."

And they haven't. Reducing taxes has not led to increasing revenues. It has led to an explosion of deficits. Time and time again, Republicans have promised that tax cuts for the rich would increase productivity and magically raise government revenue. It hasn't. The fact that they promoted this theory as "trickle-down economics" should have been enough to turn people off. What good comes in a trickle? Imagine marketing a faucet as a trickle-down faucet? *Eventually* I'll get a glass of water? I'm thirsty *now*!

Quenching my thirst was never the point, though. Justifying tax cuts was. That's all Ronald Reagan cared about. You could argue he got into politics just for that purpose. "As a B-list Hollywood movie star during the 1940s, Reagan faced the exorbitant tax rate of 91% (rates had been hiked to fund America's war effort). 'You could only make four pictures and then you were in the top bracket. So we all quit working after four pictures and went off to the country,' Reagan once remarked."[1]

How patriotic. Of course, GOP patriotism became less and less about what was good for the country and more about what was good for them and their donors. Reagan's tax cuts ushered in this new era. Despite being doodled in 1974, it took the receptive ears of one Ronald Reagan to make Laffer's dreams come true. As far as Ronald Reagan was concerned, a bar napkin with no data points was all the statistical analysis he needed to push through the largest tax cut in history. With two Republican sponsors in Congress, the Economic Recovery Tax Act of 1981 (ERTA) became law.

Rather than usher in an era of pronounced economic growth and a bevy of tax revenue, the deficit ballooned the year following ERTA's enactment. Skyrocketing interest rates ran with the exploding deficit as the rates surged from 12% to 20%.[2] Borrowing, which is a major driver of economic activity, became prohibitively expensive. Consequently, the largest tax cut in history drove the economy into a recession. It was the second dip of the 1978–82 double-dip recession.

So much for tax cuts increasing economic activity *and* tax revenue. They did neither. In actuality, they reduced both. Before the ink was barely dry on ERTA, Congress passed TEFRA in 1982. The Tax Equity and Fiscal Responsibility Act rolled back most of the personal tax cuts Reagan had championed. But it was too late for the deficit and for our republic. By the time Reagan left office, the national debt had tripled.[3]

Not the national *deficit*, which is what we owe in any given year when revenues are less than what we spend. Reagan was deficit spending beyond belief. Because he was such a profligate spender and tax cutter, the *total debt* we owe tripled. Perhaps more damaging was the baton he passed on to his fellow Republicans. Despite overwhelming evidence to the contrary, Republicans have fully embraced the myth that cutting taxes on the wealthy will trickle down to everyone else and transform deficits into surpluses. Like the game Pond Scum, we want to believe—despite evidence to the contrary.

Fantasy begets more fantasy. True belief obliterates facts. Otherwise, trickle-down economics would be a zombie lie that would no longer be feasting on the American middle class. For if trickle-down economics did in fact trickle down, you would think after nearly 40 years, a little something would have run down our collective legs by now. It hasn't. As you can see in the upcoming chart, the top 0.01% have taken almost all of the economy's gains since Ronald Reagan was elected. Only the top 1% has performed better than overall economic growth, with only 10% matching it. The bottom 90% have been left behind.[4]

Just like in Pond Scum. Not only have the rich prospered, they have done so at everyone else's expense. They gave us their worst cards and took our best. According to Alan B. Krueger, professor of economics at Princeton University, "Since 1980, more than 100 percent of the total growth in income in the United States has gone to the top 10 percent of families. A whopping two-thirds of all income gains have gone to the top one percent. The bottom 90 percent saw their combined income actually shrink."[5] Watching as their wages stagnated, U.S. workers have not seen an inflation-adjusted increase in their pay since 1978.

Rather than "trickle-down," perhaps Republicans should call their bar napkin economic theory "gusher-up." Not only do the wealthy pay less in taxes, we're giving them our economic gains so they can pay less. In their defense, it's expensive being rich. Sending children to Ivy League universities is getting prohibitively expensive—especially when you have to factor in room, board, books, and bribery. This can be costly, but not as pricey as *legal* bribery. Bribery is for the one percent, not the point-one percent. Just ask Jared Kushner. Knowing his son couldn't get into Harvard on his own merits, Jared's daddy pledged $2.5 million to Harvard. Somehow, little Jared got in. I guess they were impressed by the 2.5 million reasons Jared gave on his application for why he should attend their prestigious university.

Impressive as it is, it's only something the very wealthy can afford to do. Even without having to save in a 529 Bribery Fund, the actual cost of college is no longer realistic for the wage-stagnating middle class, further widening the gulf between the haves and the have-nots. Without a college education, even the pretense of being able to rise above your station is pure myth. Now, even the prospect of sitting at the table and being Pond Scum may not be achievable. Imagine being so far down the socioeconomic hierarchy you can't even dream of being Pond Scum!

Conceptually, it's easier to understand when taken in context of the larger goal: creating a permanent underclass. When Republicans unleashed their middle-class-destroying tax policy, they were channeling their inner Gore. Not Al, mind you, but one that personifies the success of the few at the expense of the many. While it may not make for a good bumper sticker, it encapsulates the GOP's ideology.

"It is not enough for me to succeed. Others must fail." According to Gore Vidal—and Republicans—that is the true measure of success. Had the GOP dropped the pretense of an economic justification for their policy, it would at least have some legitimacy. Tax cuts for the wealthy don't lift all boats. Only yachts. They don't pay for themselves, either. Economically, it doesn't work. Philosophically, it does. Being marked by cunning, duplicity, and bad faith, it is truly Machiavellian and worthy of Gordian praise.

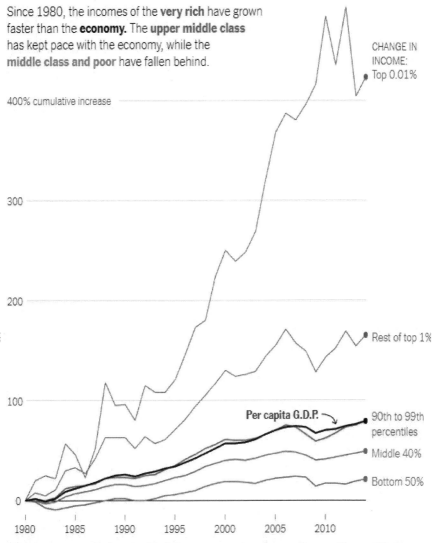

Since 1980, the incomes of the **very rich** have grown faster than the **economy**. The **upper middle class** has kept pace with the economy, while the **middle class and poor** have fallen behind.

CHANGE IN INCOME:
Top 0.01%

400% cumulative increase

300

200

Rest of top 1%

100

Per capita G.D.P.

90th to 99th percentiles

Middle 40%

Bottom 50%

0

1980 1985 1990 1995 2000 2005 2010

Note: Incomes are after taxes and include government transfers. · Sources: Thomas Piketty, Emmanuel Saez and Gabriel Zucman (incomes); Bureau of Economic Analysis (G.D.P.) · By The New York Times

Source: David Leonhardt, "How the Upper Middle Class Is Really Doing," *The New York Times*, Feb. 24, 2019.

Before Reagan, Republicans could actually have been considered fiscally conservative. But like the environment or our collective resources, there is little they conserve. There is also little they serve other than themselves or their donors. "Conserve-themselves" would actually be a more apt moniker for the politicians in today's Republican Party. They certainly don't serve their constituents. If they did, we would all be better off with Republicans in charge. But we're not.

Contrary to what you've been told, Democrats are better for the economy and the stock market. Under their stewardship (when there has been a Democratic president), the GDP growth rate was 4.33% versus 2.54% for Republicans. The stock market favored Democrats by returning 8.35% versus 2.70% (as measured by the S&P 500). Finally, the pain of recession was far less, with 1.14% of quarters in recession under Democratic leadership versus 4.56% under a Republican president.[6] This is over a 64-year period.

Even more amazing is how the "job creators" fared at actually creating jobs. According to Michael Tomasky of *The New York Times*, "From John Kennedy through Barack Obama—56 years during which, as it happens, we had a Democratic president for 28 years and a Republican president for 28—we saw more than 50 million jobs created under Democrats and just 24 million created under Republicans."[7] What about the "job creation" under Trump? His pre-pandemic average of about 175,000 jobs a month was less than President Obama's second term.[7] Valuable information. Unfortunately, since it wasn't written on a bar napkin, Republicans probably aren't familiar with it.

They're also not familiar with it because facts are inconvenient. And nothing needed to trickle down. With Democrats in charge of the economy, a rising tide does lift all boats. That is why Republicans are such horrible stewards of our economy. They know a rising tide lifts all boats but prefer it when it only lifts *their* boats. Part of the reason is that they feel richer when their boats rise while others sink—even if their boats are smaller than they could have been. Or as Gore Vidal would say, "It is not enough for me to succeed. Others must fail."

Relative success is entrenched in Republican orthodoxy. It's one reason they're incapable of delivering on their economic promises. Not inconsequentially, either. It is a driving force behind the growing inequality in our country and the fact that only a few reap the rewards of our capitalistic system. When Karl Marx called religion the opiate of the masses, he could just as easily have said it was capitalism. Under the guise of an equal playing field—one where anyone can get ahead—only a few have. Wealth becomes entrenched, and the wealthy have no interest in making what they have available to everyone—just like in the game Pond Scum. Once you're at the head of the table, you'll do anything to stay there.

Structural inequality coupled with vanishing upward mobility makes the American Dream achievable only in our sleep. Being born in America, we have been raised to believe we live in the land of opportunity. However, those opportunities are becoming increasingly rare as fewer and fewer Americans enjoy the economic benefits being offered. Rather than being the example for other countries to follow, we are increasingly being the example to avoid.

"America is further toward the high-inequality, high-immobility end of the scale than other advanced economies. Higher income inequality goes hand in hand with lower upward mobility in America, research by Harvard economists, Raj Chetty, Nathaniel Hendren and others has shown."[8]

When the economic spoils go to the one percent of the one percent, there's not much left for the rest of us. Anything that does trickle will be quickly scooped up by those next in line. This means that for the vast majority of Americans, what they have ends up trickling up. In a zero-sum game, they lose. Otherwise, if supply-side economics worked, all of the economic statistics listed above would prove the opposite. But it doesn't, and there is a simple economic rationale behind it. There aren't enough wealthy people to generate the economic activity necessary to fuel a nearly $20 trillion U.S. economy. Considering there are roughly 80 people that have as much wealth as the world's 3.6 billion poorest people, no matter how gluttonous they are, 80 people can't consume as much as 3.6 billion can.

That consumption gap is why trickle-down economics doesn't work. There is only so much trickling down 80 people can do—especially when they save rather than spend. There's an inverse relationship between taxes on the wealthy and their savings habits. Reducing their taxes increases their savings and vice versa. Little evidence shows any impact on their spending. Increased spending is what we need from them to justify their tax cuts and boost the economy.

In some respects, they act like corporations. Just like wealthy individuals aren't interested in spending their tax cuts to help the economy, neither are corporations. Apple took the recent GOP tax cut and turned it into a $100 billion stock buyback program.[9] They weren't alone. The Welfare for the Wealthy Tax Act of 2018 ended up with corporations buying back nearly $1 trillion of their own stock. They didn't spend their tax welfare checks on new workers or new equipment. They're beholden to shareholders, not society. They will do what's in their shareholders' best interest with little regard for anything else.

What's in their best interest? It's making those 80 people richer with stock buybacks and dividend increases—which ends up benefitting the 80 at the expense of the many. Without increasing economic activity or tax revenues, the government becomes poorer and so do the rest of us. Any short-term boost in economic activity won't last. Eventually, tax cuts will have to be paid for. The only thing that trickles down is the bill—right to the middle class in the form of tax increases or benefit cuts. The market knows tax cuts lead to deficits. Which lead to higher interest rates. Which lead to economic downturns.

If Republican presidents are bad for the economy, why are Democratic presidents good? With or without knowing it, they stumbled upon a bedrock principle of economic expansion. Give money to those who have the least and they'll spend the most. It's called elasticity of demand.

Take my family, for example. Taxes have little to do with our spending. A tax increase or decrease doesn't make much of a difference in our spending, and we're far from a member of the Elite Eighty. Theoretically, the tax cuts to corporations were given so they would increase wages. Increasing wages is a prerequisite for an increase in consumer spending. That didn't happen with the most recent corporate tax giveaway—not to mention the others. Companies are using their tax cut to give money back to shareholders. In other words, to savers, not spenders. Which brings us back to elasticity of demand.

As an economic term, elasticity of demand means what it says. If someone has inelastic demand, it means an increase in income won't have a big impact on their spending. On the other hand, someone with elastic demand means a change in income has a big impact on their spending. Put another way, if I give a dollar to someone making minimum wage in the form of a tax cut or pay raise, chances are they'll spend most or all of it. They have elastic demand. Like a rubber band, it's very expansive.

Conversely, if I give a dollar to a robber baron, he won't notice the difference. He has inelastic demand, like a thumbtack. To get the economy moving, we need to put more money in the hands of those who will spend it. This increases demand, which is a signal to corporations to invest and hire more workers. This puts upward pressure on wages, which increases economic activity and tax revenues. It is the opposite of what Republicans espouse.

While some of this disconnect can be attributed to Corporate Stockholm Syndrome, part of it has to do with their value system. Wealthy Republicans, who call the shots for Republican politicians, value comparative wealth over absolute wealth. Under Democratic presidents, economic expansions tend to be broader, deeper, and longer, with more jobs created. Economic contractions were also shorter and the stock market performed better. The problem with valuing comparative wealth over absolute wealth is that if you're doing better, but still not as well as I am doing, I might feel less wealthy because you've closed the gap a little bit.

The pie may be growing, and I may be getting more than my fair share, but it *feels* like less. I may be better off on an absolute level under Democratic stewardship because the economy and stock market are growing more robustly. However, if a Republican is going to cut my taxes disproportionately relative to yours and cut back on government spending that benefits you, I may feel better off—in part because you're worse off.

That's essentially what Gore Vidal was saying. Wealth is not just a number; it's a feeling. That's why feelings and economics don't mix. Neither does wishful thinking. While it sounds good to envision a world where prosperity trickles down and magically creates prosperity and balanced budgets, it is nothing more than wishful thinking. Allowing bar doodles and fantasy to become economic doctrine can only lead to one place. It is the same place that befell the Roman Empire. It was a historic fall from grace that seemed—to anyone not paying attention—to come out of nowhere.

Chapter 4: The Nine

Homeownership is a quintessential part of the American Dream. Owning a piece of property is like owning a piece of America. It allows you to reminisce about the true meaning of property ownership and transport yourself back to a time when property owners were conveyed rights only available to them—like voting. In the early history of the U.S., most states allowed only white male adult property owners to vote. This is the indelible link between owning property and having the freedom that defines being American.

A freedom—it turns out—that can be expensive. As any homeowner can attest, the freedom of owning a home is anything but free. Just ask any two out of three people you meet. With nearly two-thirds of Americans owning homes, it's safe to say they'll probably all agree on one thing. New home, old home, or something in between: homes are called money pits for a reason. No matter your circumstances, there's always something to buy, fix, or improve upon. Just maintaining a home can be expensive—I never knew how expensive until I became a homeowner.

When it comes to home repairs and maintenance, there are two ways to go. You can do it yourself or you can pay someone to do it for you. If a home repair has anything to do with water or electricity, I tend to choose the latter. After experiencing a few too many close calls with live wires, I knew it was time to hire an electrician when using most of our outlets ended up tripping our circuit breakers.

After calling several companies, we hired Lance from Electricians 4 Freedom. Not that he was our first choice; he just happened to be the only reasonably priced electrician who could start on short notice. But he made me a little nervous. He spent most of his time complaining about "Big Electric," whatever that was, and how they were always trying to tell him how to do his job.

As the son of an electrician, he told me it was in his blood. He didn't need Big Brother setting rules and regulations for guys like him. According to Lance, too many electricians had fallen under the spell of Big Electric. He kept referring to them as "commies" and "un-American." Lance assured me he was more like our founding fathers and was trying to free customers like me from oppression and tyranny. In other words, to get out from under the thumb of Big Electric.

He seemed patriotic enough. When Lance showed up early for our appointment, I got a good look at his custom Ford F-150. It was retrofitted with dual exhausts and the body was wrapped in an American flag. It matched the flag on the lapel of his shirt. *What could go wrong?* I thought. Electricians are all the same, more or less. Even though he hated Big Electric, surely, he abided by their constitution. So, we hired him.

As promised, Lance's flag-wrapped truck pulled up to the curb right on time. He greeted me wearing his custom-made shirt sporting his company logo and of course a flag pin on his lapel. He wanted to get right to work, and he made it clear my only job was to stay out of his way. No lookie-loos on this project. I must confess this was difficult for me. Whenever a repairman is at our house, I like to see what they're up to and learn a little something in the process. Not this time.

Feeling a little anxious, I decided to run out for some coffee. I know caffeine isn't known for taking the edge off, but I needed a distraction. With all the banging, beeping, and drilling I heard, I decided against asking Lance what he wanted. I'd grab him a coffee and work under the assumption that everyone loves a latte. I wasn't in a hurry to get back, so I decided to take my time getting our drinks.

I was gone for a little more than an hour. When I turned into our neighborhood, I couldn't believe what I saw. There was nothing but smoke and the charred remains of what used to be my home. In a daze, I ran toward Lance with my car keys in one hand and a coffee tray in the other.

"Are you okay?" I blurted out.

"I'm fine," he replied as he reached over and grabbed a latte. "I probably should have had one of these earlier."

"What happened?!?" I stammered, feeling like my legs were collapsing under the weight of my body.

"Your house burned down," he stated matter-of-factly, as if the carnage in front of me wasn't obvious enough.

"I can see that, Lance!" I shouted as concern gave way to anger. "How did this happen? What kind of electrician are you?"

"Electrician? What makes you think I'm an electrician? I'm a fireman."

With that, Lance stopped to admire his handiwork. Then he closed his eyes and took a deep breath.

"You know what that smell is?"

"That's freedom."

※　　　　※　　　　※　　　　※　　　　※　　　　※

For me, hiring Lance would be like voting Republican. How can anyone be good at something they hate? Anyone who hates what they do or who they do it for can't be good at their job. Lance hates Big Electric, so burning down my house was a foregone conclusion. Republicans hate the government, so how can they be good at running it? When they tell us government is terrible and dysfunctional, they have no other option but to make sure it is. It's no longer a self-fulfilling prophecy. It's self-preservation.

When Republicans tell us government is the problem, it's because they want it be. Yet it wasn't always this way. Republicans used to claim to want government to be small—but effective. That ended thanks to Ronald Reagan. Famously, Reagan uttered the following one sentence and nine words that would be a clarion call for his party:

The nine most terrifying words in the English language are: I'm from the government, and I'm here to help.

This has been the Republican mantra ever since. Just like Lance disdained Big Electric, Republicans loathe government. When they undermine the government, it is by design. If government is effective, it undercuts one of their main talking points, at the same time endangering their ultimate objective. That can be summed up by anti-tax and anti-government zealot Grover Norquist when he said: "I don't want to abolish government. I simply want to reduce it to the size where I can drag it into the bathroom and drown it in the bathtub."

Ironically, he said this in 2001 just as Republican George W. Bush was about to break the debt clock. Engineering runaway deficit upon runaway deficit, government was certainly not reduced. It turns out Republicans love Big Government; they just don't want to pay for it. They're like frat boys in Vegas with someone else's credit card—running up a bill they'll never have to pay. If Grover ever gets to fulfill his dream of drowning the government, he'll have to choke on a lot of Republican red ink first. And find a much bigger tub.

Because deficits are never a problem when Republicans are in charge. As long as taxes for the wealthy remain low, deficits are allowed to grow. Then Republicans can attack government and the deficits these low taxes create, hoping to chip away at the safety net by cutting spending at the margins. Spending to help the public is the problem.

That's why Republicans were near universal in the condemnation of deficits during Obama's presidency. Republicans were deficit hawks when they thought government purse strings would be opened to help the average American recover from the Great Recession—the one they started. But they had no problem with a deficit-destroying tax cut for the wealthy in the midst of an economic boom in 2017.

At the end of the day, what they fear most is a government run by the people and for the people—a government that helps the average American. They worry about what would happen if government provided services to the public in an efficient manner—one that voters loved. Imagine if the 2017 $1.5 trillion Republican tax cut had been used to bail out homeowners in 2008 when it was needed the most. Imagine how much healthier our middle class would be. Republicans have, and it terrifies them.

That's why Republicans scream "Socialism" at the top of their lungs every time the government does anything of value. As long as they link the two together, their hope is that enough Americans will equate the two. Counterintuitively, the people who need it the most will fight it the hardest. As long as they believe good government equals socialism, they'll continue to view the government as the enemy, a never-ending socialist plot. One where the government takes over the means of production of anything and everything.

The Republican socialist propaganda machine keeps enough voters from somehow realizing that they cherish most of what government does. Social Security and Medicare top that list. Reagan's biggest fear was voters recognizing how much they benefit from government. In addition to not wanting to pay taxes, it may have been the reason he ran for president in the first place. Years before he was elected, he was practicing his pitch, warning against the impending perils of a socialist takeover. Socialism became a bogeyman Reagan and his fellow Republicans could wield—and still do, for maximum effect.

Ever since the New Deal, Republicans have been trying to dismantle the social safety net. They view Social Security and Medicare as government handouts even though everyone pays into both. Republicans fear voters may figure out Social Security and Medicare are well-run, well-liked government programs and want more. That was the impetus behind Ronald Reagan's Radio Address on Socialized Medicine, recorded in 1961. Nearly 20 years before he became president, he was planting the seeds for the dismantling of Social Security and Medicare.

His address is important for several reasons. It linked government-run programs with the evils of socialism. Most Americans believe we fought our World Wars against socialism. There was little distinction between socialism, fascism, or any other type of government—especially one that ended in an "ism."

Socialism was the enemy and anything socialist was a threat. But what Reagan did was even more insidious. He linked socialism to liberalism. Reagan knew he needed to domesticate a well-known foreign foe. Decades before ascending to the highest office, he tried to link good governance with socialism—in the process, creating an American enemy. It was one Republicans could attack for political gain to further their elitist agenda. The following is from Ronald Reagan's Radio Address on Socialized Medicine.

Now, back in 1927 an American socialist, Norman Thomas, six times candidate for president on the Socialist Party ticket, said the American people would never vote for socialism. But he said under the name of liberalism the American people will adopt every fragment of the socialist program.

Now, the American people, if you put it to them about socialized medicine and gave them a chance to choose, would unhesitatingly vote against it.

Reagan deftly linked American opposition to Medicare with their opposition to socialism. Linking socialism to liberalism, he nimbly blacklisted both, tarnishing government in the process. Later, Reagan went in for the kill. The following are several relevant passages that form the bedrock of today's Republican Party's position on Social Security and Medicare.

"One of the traditional methods of imposing statism or socialism on a people has been by way of medicine. It's very easy to disguise a medical program as a humanitarian project. Most people are a little reluctant to oppose anything that suggests medical care for people who possibly can't afford it.

So, with the American people on record as not wanting socialized medicine, Congressman Ferrand introduced the Ferrand Bill. This was the idea that all people of Social Security age should be brought under a program of compulsory health insurance. Now this would not only be our senior citizens. This would be the dependents and those who are disabled. This would be young people if they are dependents of someone eligible for Social Security.

Now the advocates of this bill, when you try to oppose it, challenge you on an emotional basis. They say, "What would you do, throw these poor old people out to die with no medical attention?" That's ridiculous; and of course, no one has advocated it. As a matter of fact, in the last session of Congress a bill was adopted known as the Kerr-Mills Bill. Now without even allowing this bill to be tried, to see if it works, they have introduced this King Bill which is really the Ferrand Bill.

What is the Kerr-Mills Bill? It is a frank recognition of the medical need or problem of the senior citizens that I've mentioned. And it is provided from the federal government money to the states and the local communities that can be used at the discretion of the state to help those people who need it.

Let's take a look at Social Security itself. Again, very few of us disagree with the original premise that there should be some form of saving that would keep destitution from following unemployment by reason of death, disability, or old age. And to this end, Social Security was adopted. But it was never intended to supplant private savings, private insurance, pension programs of unions and industries."

The hypocrisy of his speech is remarkable. Instead of having Social Security support senior citizens, he calls upon unions. These are the very unions he and his party have done everything in their power to dismantle. Starting with Reagan's takedown of the FAA, Republicans have been union-busting ever since. Unions were taken down, and with them, their pensions. Pensions that used to provide a solid middle-class retirement are a thing of the past. Without strong unions and a significant minimum wage—to put a floor on earnings—most Americans can't save enough for an emergency, let alone retirement. In fact, half of all people on Medicare had incomes less than $26,200 in 2016.[1]

None of that will prevent Republicans from dismantling the most enduring and endearing part of the New Deal. It's already happening, and the blueprint was provided in Reagan's speech. When he mentioned the Kerr-Mills Bill as a solution, it was a prelude to today's block grants. Block grants are a way for the federal government to shirk its financial responsibility. Rather than paying for a federal program, the government gives a specific dollar amount (block grant) directly to states and local communities. This money can then be used at the discretion of the state to help those people who need it.

Once it's a state program, it's out of the federal government's hands. That's the problem and that's why Republicans support it. If Social Security were a block grant, your state may or may not pay you your full Social Security benefit. Republicans are trying to get Medicaid to be a block grant first. Turning Medicaid into a block grant would ultimately mean cuts in services to people who need healthcare the most and are the most vulnerable. The math is simple. A state gets a "block" of money from the government. If the services they provide with that money exceed the amount of money they receive, they either raise state taxes or cut back on services.

Since poor people don't vote and have been stigmatized as "takers," raising taxes seems unlikely. Especially raising taxes at the state level for healthcare for the indigent, particularly in red states. That's one of the reasons so many Republican states refused to accept Medicaid expansion. Rather than help their most vulnerable citizens, they turned down federal money. According to Rachel Garfield, Kendal Orgera, and Anthony Damico, from the Henry J. Kaiser Family Foundation, "Nationally, more than two million poor uninsured adults fall into the 'coverage gap' that results from state decisions not to expand Medicaid."[2]

That's two million working poor without access to healthcare. Garfield, Orgera, and Damico further state, "Under the ACA, Medicaid eligibility is extended to nearly all low-income individuals with incomes at or below 138 percent of poverty ($17,236 for an individual in 2019)."[2] Expanding Medicaid was directed at those too poor to pay for healthcare, but not poor enough to get Medicaid. Hence the need for expansion. They're working; they just don't earn enough to pay the bloated costs of healthcare.

These working poor would seem to be exactly the kinds of people the government should help. Even without any bootstraps to pull themselves up by, helping the less fortunate is not something Republicans are interested in. Ideologically and strategically, it is something they diametrically oppose. Expanding Medicaid can only lead in one direction: further expansion. When you do one thing well, voters are going to expect another. And another. And another.

Besides, expanding Medicaid would prevent it from becoming a block grant program. In turn, this would ruin the chance to block grant or privatize Social Security. Convincing the average American that Social Security and Medicare are part of a larger socialist conspiracy is no longer a practical option for Republicans. They reserve that for everything else the government does that people might like. It is precisely because Social Security and Medicare are two of the most popular government programs in existence. That's the problem for Republicans. How can you dismantle something that everyone wants? How can you take away the only retirement benefit many retirees depend on?

You drown it in Grover's bathtub. Without knowing it, this is exactly what Ronald Reagan did—or at least what he laid the groundwork for. Reagan's legacy lies in what he did, and more importantly, what he emboldened others to do. His blueprint did the most damage. His domino set the others in motion. That's why conservatives love him. Because of Reagan, dismantling Social Security is a real possibility.

It's possible because Reagan pulled off one of the most extraordinary heists in American history. With an assist from the architect of the Great Recession, Reagan orchestrated one of the greatest frauds ever perpetrated against the American people. Alan Greenspan, whose monetary policy helped lead to the housing collapse when he was the head of the Federal Reserve, was his co-conspirator. Everything, of course, circled back to tax cuts. To anyone who knew better, Reagan's tax cuts did not increase tax revenue.

Contradicting supply-siders' claims, reality proved that lowering taxes did not increase tax revenue. Rather, lowering taxes reduced tax revenue dramatically. Part of the supply-side con was that David Stockman, Reagan's Budget Director, manipulated the budget forecasts that were generated from the Office of Management and Budget. Before the changes, as expected, the computer forecast that Reagan's tax cuts would generate massive budget deficits for years.[3]

Selling budget-destroying tax cuts would never get through Congress. That's why David Stockman rigged the computer at the Office and Management and Budget. A change here and a tweak there and *voila*, red ink changed to black. Stockman's objective was to get the tax cuts passed, not to worry about the consequences. He knew cutting taxes was easy; raising them was hard. Unfortunately, the real world is not so easily manipulated. Tax cuts don't pay for themselves. A tax cut today is a tax increase tomorrow. Or a benefit cut if Republicans are in charge.

The problem for Reagan was his tax cuts were so unsustainable, he couldn't wait for tomorrow. Further complicating matters was the fact that Republicans' demonization of government created an atmosphere of distrust. Voters didn't trust the government with their money, so the less of it they got, the better. But Americans did trust Reagan, which was his bailiwick. He had an uncanny ability to sell the American people on his honesty and good intentions, even when he possessed neither. It enabled him to get out of one mess and into another scot-free.

This was a mess he created but would never be held accountable for. On the contrary, like all Republican tax cuts, the mess will be someone else's problem. Just like the frat boys in Vegas, why worry about a charge you're never going to be held responsible for? Short-term thinking leads to short-term results. The short-term thinking was, *How can we hide our tax cut losses?* The short-term results were illusory budgetary fixes and the destabilization of an institution.

Luckily for Reagan, Americans love Social Security. Otherwise, a $2.7 trillion tax hike would have been unthinkable. Perhaps even luckier for him was that no one questioned him about his 1962 album *Ronald Reagan Speaks Out Against Socialized Medicine circa 1961*. Had anyone listened to Reagan warning about the perils of Medicare and Social Security, we would have known how he really felt about "preserving" Social Security.

Vinyl enthusiasts and anyone who followed his political career knew. During the 1976 Republican presidential primary, he proposed making Social Security voluntary. Today, Republicans want to privatize it. George W. Bush tried to do just that in 2005. He failed because congressional Democrats were unified in their opposition to privatization, and Bush was reeling from the Hurricane

Katrina disaster. Privatizing—and especially making Social Security voluntary—would destroy the program as we know it. When Reagan referred to Social Security as a "welfare program," he was conveying his party's deeply held beliefs about what has turned into a lifeline for far too many senior citizens. All of this makes his feigned concern for the program that much more disingenuous.

His concern was for his own well-being. To balance the budget, Reagan needed money. Getting revenue from tax cuts proved to be mathematically impossible, just as any Economics 101 textbook said it would be. Tax increases were off the table, and so was cutting the government. Contrary to popular belief, Reagan did not shrink government. He increased the number of federal employees on the government payroll while exploding the deficit. Using the government and government spending as a punching bag didn't stop him from using both to keep the economy and his political aspirations moving forward.

With few options, Reagan knew he needed a crisis. At the time, Social Security was decades away from running into trouble. When baby boomers began to retire in 2010, nearly 30 years from Reagan's budgetary crisis, Social Security would begin to feel the strain of increased expenses and reduced revenues. So, in 1981, Reagan told Congress Social Security was "teetering on the edge of bankruptcy." He knew if he made the threat imminent, he could accelerate Social Security's demise—obfuscating his tax cut's real impact.

Ronald Reagan and Alan Greenspan convinced Congress that Social Security was in peril. In order to make it solvent, a tax increase was needed—not an income tax increase, but a wage tax increase. These taxes were supposed to be saved and invested in Treasury Bonds that were part of a trust fund. The Social Security Trust Fund was just that: a trust fund separate from the general obligations of the government that was funded through payroll taxes. Those payroll taxes then went to buy bonds that would be used in the future to pay benefits. The tax increase was supposed to be earmarked for this purpose.

Social Security had been an "off-the-books" entity. It's like your 401(k) plan. It's an "off-the-books" asset. You can't use it to pay your bills. It's for retirement. What Reagan did was allow a $2.7 trillion increase in Social Security taxes to be transferred to the government's general fund over a 30-year period of time.[3] The result was that Social Security's excess revenue was being used to pay for Reagan's tax cuts. In a 401(k) plan, any money you borrow would have to be paid back. With Reagan's tax heist, the money's been spent. It's $2.7 trillion we will never see again.

Not seeing that money paid back is a foregone conclusion. That may be Reagan's most damning legacy. You can't be good at something you hate. Reagan insisted that government was the problem. Then he made good on his promise. He conned us into believing we didn't have to pay our taxes. Now the bill is due and we're left wondering who's going to pay for it. He made us believe government was the enemy without tapering our expectations of what government should do for us. Thanks to Reagan, we want what the government gives us but don't want to pay for it.

Reagan and the Republican Party are the political equivalent of Wimpy. For the uninitiated, Wimpy is Popeye the Sailor's friend and a bit of a freeloader. He lives in the land of make-believe, very similar to the one where Republicans reside. Making decisions today, assuming tomorrow would never come. Always short of money, Wimpy's mantra was, "I'd gladly pay you Tuesday for a hamburger today." What's also important to note is that he never comes around on Tuesday.

Just like Reagan's tax cuts, today's hamburger always tastes better when someone else pays for it—especially on the Vegas Strip. The problem for America is every day is Tuesday. Republicans are nowhere to be found. And the bill is due.

Good luck collecting.

Chapter 5: POC

Close your eyes. Now, imagine you're in a white room. Everything in the room is unremarkable. The table, the chairs, even the two plants are designed specifically to make you forget them. They're intentionally nondescript. Even the mirror hanging on the wall looks like it could be any mirror on any wall. Everything is completely forgettable. What follows will not be. For better or for worse.

That's because you're in a focus group. Bland surroundings heighten your product experience. It's called a focus group because that's what the companies holding them expect you to do: focus. Not on what's around you, but on what's in front of you. Nothing should detract from what you are about to taste, touch, and feel. With distractions eliminated, all that's left are the products.

As each is introduced, there is an explanation and then an "experience." Food products are sampled and satisfaction levels recorded. Utilitarian items are passed around and judged on their functionality and whether they truly meet your needs. Luxury items are evaluated last. After "shopping" for necessities, do you still have a taste for something that may be out of your budget? Can that want be turned into a need?

That's what's being recorded on the other side. Your reactions. That forgettable mirror hanging on the wall is really two-way glass. Now, imagine being on the other side of that glass: the viewing side. Watching each and every reaction. As CEO, you want to see firsthand how consumers relate to your products. Their opinions are the only ones that matter. No one in marketing or product development can take the place of a consumer. What they want and what they'll buy are all that matters.

As the focus group closes, the products are put away. In their place come the evaluation forms. Nervously, you watch as each participant finishes their review and files out the door. Once everything wraps up, you know it will take some time for the results to be tabulated. But your optimism is high—justifiably so. There wasn't a single instance where the majority of people found a product not to their liking. There were a few complaints over pricing. Some participants wouldn't make a purchase because of it, but they still approved of the product itself.

When the outside consulting firm told you they were ready, you could barely contain your enthusiasm. Surely, the results would be positive. Too many of the participants loved your products. You saw this for yourself from the other side of the two-way mirror. Nothing could convince you otherwise. Stellar results were forthcoming. You knew it.

Until you didn't. Everyone loved almost everything. The consultants kept reassuring you of this fact, which you already knew. You watched their reactions. They all wanted your products until they were asked to fill out their feedback forms. It turned out they love your products, but they hate you. More specifically, they hate your company. Most of the participants couldn't believe the products they sampled were actually yours to begin with. Several kept coming up during the evaluation session to ask if your company really made all these amazing products.

Yet they ended up loathing the amazing products on their evaluations. A few were able to get over the association with your company and evaluate your products on their own merits. Unfortunately, most didn't. It turned out your competitor had been running a smear campaign against you. None of their marketing dollars were going toward promoting any of their own products. They actually didn't even care about sales. Everything they did was geared toward tearing you down—a total hit job. They viewed success through your failure.

Without any real products to tout, they owned little more than a bunch of empty slogans. They claimed to be for personal responsibility but didn't take responsibility for the damage their products caused. They preached family values, then acted like The Addams Family. They asked you to tighten your belt because their belts can no longer hold back their bellies. They claimed to be pro-

America as they dismantled democracy and undermined the Constitution.

Your competitor is the Republican Party. They've been running a decades-long smear campaign against you and the government. And that's how they win elections. Not on the merits of their own ideas. They know better than to run any campaign on the worthiness of their own products. They know what happened in that focus group. Just as all those participants loved your products, the majority of Americans overwhelmingly approve of government. That's a problem for Republicans.

Americans love Social Security, Medicare, and the military. In other words, they love government. Because over two-thirds of government spending is in these three areas alone, that's a safe assumption. According to the Congressional Budget Office, 2017's federal budget was roughly 29.3% Social Security ($939 billion), 18.4% Medicare ($591 billion), and 18.4% Defense (590 billion).[1] That totals 66.1%.

While you can argue 66% doesn't get you to "love" territory, it's certainly a passing grade. Add in veterans' benefits, the ability to fly in planes that don't crash into each other, safe food, drivable roads, and non-collapsing bridges, and even the rightest of right-wingers would have to concede the government gets at least a C+. Going through the budget line-by-line could get government's approval rating even higher. Certainly high enough for a second date.

This is the reason Republican politicians spend so much time demonizing government. If government is bad and is the enemy, it can't possibly do anything worthwhile. It's the reason so many Republican voters are always demanding, "Get your government hands off my Medicare," as they rail against socialized medicine. Republican politicians are happy to let them believe the government-run program of socialized medicine, also known as Medicare, is somehow not government-run. Republican politicians believe being uninformed is good. Being misinformed is better. Being radicalized is best.

When Reagan became president, it became known as the Reagan Revolution. Reagan knew revolutions needed enemies—enemies that needed to be defeated. Having the government embody what the Republican Party was fighting against was a start. Demonizing the government was easy. For Republicans, the government was the enemy.

It was a faceless enemy, however. Now that Republicans had created the notion of the government as the ultimate purveyor of evil, they needed to go one step further. They needed to make sure government was defeated, just like in a war. Having government fail was the only way for Republicans to succeed. You can't be at war with an abstract thing. Being at war requires being at war with other people.

When Reagan uttered the nine most terrifying words in the English language, it was the first shot of the Reagan Revolution. The target was none other than government itself. It's easy to hate faceless bureaucrats. Everyone has a government horror story. To be successful, the Reagan Revolution needed to have a battlefield filled with enemy combatants. That became anyone who would have the temerity to declare government can be a source of good.

Ronald Reagan famously declared that there was an Eleventh Commandment. He used this phrase during his 1966 campaign for governor of California. Reagan's Eleventh Commandment reads: "Thou shalt not speak ill of any fellow Republican." Uttering these words was Reagan's way of forming his cavalry. Prior to launching an invasion, one must first galvanize their own troops. Reagan began laying the groundwork for the pervasive "us-versus-them" environment we live in today long before he became president.

In doing so, he was caricaturizing and naming his enemy. Implicit in his Eleventh Commandment was that one *shall speak* ill of Democrats. This was also what he was doing in his 1962 album *Ronald Reagan Speaks Out Against Socialized Medicine*. Tying socialism, which we fought wars against, to Medicare smeared Medicare's supporters as socialist and implicitly un-American. According to Reagan, if you support anything he deemed as socialist, you were the enemy. The implication is that Democrats are socialists. Socialists are un-American. Therefore, by default, Democrats must be un-American.

Yelling and labeling Democrats as socialist has been a defining feature of the Republican playbook ever since. It is an integral part of their advertising plan—claiming the mantle of being pro-America while Democrats are un-American. While it is demonstrably false, it has been one of their more effective marketing strategies. And Ronald Reagan was not alone in creating this falsehood. Perhaps the greatest architect behind the dismantling of our functioning government was trumpeting this destructive rhetoric nearly as long as Reagan himself.

If there was one thing this charlatan knew, it was united we stand, divided we fall. A divided nation was one that could be manipulated. Dividing a nation as resilient as ours would take time, but he knew it had to be done. For if nothing else, he was prescient. He saw the writing on the wall. He knew Republicans couldn't beat Democrats with their ideas. Just looking at trickle-down economics proved that point. He knew to beat Democrats, Republicans had to attack them personally. Make them the enemy. Once he did that, he could begin tearing down government itself.

Newt Gingrich surmised the best way to take down government was to tear down Democrats. He did this with reckless abandon. Regardless of facts, fairness, or civility, Gingrich launched personal attacks against his "enemies." Gingrich laid out his game plan before a group of college Republicans in Atlanta before winning his 1979 seat in Congress.

"I think that one of the great problems we have in the Republican Party is that we don't encourage you to be nasty. We encourage you to be neat, obedient and loyal and faithful and all those Boy Scout words, which would be great around the campfire, but are lousy in politics."[2] His relentless assaults would provide the blueprint for countless Republicans and is the genesis of the demise of our civic—and civil—discourse.

As intended, Gingrich wanted politics to be nasty, not colloquial. In his eyes, Democratic colleagues became enemies. Attacking Democrats was the only way to win elections. That's why he enlisted his fellow Republican House members in his quest to pollute our politics. "Gingrich encouraged them to go after their enemies with catchy alliterative nicknames—"Daffy Dukakis," "the loony left"—and schooled them in the art of partisan bloodsport. One memo, titled "Language: A Key Mechanism of Control," included a list of recommended words to use in describing Democrats: *sick, pathetic, lie, anti-flag, traitors, radical, corrupt.*"[3] Ronald Reagan may have made government the enemy, but Newt Gingrich put a face on it. Because he knew how to. Because of Newt Gingrich, half our country views the other half as enemy combatants.

Back in 1979, after his electoral victory, Gingrich went on a fledgling network called C-SPAN to test drive his new theory. He led a group of other young Republicans on the air to defame then-Democratic Speaker Tip O'Neill and other Democratic lawmakers of putting "communist propaganda" in the Speaker's lobby.[4] Gingrich knew that calling Democrats *communist, socialist, fascist,* or anything ending with an "ist" or "ism" was tantamount to labeling them as un-American. It was a political scarlet letter. Once it was affixed, it was nearly impossible to remove. Even more effectual, it labeled everything you stood for as well. Linking Democrats to government enabled Gingrich to neuter it, then tear it down.

This is precisely what he did. Obstructionism became the governing philosophy of Republicans when Newt Gingrich took over the House of Representatives. Long before John Boehner shut down the government during Barack Obama's presidency, Newt Gingrich was doing the same to President Clinton. Governing through compromise became taboo. Republicans worked to make sure government was no longer representative of the people. If there's a theme, it's that Republicans don't view constitutionally elected Democrats as valid. They thwart the majority when they are in the minority and steamroll the minority when they are in power.

Cynically, Gingrich used his powers as Speaker for his and his party's self-enrichment. The shameless partisanship Republicans exhibit in their daily quest to put party over country is nothing more than a continuation of the Gingrich Doctrine. While disparaging government largesse, Gingrich was stuffing his pockets with government money through earmarks. Politicians use earmarks to pad spending bills that benefit their constituents. It is considered the epitome of government waste and is derisively referred to as "pork-barreled legislation."

And there was none porkier than Newt Gingrich. Rallying against big government as he gorged himself at the earmark trough, the anti-socialist crusader set in motion the largest socialist spending spree in history. Under his tutelage and direction, spending on earmarks doubled during his tenure, rising from $7.8 billion in 1994 to $14.5 billion in 1997.[4] Unsurprisingly, they were not evenly distributed.

Gingrich drafted a memo entitled "Proposed Principles for Analyzing Each Appropriations Bill." It instructed the chairmen of the House Appropriation subcommittees to ask, among other factors, if "Among them, 'Are there any Republican members who could be severely hurt by the bill or need a specific district item in the bill?'"[5] In doing so, Gingrich weaponized appropriations while undermining our democracy. Using taxpayer money to get

Republicans reelected was apparently his version of a functioning government.

Of course, there was no other reelection more important to Newt Gingrich than the reelection of Newt Gingrich. Being the head pig in charge, he made sure he always got fed first. Gingrich represented Cobb County, Georgia. Cobb County received more federal dollars per resident than any other suburban county in the country in 1995, except for Arlington, Virginia, home of the Pentagon and other federal agencies, and Brevard County, Florida, home to Cape Canaveral and the Kennedy Space Center.[4] As he kept ringing up the cash register, he proved his point. Government spending was a socialist handout. The money going to Cobb County, Georgia was coming from one of the biggest socialists in Congress: Newt Gingrich.

No wonder Republicans haven't been able to shrink government. With these socialists in charge of the purse strings, they're never going to get government into that tub, let alone drown her. Republicans are the first ones to rail against government spending as they jam their pockets full of our tax dollars. Shamefully, they don't see the irony in this.

They only have themselves to blame. How can they take down the government when they turned it into a revenue-sucking colossus? Starving the beast wasn't going to work when you turned it into the Kraken. If government was to be drowned in a bathtub, it would have to be neutered first.

Doing this required the undermining of our very democracy. Once again, Republicans turned governing into warfare.

Representative government would have to go. Republicans see no need for two-party rule to begin with. Dismantling it fell to yet another Republican Speaker of the House who set the wheels in motion.

It was the disgraced 51st Speaker of the House of Representatives: Republican John Dennis Hastert. He ignominiously represented Illinois's 14th congressional district from 1987 to 2007. The damage he did was not just to our democracy. He was found guilty of illegally structuring bank withdrawals to buy the silence of a former student he sexually abused. Judge Thomas M. Durkin of Federal District Court rebuked him at his sentencing as "a serial child molester."[6] While nothing is as atrocious as harming a child, he left a stain not only on society but on our Constitution.

During his unprecedented stewardship, he worked tirelessly to undermine democracy. His crowning achievement was a rule that fellow Republicans treat as law. It was his namesake: The Hastert Rule. The Hastert Rule is by its very nature undemocratic. It is known as the "majority of the majority" rule. Republicans use this rule to usurp the will of the minority along with their constituents. Under the made-up rule, the Speaker will not allow legislation to be voted on unless a majority of the majority party supports the bill. What this means in practical terms is that Republicans will not allow any legislation to pass unless a majority of Republicans support it. If it can't pass with only Republican votes, it never gets voted on.

Essentially, Republicans enacted one-party rule in the House of Representatives. Previously, legislation could be passed with a majority comprised of Democrats and Republicans. As intended.

Now, only legislation that had enough Republican support to pass would get a vote. Countless pieces of legislation that had enough support to become law were never even voted on. Republicans didn't want legislation passing with bipartisan support. They would rather have legislation that would benefit the country wither on the vine than to share any credit with their enemies. Democrats, on the other hand, believe in democracy and the will of the people.

When Nancy Pelosi was elected Speaker of the House in 2007, she shared our founders' view of government for the people and by the people. Asked about the Hastert Rule, she took an America-first view. She placed country over party. "I'm the Speaker of the House," Pelosi told reporters. "I have to take into consideration something broader than the majority of the majority in the Democratic Caucus." Rules that undermine democracy have no place in the Democratic Party. That was evident when the House approved an Iraq War supplemental bill. There were twice as many supporters from the minority as from the majority. The final vote tally was 280-142, with 194 Republicans voting for passage and only 86 Democrats approving.[7]

Paradoxically, Republicans' view on majority rule only applies when they are in the majority. This mindset continues to undermine our government, and it almost undid the global economy. Despite their role in the financial crisis, the party of personal responsibility fails to take any responsibility for nearly taking down the banking system and our country with it.

In 2008, the global economy was in shambles. It was on the brink of collapse largely due to Republican policies. Runaway, unregulated capitalism pushed the economy to the edge of a depression. Initially, Congress and President Bush passed the Troubled Asset Relief Program in October of 2008. It was a stopgap measure to stabilize the economy. Government, i.e., taxpayers, would buy the most toxic financial assets to stave off a potential collapse of the banking system.

But it wasn't enough. After President Obama was inaugurated, the country was hemorrhaging jobs. Democrats refused to sit idly by and let the dominoes Republicans set in motion take down the global economy. Controlling the presidency and both Houses of Congress, it was up to them to once again clean up a Republican mess—one that was getting worse.

By February of 2009, the economy was losing 750,000 jobs per month. At that rate, the only people employed would be politicians. Rather than allow another Great Depression, Democrats put together a stimulus package to save the economy. It was a nearly trillion-dollar package of tax cuts, state aid, and infrastructure spending that was considered essential to economic survival—which is why it received virtually no Republican support. Only three Republican senators and not a single Republican member of the House voted for the 2009 stimulus bill.[8]

Once again, they put party over country. Democrats bailed out Republicans and watched as Republicans bailed on America. Gaining and holding on to power was all that mattered to them—at any cost. Republicans knew a rapidly recovering economy would help Democrats as the party in power. Rather than allow that to happen, they continued to follow their One-Party Doctrine. Never was this more evident than when Mitch McConnell used his minority status to destroy the Senate.

Government had ceased to become a vehicle to enact the will of the people. Under Republicans, it was used to enforce the will of the few. When in the majority, they enforced this will with reckless abandon. In the minority, Republicans prevented government from functioning as it was designed to do by our founding fathers. When government is broken, the party in power will be blamed regardless of who is responsible. Newt Gingrich realized preventing the government from functioning was the quickest way to gain power. Mitch McConnell institutionalized that legacy.

Dysfunction in the House of Representatives is almost expected. It's an institution with 435 members. Each member faces reelection every two years. With Newt Gingrich having enacted his scorched-earth Gingrich Doctrine, civility in the House became a relic of a bygone era. Unimaginably, when the Tea Party took over in 2010, things got worse. They didn't even abide by the Hastert Rule. They only wanted legislation that the minority of the majority wanted. Provided, that is, the minority was the Tea Party and the majority were Republicans.

The Senate was supposed to be different. There are two senators from every state and each term is six years. Therefore, senators are not perpetually running for reelection. This should facilitate bipartisanship. Such an atmosphere was intended to elevate these government employees above the political fray. It is the reason the Senate had often been called "the greatest deliberative body."

"Had" is the operative word. It was only a matter of time before the Gingrich Doctrine infected the Senate. Newt Gingrich launched a tribalism that pervaded and contaminated every facet of our government. With the House of Representatives broken, it was only a matter of time before the Senate followed suit. When Mitch McConnell, the minority leader of the Senate at the time, said Republicans' sole mission would be to make President Obama a one-term president, it began.

Republican Senator Robert Bennett's account of what McConnell told fellow Republicans after Obama's election was as follows. "Mitch said, 'We have a new president with an approval rating in the 70 percent area. We do not take him on frontally. We find issues where we can win, and we begin to take him down, one issue at a time. We create an inventory of losses, so it's Obama lost on this, Obama lost on that.'"[9]

If America wins, Republicans lose. But when *Republicans lose, America wins.* For they are not interested in what is good for the country—only for what's good for their party. That's why in the midst of the greatest economic catastrophe since 1929, all they cared about was taking down a popular president. Republicans' only reason for existence became to obstruct—not just economic progress, either. By 2013, 79 of President Obama's nominees had been blocked by Senate filibusters, compared with 68 in the entire previous history of the Republic.[10] That means in a mere four years, Republicans had blocked more nominees than in the prior 230-year history of our country.

The conserve-themselves party was in full swing. And they were bitter. Despite their best efforts, the economy and the stock market vastly improved. Thanks to the Federal Reserve, interest rates were lowered and liquidity was injected into the system. Under normal circumstances, government spending would have increased as well, creating an even more robust and broad economic recovery. If not for the GOP.

Had Republicans placed country over party, our recovery would have been swifter and deeper. It goes back to Economics 101—a class the Republican Party might want to retake. Because understanding basic economics is critical if you are to be in government. Economics 101 teaches us that consumer spending drives the economy. It is roughly two-thirds of Gross Domestic Production (GDP). After the great recession, consumer spending plummeted. As job losses mounted, consumer spending nose-dived. Had any Republican congressmen taken Introduction to Economics, they would have known how to fix the economy.

GDP equals consumer spending (C) plus government spending (G) plus business investment (I). It then subtracts out or adds in net exports. Net exports equal exports minus imports (X - M). The final formula is: GDP = C + G + I + (X - M). Since the recession was global, consumer spending, business investment, and exports were all down. This left government spending as the lone hope for an economic recovery.

Since our government's budget is not like a family's, spending can be increased in times of trouble. While families can't print money or borrow at nearly unlimited levels, the government can. That's what should have happened. The "G" of government spending needed to increase to make up for the lowered "C" of consumer spending to get GDP back on track. Because of Republican obstruction, government spending was prevented from increasing to make up for the lost revenue from falling spending from consumers, businesses, and exports. In other words, Republicans made the Great Recession worse.

To put it in layman's terms, suppose you can't pay your bills. You approach your boss and ask for an early raise. After hearing about your predicament, he decides to give you a *pay cut*. His rationale is that you should be punished for spending more than you make. As this scenario played out across the country, everyone got poorer. When Republicans refused to stimulate the economy, they had a similar rationalization. Someone needed to be punished, and they weren't going to increase the deficit to help out anyone other than bankers. The ones that created the mess to begin with. The ones we bailed out.

Cynically, the national debt Republicans were suddenly so concerned about was there largely because of their economic policies. They weren't very concerned when Bush broke the debt clock. They don't really care about deficits or the debt. Their real goal was to prevent President Obama from getting reelected. In order to achieve their ultimate objective, not only did Republicans prevent the economy from fully recovering from the Great Recession, they actively suppressed growth.

Under the ruse of being worried about deficits, Republicans held the economy hostage. They continually threatened not to raise the debt ceiling. To do so, Republicans demanded spending cuts. Giving in to these demands would have helped them politically because spending cuts would have killed our anemic recovery. They would have blamed this on President Obama. Never ones to be forthcoming, they hid their thinly veiled intentions behind their nonexistent concern over our debt.

In doing so, they lied to the public about what the debt ceiling represents. The debt ceiling is a legislative limit on the amount of national debt that can be incurred by the U.S. Treasury. It limits how much money the federal government may borrow. However, it only needs to be raised because we've already spent the money. That's why not raising the debt ceiling can end in default. Defaulting on debt means you don't pay what you owe.

Republicans wanted Americans to believe it represented future spending instead of spending *they* already approved. Essentially, Republicans didn't want to pay their bills. Big surprise. They approve spending and cut taxes. Tax cuts starve the government of the revenue needed to pay for the spending. When government needs to borrow to make up for the tax cut gap, Republicans threaten to shut down the government.

It's like telling a friend, "I can't pay you back because you were so irresponsible to lend to someone like me money in the first place. You should have known better. You really need to get your spending in line." The fallout from treating a friend like that is a lost friendship, which you may or not be able to fix. The damage Republicans did to our economy can't be. October 2013 is a case in point of what their lack of patriotism can cost us. When Republicans created a fiscal crisis over the debt ceiling, it was later shown to subtract nearly one percent from U.S. GDP, equaling nearly 150 billion dollars and an estimated 750,000 lost jobs.[11]

That's money and income lost forever. But the damage and economic pain they caused wasn't enough. Despite their best efforts to undermine the economic recovery, they couldn't. Republicans slowed it down; this led to lower tax revenue and higher deficits. They held it hostage, leading to job losses and billions of dollars of lost economic output. But they couldn't prevent the recovery. They couldn't prevent the recovery they hoped would prevent President Obama from getting reelected. But Republicans weren't done inflicting pain on our country.

Elections and the Constitution only matter to Republicans when it is convenient and suits their agenda. When it doesn't, they are summarily dismissed. Nothing exemplifies this more than when Mitch McConnell usurped the powers of the presidency, single-handedly invalidating the election of 2012. The year Barack Obama was elected President of the United States for a second term.

Voting for president entails authorizing that person, through each vote and the cumulative will of the people, to execute all of the powers of the presidency. One of the most important of these powers is deciding who sits on the highest court in the land. Part of the separation of powers specifies that the Senate's role is to "advise and consent." The duly elected president has the sole and ultimate responsibility of selecting a nominee to the Supreme Court.

When Antonin Scalia died on February 13, 2016, that is exactly what President Obama did. He fulfilled his constitutional duty, as our founding fathers dictated. The duty 51.1% of the country elected him to fulfill. A duty 65,915,795 Americans entrusted him to perform. Nearly 66 million votes were cast with the understanding that he would do his job and the Senate would do theirs.

But instead of "advise and consent," Mitch McConnell decided to obstruct and usurp. Flagrantly violating his constitutional duties, not only did he refuse to have a vote on President Obama's nominee Merrick Garland, he wouldn't even let him meet with the Judiciary Committee. His intent was obvious. Merrick Garland was qualified for the Supreme Court and Republicans were on record saying so. In fact, Republican Orrin Hatch, who has served as chairman of the Senate Judiciary Committee on three separate occasions, once said there was "no question" Merrick Garland could be confirmed to the Supreme Court.

Instead, his nomination lasted 293 days without a single meeting or hearing. Following in Dennis Hastert's footsteps, Mitch McConnell created another felonious rule nowhere to be found in the Constitution. Claiming it was an election year, he refused to hold any hearings. Prior to 2016, that was never an issue. Starting with George Washington in 1796 and ending with Ronald Reagan in 1988, there have been 13 Supreme Court vacancies filled during an election year. Miraculously, since 1955, every Supreme Court nominee confirmed during a period of divided government has been nominated by a Republican president and confirmed by a Democratic Senate.[12]

By not allowing a hearing or vote on Merrick Garland, Mitch McConnell violated the Constitution. Specifically, Article II, Section

2, which authorizes the Senate to advise and consent. Over 350 law professors asserted it is a dereliction of that constitutional duty.[12] But it is so much worse. Mitch McConnell's singular reason for refusing to fulfill his constitutional duties was his intent to undermine a United States election.

Had Republicans held hearings and voted on Merrick Garland's nomination, they would be held accountable for those votes. Voting against an imminently qualified candidate would be something Republicans would not be able to justify. It may have cost them the Senate and the Presidency. Instead, Mitch McConnell assumed the duties of the Commander-in-Chief. In doing so, he stole nearly 66 million votes. From a man who only received 806,787 votes in 2014, it's quite the felony.

It's like Mitch McConnell decided that the votes of a white guy from Kentucky were worth more than a black man from Chicago. That his 806,787 votes were worth more than President Obama's 65,915,795. That each one of his votes was worth 82 times more than each one of our president's votes. Mitch McConnell acted like Kentucky elected him president—not just of Kentucky, but of the whole country. Another white-collar crime gone unpunished.

And it's a crime we are continuing to pay for. Unfortunate as that was, McConnell's disdain for democracy and disregard for the will of the people would only get worse. With Ruth Bader Ginsberg's passing on September 18, 2020, Mitch McConnell immediately said Trump's Supreme Court pick would get a hearing. Six weeks away from the election on November 3. Her confirmation would be occurring eight days before election day. Illustrating, once again, that

Republicans look at elections as minor irritants standing in the way of their agenda. Theft and immorality are weapons they wield in their quest for power.

None wield them better than Mitch McConnell. The fact that Mitch McConnell would steal from the American people should come as no surprise. Stealing is second nature to him. Mitch "the Moocher" McConnell is one of the biggest welfare queens in the Senate. The self-professed small government conservative embodies today's conserve-themselves party. Taking more than he gives and getting way more than his fair share, his grand larceny is the only thing keeping his state afloat. In 2017, Kentucky received $40 billion more from the federal government than it paid in taxes—about one-fifth of the state's G.D.P.[13]

Without government handouts, Kentucky wouldn't be able to survive. You would think there would be a little gratitude. Instead, Mitch McConnell and the Republican Party continue to undermine our democracy and all that it stands for. Their attacks on America, its institutions, and its founding principles all threaten our very republic. We sit idly by, falsely assuming our democracy is so strong it can withstand any attack. We don't realize that when democracies die, it is a slow, gradual death. Dismantled stone by stone. Out in the open. By the time you realize how sick the patient is, they're dead.

One day, when America's postmortem is written, it will revolve around Mount Benedict Arnold. Four Americans who betrayed our country for their own narrow interests. The Four Horsemen of the Democalypse (the dismantling of our Constitution and our democracy). Ronald Reagan, who made government the enemy. Newt Gingrich, who started a political civil war. Dennis Hastert and Mitch McConnell, who broke our government from within the halls of Congress.

Democracy is not guaranteed, and ours is quickly fading away. Little by little, the damage done to our institutions is becoming irreparable. If you want to know why civility is dead, ask Newt Gingrich. If you want to know why government no longer represents the will of the people, ask Dennis Hastert (or visit him in prison). If you want to know why the Senate is broken and beyond repair, ask Mitch McConnell. If you want to know why our democracy has failed and America is not "great again," ask all the Republicans who made it this way. Then ask yourself: what am I going to do about it?

Patriotism is the last refuge of the scoundrel.
—Samuel Johnson, 1775

Chapter 6: Monte

America has a long and storied history with con men. They come in all shapes and sizes. In the 1800s, it wasn't uncommon for one to ride into town on a horse-drawn wagon. Once they arrived, they would set up shop in the center of town and the show would begin. The master showman would leap onto a bevy of boxes, pre-arranged for maximum effect. He would then bellow to the crowd, "Come one, come all! Gather round while you still can. I have the cure for what ails you. Only I have what you need. But like my remedy, I'll be gone by the morrow!"

One by one, the townspeople would approach the back of his wagon to seek a cure for their problems. Out of earshot of their neighbors, the con man always had the cure. No matter the ailment—headache, backache, pneumonia, cholera, or typhoid—only he had the antidote. Just as he predicted, by morning, his wagon was empty and he was on his way. Knowing he would never pass through town again, he didn't worry about what his snake oil might do. Or the fact his snake oil didn't contain any snake oil to begin with. It was too expensive.

Over time, con men got more sophisticated, but the con remained the same, whether it was Charles Ponzi, Bernie Madoff, or the street corner hustler playing Three-card Monte. All the con man wanted to know is: how can they separate you from your money without you knowing what happened? Like a magician, they need you to be distracted. Keeping you looking in the wrong direction is the key to the con.

Republicans want you looking the other way, too. They want you focused on what they say, not what they do. Above all else, they want you ignoring the warning label. "Warning: The Surgeon General Has Determined That Voting for Republicans Is Dangerous to Your Health." Common side effects may include but are not limited to: loss of health insurance; bankruptcy; destruction of the planet; loss of life; the undermining of democracy and the dismantling of the Constitution.

Think of Republicans like the Marlboro Man. When tobacco companies were trying to market their product, they had a dilemma. As far back as 1950, a link between smoking and lung cancer was established. Promoting cancer, black lung, emphysema, tracheal removal, or even death didn't seem like a winning marketing strategy. Instead, tobacco companies lied about the damage their products were known to cause.

Cigarettes were marketed as "cool." The Marlboro Man embodied this sentiment. Mascots like Joe the Camel were used to entice children to smoke. In the early years of cigarette advertising, they even boasted that "more doctors smoke camels" and "as your dentist, I would recommend Viceroys." Would you go to a dentist that recommended you smoke Viceroys? Marlboros, maybe, *but* Viceroys?

Neither would I. Neither would all the states that sued the tobacco companies. It turns out, contrary to what the tobacco companies would lead you to believe, cigarette smoking is deadly. States began to notice as they bore the medical costs of smoking. That's when they banded together and sued the tobacco industry.

Tobacco use was directly responsible for the health problems of their residents. These health problems morphed into a significant financial burden for the state. The states' argument was simple: you (the tobacco companies) caused our health crisis. You pay for it. Which they did to the tune of over $206 billion paid out over 25 years.[1] As part of the settlement, tobacco companies were also restricted in their marketing. Smoking was deadly, and tobacco companies were no longer allowed to pretend otherwise.

As more and more information came to light, fewer and fewer people took up smoking. Fewer and fewer places even allow smoking. People of a certain age remember smoking in airplanes. The absurdity of having a smoking section in an enclosed metal tube would be laughable if not for the consequences. Smoking's toxic for the smoker and for anyone near them. In an airplane, that means everyone. It's not like rolling down the window is an option. Even if it were, secondhand smoke can be just as deadly as firsthand smoke.

Just like voting. I may not vote Republican, but I'm sucking in the deadly secondhand votes of those who do. Republicans allowing bears, wolves, and their cubs to be slaughtered may be the most humane thing they end up doing. I could avoid going to a bar or restaurant that allowed smoking; I can't avoid living on this planet. There's nowhere else to go. Until Elon Musk gets us to Mars, I'm stuck here forced to breathe in secondhand Republicanism.

Someday soon, we may wax nostalgic about the quick death of the Alaskan wildlife. Having been murdered in their dens after hibernating or shot suddenly from overhead at least would be quick, unlike what's happening to us. We're like the proverbial frog in the pot—thinking we're in a warm bath until we realize we're boiling to death. When we do, it's too late. Every time another environmental regulation is torn down, we get one step closer to that fate. With the pro-pollution party in charge, it's accelerating our demise and that of our planet.

Regulations are being dumped left and right. Whether it's allowing methane leaks on public lands or coal runoff into rivers, our environment is becoming less and less safe. It's no longer theoretical. We can all see the damage climate change is causing. It's all around us. How high must the floodwaters rise before Republicans see it too? As long as dollars continue to float, we have a way to go.

There's a reason Republicans don't believe in global warming. They're paid not to. Receiving nearly all the oil and gas company's lobbying money buys their ignorance. Paradoxically, they claim it isn't because of the campaign contributions they receive; it's because they're for deregulation. It makes for a good campaign slogan. "Get the government out of the way of free enterprise."

With government being the enemy, it's an easy sell. But what Republicans want is for government to get out of the way so corporations can pass their costs on to the rest of us. Businesses have expenses. One of the ways to maximize profits is to get someone else to pay those expenses. When corporations pollute the environment, the rest of us pay for it. Pollution creates environmental hazards and healthcare costs that are imposed upon us—"us" being taxpayers. That is why Republicans are against regulations. They want you focused on something else as they separate you from your money so they can hand it over to corporations.

Republicans are not really for deregulation. They're for corporate welfare. That's why it's so onerous to become a beautician in one of the reddest of red states. In Texas, the number of course hours required to get a license for various cosmetology licenses is daunting: operator license requires 1,500 hours, shampoo certificate requires 150 hours, esthetician and manicurist license requires 1,200 hours, manicurist license takes 600 hours, and an esthetician license takes 750 hours.[2] After a lifetime of washing my own hair, is another 150 hours for a certificate really necessary? Four weeks of shampoo training? Really. Shouldn't government get out of our shower?

Clearly, Republicans think otherwise. They see where things could lead. Soap. Eye. We've all been there. Luckily, the finance industry poses no such risks—at least as far as Republicans are concerned. When it comes to regulating financial companies, they are busy trying to dismantle consumer protections that were put in place after the Great Recession. Given the stakes, you can see why. They're protecting us from a bad shampoo and rinse but not from a bad mortgage. Considering increasingly lax underwriting standards—i.e., regulations—caused the greatest economic damage since the Great Depression, maybe they *should* get out of our shower and into a bank.

While Lance from Electricians 4 Freedom might have burned my house down, deregulation nearly burned down the entire economy. The Great Recession (from roughly December 2007 to June 2009) saw eight million Americans lose their jobs, the foreclosure of almost four million homes each year, and 2.5 million closed businesses.[3] Add in the bailout, and deregulation cost us trillions and trillions of dollars. So why are Republicans so worried about regulating cosmetologists and deregulating the banking industry?

Obviously, Republicans want to make sure that when you lose your house, you've been properly washed and waxed. Being homeless and jobless is bad enough. *Looking* homeless is a line too far for Republicans. They want you to look good standing in line to get unemployment benefits—the ones they would like to do away with. Is it possible Republicans are really more worried about a bad haircut than a toxic mortgage?

Perhaps, but unlikely. They just don't want you looking there. Most likely, their chameleon-like position on regulation has more to do with money. Requiring licenses generates fees that go to the states imposing the regulations. And these regulations aren't being fought by the (nonexistent) haircutter's lobby. Meanwhile, the banking industry has an army of lobbyists fighting to do away with regulations. In fact, according to OpenSecrets.org, in 2018, commercial banks spent $66,176,918 lobbying Congress. That's money that can buy a lot of votes—and ignorance.

It has been money well spent. Republicans' stand on deregulation boils down to who's getting paid and who's doing the paying. If regulations force corporations to pay their own expenses, they'll oppose it vociferously. Whether it's toxic rivers or toxic mortgages, taxpayers are expected to foot the bill. Just like we bailed out the banking industry, we'll be expected to bail out the fossil fuel industry—literally with buckets. Global warming's increasingly astronomical costs will be something we bear, not the companies that caused it.

These are costs borne with no share of the profits. In other words, it's privatizing profits while socializing expenses *and* losses. Having government pay private expenses is worse than socialism. At least with socialism, everyone gets something. Rather, this is crony capitalism. Crony capitalism allows businesses to thrive not because they are rewarded for taking risks. They thrive because of money spent developing a network of business and political connections.

Risk becomes a function of lobbying clout. Monetarily, there's an inverse relationship between risk and political donations. The larger the donations, the less risk, and vice versa. That's why lobbyists are practically a fourth branch of government. Instead of promoting capitalism, where individual risks are individually rewarded, crony capitalism reigns. Crony capitalism, or crapitalism, is the opposite of free-market capitalism. It's subsidizing someone else's risk with taxpayer dollars without any benefit.

How did capitalism morph into crapitalism? By taking the "r" from "Republican" and inserting it where it doesn't belong, then following the money. Lobbyist dollars are the main reason Republicans argue companies should be able to "self-regulate." Under the guise of free-market transparency, they argue companies will lose market share if they don't. I wonder if they use the same logic with their children. Are their teenagers allowed to self-regulate? How many Republican politicians decide to leave their kids alone with the keys to the car, an unlocked liquor cabinet, and access to their bank accounts? Then they go away for a month assuming everything will be fine. After all, the children certainly know the marketplace will punish them if they don't act a certain way.

Self-regulating children are like self-regulating companies. After a month, the liquor's gone, the house and car are trashed, and the bank account is empty. It's what they do. Just like the scorpion and just like corporations, it's in their nature. Self-regulating teenagers doesn't work because number one, they *always* think they'll get away with it. They're also wired for short-term pleasure over long-term consequences. Just like companies. Take away the consequences, and probability and statistics dictate the rest. Doing the right thing voluntarily is the triumph of hope over experience.

That is the reason we need regulations. They're incentives for doing the right thing. Without any, companies will pursue short-term profit maximization regardless of societal expense or consequence. The godfather of crapitalism espoused this very notion on September 13, 1970, in *The New York Times Magazine*. Milton Friedman, an American economist, wrote an essay titled "The Social Responsibility of Business is to Increase Its Profits." That, according to Friedman, that was their *only* responsibility.

This kind of thinking transformed capitalism into the Darwinian, win-at-all-costs, toxic, zero-sum world we live in. Having the sole goal of maximizing profits creates perverse incentives. If dumping toxins in a stream is cost-free and increases profits, the incentive is to continue polluting. Whereas crapitalism perverts incentives, capitalism creates them. The same polluter who is required to pay their own expenses would be incentivized to reduce their costs—i.e., stop dumping toxins into streams. Reducing costs and increasing efficiencies is the hallmark of capitalism. Shirking costs is the backbone of crapitalism. It's Republicans' version of shared sacrifice.

Contemporaneously, this forms the foundation of their tax orthodoxy, which is little more than legislating tax avoidance. Yet another area where Republicans put party over country. Fiscal responsibility is just an empty political slogan they use to get elected and to get you to look the other way. Rather than advocating for a fair tax system, they would rather have corporations pay as little tax as possible. Doing so allows them to maximize profits. It's also another taxpayer subsidy. As brilliant as Steve Jobs was, Apple thrived because of all the benefits that were bestowed upon him from being an American.

Apple's intellectual property is protected under United States patent laws. Their physical stores from United States law enforcement. The country from our military. Apple's products go to market on United States paid roads and bridges. United States infrastructure allowed for the communication systems enabling an iPhone to make calls and surf the internet. Without any of these, the revolutionary iPhone couldn't have been made in the United States—and perhaps not made at all. Our collective and cumulative resources (paid for by our taxes) help pay for Apple (along with countless other companies) to make the products they do, distribute them, and succeed in a uniquely American way. How did Apple repay us?

Part of the collective agreement supporting this arrangement is an implicit understanding that Americans succeed in part because of the benefits of being an American. Such benefits are paid for by all of us. In return, the agreement is that you pay it forward. Pay for benefits that allow capitalism to flourish. Acknowledging these benefits and being willing to pay for them is essential to the functioning of our economy.

Under capitalism, that is. Crapitalism is another story. Lurking behind crapitalism is a belief that those at the top shouldn't pay their fair share—or any share, for that matter. Hiding behind the term "job creator" is the mythology that businesses became successful without any of the help they actually received along the way. It's a convenient way for Republicans to justify tax cuts for corporations and the wealthy—aka, their donors.

Again, it comes down to who paid and who's going to get played. Instituting a regressive tax structure becomes freeing the "job creators" to create wealth and have that wealth trickle down to the masses. The problem is, the only thing that trickles down are deficits. Trickle-down economics, along with most other bar napkin doodlings, have been discredited time and time again. But it's getting worse. Under the motto of "the only thing we're responsible for is our shareholders," corporations took the most recent Republican tax cuts and used them to increase dividends and stock buybacks.

Using taxpayer money to support individual stockholders is crapitalism at its finest. Without being used for plants, equipment, or hiring, businesses are ensuring future tax revenue will be reduced as well as current tax revenue. By not investing in the above, there aren't more workers generating more tax revenue. Neither is there the possibility of increased production. Rather, the money went to the pockets of individual shareholders at taxpayer expense, transferring wealth to those with the most precisely because they are well-off enough to own stocks.

With an expected $1 trillion being expected to go to stock buybacks and dividends, Apple led the way when they announced a $100 billion share repurchase program. This is why the government's deficit is over $1 trillion dollars a year, with nearly $22 trillion in total debt. Instead of even trying to match revenue and expenses, Republicans would rather slash taxes and watch the deficit explode. Fiscally responsible Republicans are like unicorns. I've heard of them. I've seen them in fairy tales. But I've never actually seen one. Yet somehow, the myth will not die.

When Reagan was elected, he slashed taxes, insisting that reducing taxes would increase tax revenues. It didn't. The federal debt ballooned under his stewardship. He added $1.412 trillion in annual deficits, which increased 142 percent, putting us on the path to crippling debt.[4] All of this would have been even worse had he not pilfered nearly $3 trillion from the Social Security Trust Fund.

Future unicorns did no better. His successor, George H.W. Bush, managed to increase the debt by 52% in only four years. Thankfully, we elected a Democrat to stop the hemorrhaging. Bill Clinton increased the debt by only 37% in eight years. Even more impressively, his last four budgets were not only balanced, but ran surpluses. That meant the national debt was being reduced as a result of the annual surpluses we were running. Bill Clinton was paying off Reagan and Bush's spending.

Unfortunately, Republicans saw Clinton's balanced budget and thought, *How can we wreck that?* Because they view surpluses and deficits as the same thing. Having either is a perfect time to cut taxes—for the plutocracy. Which is what George W. Bush did. He inherited a declining federal debt and budget surpluses. Under his economic tutelage, he turned the surpluses to deficits and increased our debt by 86%. In the process, he broke the national debt clock. It was not equipped to handle a $10,000,000,000 figure.

Of course, George W. Bush did more than leave us with over $11 trillion in debt. He left us with two wars and the near collapse of the global economy. That is why President Obama's 78% debt increase looks so mild in comparison. The annual debt increase under President Obama was lower than any Republican president from Reagan onward. And it was done on the precipice of a near depression. With the economy losing nearly nine million jobs during the Great Recession, tax receipts plummeted. Yet even under such extreme circumstances, Obama would have been considered the most fiscally responsible Republican in my lifetime.

He would have looked even *more* financially astute had he adopted George Bush's fuzzy math. Always looking to reduce the actual cost of their policies, Republican presidents rely on misleading accounting to hide the true cost of their deficit projections. Reagan famously did it to hide the cost of his tax cuts. George Bush did it to hide the cost of his wars, among other things. That's why his tax cuts had a sunset provision, meaning they would expire in ten years. Without the understanding they would expire, the tax cuts would not have made it through the budget reconciliation process. Once again, the con was on.

Because they were so financially damaging, Bush's tax cuts were only allowed to wreak havoc for ten years. Sunsetting was the only way to get them approved because after ten years, the financial damage was too great. President Obama banned these accounting gimmicks. By accounting for the spending on the wars in Iraq and Afghanistan, Medicare reimbursements to physicians and the cost of disaster responses, along with lower actual revenues from the alternative minimum tax, his budget was projected to be $2.7 trillion deeper in the red over the next decade than it would otherwise appear.[5] Had he used Republican math, Obama would have been *even more* fiscally responsible compared to his Republican predecessors.

That's why Democrats are better for the economy *and* the stock market. They understand math and economics, creating more jobs in the process. Under their stewardship (when there has been a

Democratic president), the GDP growth rate was 4.33% versus 2.54% for Republicans. The stock market favored Democrats by returning 8.35% versus 2.70% (as measured by the S&P 500). Finally, the pain of recession was far less, with 1.14% of quarters in recession under Democratic leadership versus 4.56% under a Republican president.[6]

Understanding the cult of Republicanism is important in understanding this gap. At this point, it's safe to say the Republican Party is a cult posing as a political organization. According to Merriam-Webster, a cult is defined as: "great devotion to a person, idea, object, movement, or work (such as a film or book)." Devotion is the key ingredient. Republicans are devoted to a movement—one based on ideas and feelings rather than facts, science, math, or economics. Not theories, but thoughts. When experience disproves these thoughts, it doesn't matter. Facts become fiction and fiction, fact. Or, even worse, alternative facts.

Exhibit number one is trickle-down economics. Despite being disproven over and over in the real world, Republicans continue to adhere to this failed economic fantasy. They then justify it in a uniquely Republican way: because it was written on a bar napkin. No data, no worries. No proof, no problem. They were told what to believe, and that's all there is to it. Devotion. The same holds true for their political doctrine. It rests in the same nebulous place as trickle-down economics.

Rather than turn to a great political mind, they turned to a fiction writer. Nothing could be more apt than relying on fiction, hoping it turns into reality—and wishful thinking is the hallmark of the Republican Party. It may be the defining reason they have strayed so far from their conservative roots. Once you realize Republicans' intellectual hero is Ayn Rand, their thinking makes more sense. Ayn Rand was born in communist Russia in 1905 and moved to the United States in 1926. While today's Republican Party can't get enough Russian influence, Ayn had had her fill.

Her disdain for Russia and government was the centerpiece of her novels—one novel in particular, her fictional book *Atlas Shrugged*. It's based on a philosophical system she created called objectivism. It's not an economic or political theory, but one of philosophy. Generally speaking, philosophy is a way of thinking about the world, the universe, and society. Philosophical thought is often general and abstract. Devoid of facts, philosophy engages one by thought experiments without definitive conclusions. *I think, therefore I am.*

Rand's philosophy came through loud and clear in her novels. She depicts a failing United States where industrialists have abandoned their wealth and country due to excessive regulations. Without these true patriots, America devolves into chaos. The most vital industries collapse, leading to a dystopian America. Without them, everything unravels.

If this sounds familiar, it's because her novel has become part of Republican orthodoxy. Holding up her work of fiction, they use it as the basis for their worship of "job creators." As for the hardworking Americans doing the heavy lifting for these job creators, they should be happy just to have jobs. Otherwise, Rand makes it pretty clear where we're headed. Those sensitive tycoons, if forced to consider anything but their own selfish interests, will take their ball and go home—plunging us into dystopia. All because we failed to worship the heroic job creator sufficiently.

Which begs the question: shouldn't we worship all job creators equally? If Republicans truly value job creators, why don't they worship the largest one in the country? The same one that created their jobs: the U.S. government. Maybe Rand was right. Giving jobs to the ungrateful is a mistake. One person in particular embodies this thanklessness. Considering everything government has given him, it's even more remarkable. Not only did the government create his job, one could argue it created him.

Former Republican Speaker of the House of Representatives Paul Ryan knows far too well how government creates jobs. It's created all of his. Paul Ryan has been on the government dole since he was in high school. After his father passed away when Paul was 16, he received Social Security benefits, which were used to pay for his college. Upon graduation in 1992, he got a job as a legislative aide. From there, he never looked back. His lips were so firmly wrapped around the government teat, his biggest fear was losing *his* spot at the government trough.

Like former Republican presidential nominee Mitt Romney said, there are those "who are dependent upon government, who believe that they are victims, who believe the government has a responsibility to care for them, who believe that they are entitled to healthcare, to food, to housing, to you-name-it." In other words, people like Republican Paul Ryan. Without a hint of irony or self-awareness, he railed against the government safety net, claiming he only wanted to slash benefits so it didn't turn into a hammock. Like the one he's been lounging in his whole life.

It's a hammock he never intends on leaving. Though Paul Ryan is an ex-representative, he's not retiring like you or I would be. He's certainly not retiring when you or I would, either. Paul Ryan retired at 48. He was preparing for a pre-50 retirement while he was proposing to raise the retirement age for everyone else to 70. Considering the amount of his taxpayer-funded pension, it looks like he traded in his hammock for a golden parachute. Paul Ryan, when he turned 50 in January of 2020, was eligible to receive nearly $85,000 a year from a taxpayer-funded pension.[7]

That's a lot of government cheese—for him, at least. Paul Ryan perfectly encapsulates the difference between Democrats and Republicans. The major distinction is that a Republican removes the ladder *after* they get on the lifeboat—which is exactly what Paul Ryan and his Republican counterparts intend to do. While he may not be in Congress to see it to fruition, he helped do his best to ensure we wouldn't have a ladder when we retire. That may be the reason Paul Ryan left Congress. Not only did he remove the lifeboat ladders, he sunk the lifeboats. Once he was safely on his government-funded yacht, that is. Thanks to Paul Ryan, Republicans may realize their dream of drowning government—and Grandma—in the bathtub after all.

It's been their fantasy since 1933 to undo the New Deal. That's what you call playing the long con. Suddenly, their allergy to facts and sound economic theory makes more sense. It also explains why a Russian novelist is a defacto Republican hero. It's not because she has sound economic or political theories and research to back them up; it's because she doesn't. Coming from Communist Russia, Ayn Rand has what Republicans want: a hatred of government and a made-up philosophy to justify it.

That's why Republicans love deficits. Economics 101 says tax cuts should be stimulative. When economic growth is slow, cutting taxes helps improve spending and GDP. During boom times, taxes should be increased to save for a rainy day. Unfortunately, Republicans don't adhere to a real economic theory. It's more like relying on the tooth fairy to pay your family's bills. Or consulting a witch doctor.

When confronted with Ronald Reagan's tax plan of cutting taxes for the wealthy and having it "trickle down," George H.W. Bush famously said of Reagan's tax plan, "It's voodoo economics." At least one Republican got it. Unfortunately, one back in 1980 isn't going to cut it. Relying on voodoo is why Republicans can't balance a budget. They live in an Ayn Rand novel while the rest of us live in the real world. It's like *The Truman Show* for Republicans. In the real world, cutting taxes for the wealthy reduces economic output *and* lowers tax receipts. It's the worst of both worlds. Even more troubling, it makes us unsafe economically. Ultimately, this is the point.

Dismantling government is only possible if there's no more money. Republicans always talk about "starving the beast." Again, the metaphor conveys their true feelings. The same Republican Party that held our economy hostage under the false pretense of wanting to keep the deficit under control passed a tax cut so large it will ruin us.

Thanks to their giveaway to the wealthy, trillion-dollar annual deficits are happening now. Of greater concern is total debt. It will become unsustainable. As deficits accumulate, the Congressional Budget Office's forecasts are ominous. The CBO projects debt held by the public will rise from 78 percent of GDP (or $16 trillion) at the end of 2018 to 96 percent of GDP (or $29 trillion) by 2028.[8] It will skyrocket from there without changes to tax and spending laws.

Not surprisingly, by 2025, 99.6% of Paul Ryan's tax cuts are expected to go to the richest 1% of Americans.[9] As biased as their tax cut is, it's only going to get worse. That's why Republicans in the House of Representatives wanted to make the tax cuts permanent. Doing so would permanently cripple our country—more specifically, our government, which is what Republicans are counting on.

None other than outgoing House Speaker Paul Ryan (R-WI) said that Medicare and Medicaid were his next targets for 2018.[10] Passage of the tax bill was a self-created crisis. Never mentioning his pension as part of the problem, Paul Ryan said, "We're going to have to get back next year at entitlement reform, which is how you tackle the debt and the deficit. Frankly, it's the healthcare entitlements that are the big drivers of our debt, so we spend more time on the healthcare entitlements—because that's really where the problem lies, fiscally speaking."[10]

In other words, the taxpayer-paid pension he feels entitled to is not an entitlement. The problem is Social Security and Medicare. Somehow, the problem is something we all paid for. Social Security and Medicare are benefits we receive because we and our employers paid for them. Can you imagine if your boss told you, "Look, you're not entitled to your paycheck anymore. The company has way too much debt to keep handing out these entitlements."

In actuality, the problem is with the Republican Party. Ronald Reagan stole $2.7 trillion from Social Security because the math on his tax cuts wouldn't add up. Every Republican since has been in on the con. Cut taxes for the rich and watch the deficits explode. Eventually, the U.S. will be on the edge of insolvency and there will be no other choice but to dismantle the safety net.

Breaking the government was the first step in achieving their ultimate goal. With the government broken and our finances in shambles, Social Security and Medicare as we know it will cease to exist. Neither will make it past the next financial crisis—like the one we're in now. The fiscal path our nation is on will lead us to a place not even a Democrat can fix. This is especially true because Republicans are being led by the nesting doll of con men.

While Ronald Reagan conned America behind the scenes, Donald Trump does it in the open. His entire life has been one con nestled inside another—ad infinitum. It started with the ruse that he's a self-made man. Not only wasn't Donald Trump a self-made man, he is little more than a glorified trust fund baby. At best, he's an unmade man-child who squandered gift after gift.

His origin story fit in seamlessly with the rest of the GOP's bestseller lists of fiction. According to an extensive *NY Times* investigation, the only thing Donald Trump made with any consistency was a mess—one his father repeatedly cleaned up for him. The *Times* investigation found Donald received at least $413 million in today's dollars from his father's real estate empire. His father was paying him $200,000 a year (in today's dollars) by age 3, and he was a millionaire by age 8. After graduating from college, he was receiving the equivalent of $1 million a year from his father, a sum that increased to more than $5 million annually in his 40s and 50s.[11]

Of course, one of the main reasons Trump needed so many handouts was that he was a terrible businessman. The only thing self-made about him is his failures, which he is *very good* at creating. Losing money owning a casino is hard to do in the one business where people go *to lose* money. Somehow, Trump found a way to go broke.

Actually, anyone dumb enough to go into business with him or lend him money went broke. During a time when other casinos in Atlantic City thrived, Mr. Trump managed to lose money. He posted huge losses year after year while losing stockholders and bondholders more than $1.5 billion.[12] The gambling Trump did was with other people's money. His fortune was actually his daddy's, his stockholders', or his bondholders'.

That's why he was able to declare bankruptcy so many times and escape scot-free. Donald makes his way through life riding on someone else's coattails. When it comes to Donald's handouts, perhaps no one else funded this freeloader's lifestyle more than us, the taxpayer. When people don't pay their taxes, everyone else pays. If you think it's cool to commit tax fraud and get "one over" on the government, think again. Every dollar of taxes someone else avoids is another dollar you and I will have to pay. That means Donald owes us at least $500 million. That is the tax he should have paid on the wealth he inherited had it been accurately valued.

Instead, the value of his inheritance was greatly underreported. Donald's parents, Fred and Mary Trump, transferred well over $1 billion in wealth to their children, which should have produced a tax bill of at least $550 million under the 55 percent tax rate then imposed on gifts and inheritances. In true Trumpian fashion, the Trumps paid a total of $52.2 million, or about five percent of what should have been paid, tax records show.[11]

Having us pay his taxes isn't the only thing Trump is good at. In addition to being excellent at losing other people's money, he was adept at losing his own—or rather, the money he was given. According to the AP, in 2015, Trump's net worth had grown to an estimated $4 billion since 1987. Had he just invested in index funds, he would be worth an estimated $13 billion. Index funds were created to allow the little guy with barely any money to get a taste of investing. The mogul would have more than tripled his net worth by being average.

Average would be a step up for Donald considering he's even worse at real estate. According to John Griffin, a finance professor at the University of Texas, Donald Trump underperformed the real estate market by approximately $13.2 billion, or 57% since 1976. These numbers, as staggering as they are, would be even worse with the use of leverage. Using other people's money is something Donald Trump is very fond of. That and not paying it back.

Contrast that with a true American Patriot, John C. "Jack" Bogle. Jack Bogle, founder of The Vanguard Group, pioneered the index fund in 1976. His idea was simple: create an investment vehicle that allowed the average investor to invest in the stock market while simultaneously reducing investment costs. He also reduced the minimum amount it took to invest, which opened up investing to the masses. In the process, Jack Bogle upended the investing world, lowering costs while increasing access to all investors.

Jack Bogle wanted the little guy to be able to invest like a big shot. In doing so, it is purported that he left some $28 billion on the table. Had he followed the norm in 1976, he would have been worth tens of billions more than when he passed away on January 16, 2019. Contrast that with Donald Trump. He left billions on the table trying to prove he wasn't average. In true Trumpian fashion, his insecurities have left us all in worse shape.

Maybe a little humility would have made Don-the-Con a real billionaire—with his own money—and would have saved us the vanity grab of his running for president. No toddler I know earns $200,000 a year and claims to be self-made. Even Narcissus would have had enough modesty to glance away from the reflecting pond. But it's not the con man that's the problem; it's the *conned man*. That's us. Unlike Trump, who never looks away, it's time for us to look in the mirror.

This reminds me of something my grandmother used to tell me. "Do as I say, not as I do," which is similar to what Republican politicians keep telling us. "Believe what we say, ignore what we do." Sorry, Gran; it's time to stop believing and start watching. We need to look past the con men to the con. Follow the queen in Three-card Monte. Stop getting distracted and start realizing Republicans are good at saying the things they never do. They are terrible at governing because they don't want to be good at it. Doing otherwise isn't in their nature. It's time to start watching what they do and stop believing what they say they'll do. Before the clock runs out on us, our planet, and our country.

It's time to put away the snake oil and get rid of the airplane smoking section—once and for all.

Chapter 7: CINO

What would Jesus do? It's a question that has been asked since 1897. In the novel *In His Steps*, minister Charles M. Sheldon becomes known for posing and subsequently gifting us the query, "What would Jesus do?"[1] While a valid question, what I want to know is, could Jesus have been a Republican? That's the question I set out to answer in my next book, *What Would Republican Jesus Do?* I included the following excerpt from chapter six, page 66, in the scene just before Jesus is crucified.

✝   ✝   ✝   ✝   ✝   ✝   ✝   ✝   ✝   ✝   ✝   ✝

Jesus' trial was over. All that remained was his sentence. That was left to Pontius Pilate. Jesus' fate rested in his hands and the mob that gathered around him. They waited inside the walls of Old Jerusalem.

As the crowd grew, so did their animus. Ever the showman, Pontius Pilate fed their bloodlust. "Is this your king?" he bellowed. "Is this the King of the Jews?"

The crowd yelled back, "We have no king but Caesar! Caesar is our true king! Caesar is the King of the Jews!"

"And what do we do with false gods and false kings?" Pontius Pilate asked as he turned toward the life-sized wooden cross resting against a wall of the citadel.

In unison, the crowd began chanting, "Tie him up! Tie him up!"

With that, Pontius Pilate nodded to one of the Roman centurions standing guard. As commanded, he hoisted Jesus upon the cross while another soldier bound his wrists to the crossbar.

As Jesus struggled under the weight of what would soon be his crucifix, Pontius Pilate asked, "What kind of a God can't carry a simple cross? Surely, for the King of the Jews, this should be an easy feat."

Before forcing Jesus to walk through the city, he affixed a crown of thorns to his head, declaring, "No king should meet his death without the proper accoutrement! I bestow upon you a wooden crown fit for a wooden king."

The crowd was ravenous at this point, and Pontius Pilate began to worry Jesus wouldn't make it out of the city alive. But he did—cross in tow.

Outside the gates of Jerusalem was a knoll where the Romans crucified criminals. Anyone entering the city was forewarned. This hill looking down upon the outskirts of Jerusalem was aptly called Golgotha, which translates to "(place of the) skull."

The centurions raised Jesus' cross between those of two criminals. Then they prepared him for his crucifixion. As the centurions got ready to nail Jesus to his cross, Pontius Pilate was affixing a sign to the top of the cross that read Jesus of Nazareth, King of the Jews. It was in three languages lest any passerby miss its meaning.

With nails in hand, the centurions turned to Pontius Pilate. Before allowing a single nail to pierce his skin, he turned to Jesus and asked, "Have you any last words, King of the Jews? Is there anything you would like to tell your subjects?"

Despite being dehydrated, bloody, and nearly catatonic from fatigue, Jesus lifted his head toward the heavens. He then implored his father, "Father, forgive them, for they know not what they do." As he spoke, he unfurled his hands to make his hangmen's task easier.

Then turned to Pontius Pilate and yelled, "But I do!"

With that, the heavens parted and angels could be seen descending from all directions. Before the crowd could discern what was happening, Jesus was off his cross. The two centurions were staked through the heart and left hanging where Jesus' wrists were just bound.

Jesus yelled, "Lock and load, losers!" while directing his angels to seek vengeance against anyone who showed even the slightest hint of disrespect to his birthright as king. "I was born king and you were born peasants! How dare you question my birthright? How dare you keep me from my crown and my throne?"

As the slaughter continued, Jesus caught Pontius Pilate trying to flee. With the mere flick of his wrist, Jesus stopped him in his tracks. Touching his cheek, Jesus told him, "My friend, the end will not be so easy for you."

Simon could tell by the slight grin forming on his face that Jesus was reliving one of his fondest memories. In fact, he relived it frequently. After banishing anyone he felt betrayed him to Hades, Jesus would frequently reenact what was soon to be known as the Trojan Crucifixion—or the Master's Massacre, as the locals refer to it.

Sensing another reenactment was coming, Simon tried to distract him. Simon was squeamish around blood and gore and depending on Jesus's mood, things could get pretty medieval.

"T, have you thought about addressing your flock?" Ever since the day on the hill in Golgotha, Jesus had insisted everyone call him "T." It was short for "The One and Only." Jesus put it on everything.

Glaring down at Simon, perturbed that his daydream was interrupted, Jesus rubbed one of the blue diamonds affixing his gold crown as it tilted to the side of his head. Then he rubbed his ever-expanding belly. "What do my 'subjects' want now?" He didn't even bother hiding his disdain anymore. As far as Jesus was concerned, if his subjects didn't love and worship him before seeing the destruction he could wreak, why should he help them now? Now that they'd seen what he was capable of.

"T, they're starving. They're asking for food."

"Tell them to lift themselves up by their sandal straps."

"But they're barefoot."

"Then tell them to ask their parents for some money."

"They are. Aren't you their father?"

"Not these losers, I'm not."

Since Jesus was easily distracted, it wasn't long before he noticed the Pharisee girls tending to his garden.

"Look, Simon. See her? Every time she bends over, I can't help thinking I should go grab her by her loincloth. I can part her Red Sea and there's nothing she can do about it."

Without the reaction he was looking for, he gave Simon a dismissive huff. "Simon, where are the other eleven idiots, by the way? Don't we have a meeting?"

"We do, T, but remember there are only ten. Judas is in the dungeon being tortured until the next reenactment."

"That reminds me, I have many pronouncements to make. Have the Pharisee girl bring me some papyrus scrolls and reed. And don't forget the ink."

✝   ✝   ✝   ✝   ✝   ✝   ✝   ✝   ✝   ✝   ✝   ✝

Luckily for us (and unfortunately for my manuscript), Jesus could never have been a Republican. In fact, while Charles M.

Sheldon's novel *In His Steps* may be best known for the question "What would Jesus do?" it is his answer we should remember. He would be caring for slum dwellers, not selling steel.[1] Jesus loved the poor. He loved them so much he was to the left of Bernie Sanders. Before Obamacare, there was Jesus-care. Before food stamps, there was free bread and wine. There wouldn't be welfare without Jesus-fare, and who could forget affordable Jesus-housing?

Jesus was not only the first Jew, but the first socialist. Jesus liked free stuff and he was pretty adamant about it. He laid it out in Matthew Chapter 25. In fact, it's how he's going to judge us.

"I was hungry and you gave me food."

"I was thirsty and you gave me a drink."

"I was a stranger and you took me in."

"I was naked and you clothed me."

"I was sick and you visited me."

"I was in prison and you came to me."

Every time Republicans demonize the poor, they're demonizing Jesus. As for the repercussions of such condescension, Jesus was pretty clear about that, too. "Truly I tell you, just as you did it to the least of these who are members of my family, you did it me" (Matthew 25:34-40).

Notice how Jesus never mentions "takers" or how he doesn't want anyone lounging in a welfare hammock next to Paul Ryan? Or how the bootless should be able to lift themselves up by their bootstraps? He never mentions it because they are the oppressed, and the oppressed are his flock. As for the oppressors, they are the goats that shall be separated and judged accordingly.

The goats never see it coming, either. The more their actions contradict the teachings of Jesus, the more certain they are they will be saved. Even as they worship false gods, they are intractable in their belief. How did they drift so far off course? Innocently enough, it seems. They were led away from Jesus by one belief. Discarding all of his teachings to stand for this one thing is what blinds them. It has created the biggest chasm between them and their Lord and Savior.

Generally speaking, anything the devil is for, Christians should be against. Surprisingly, they agree on one major thing. In another excerpt from my manuscript, *What Would Republican Jesus Do?* there is an interview with the devil. It reveals just how much he has in common with many Christians.

"Thank you for taking time out of your busy schedule to sit down for this interview. Before we get started, would you like to be called Satan, Lucifer, Beelzebub, Mephistopheles, the Dark Lord, Inflictor of Pain, or something else?"

"Satan is fine."

"Well, thank you again, Satan. If it's okay, I'd like to start off with a bit of a controversial subject."

"The thornier the better."

"There's been a lot of talk amongst your followers that you are anti-abortion. With all due respect to your unquestioning desire for inflicting pain and suffering, is that true?"

"Yes."

"May I ask why? I've always believed mainstream Christianity with regard to abortion. Doesn't it inflict pain on the fetus?"

"No; otherwise, I would be for it."

"Well, isn't it taking a life?"

"No."

"So why do so many Christians oppose abortion?"

"Because they're my Christians. Not his."

"How can they belong to you when they worship Jesus?"

"Because they worship with words what they will not follow in deed. Worshipping him with their heads, not their hearts. Thwarting God's will just like I do. That's why we call them CINOs down here."

"That's the first time I've heard that term. What does it mean?"

"It stands for 'Christians In Name Only'."

"But isn't God pro-life? Aren't these Christians being pro-God by being pro-life?"

"They would be if they were pro-life."

"Isn't that what being anti-abortion means?"

"Being against something doesn't imply you're for its opposite."

"That makes sense. Could you elaborate?"

"These pretend Christians are pro-fetus. It's not the same thing as being pro-life. If they were pro-life, I'd have a real problem."

"How so?"

"Why do you think Hell is so crowded?"

"I'm not sure."

"Unwanted children. Abortion is bad for business. The best child is an unwanted child. They all end up here. If these 'Christians' were really pro-life, they'd take care of these little buggers. Instead, they expect them to lift themselves up by their umbilical cords. The best part is that they're mostly poor. The rich ones get abortions. The poor can't, but both end up here for different reasons."

"But what about the whole 'killing innocent life' thing?"

"That goes back to interfering in God's plan. When a woman gets pregnant and doesn't want to be, an angel volunteers to take the place of the baby. It stays with her and comforts her through a very difficult time."

"So do abortions kill angels?"

"Unfortunately, no. The all-knowing big guy makes sure of that. They slip back to Heaven completely unharmed."

"Now I see why you're pro-life."

"Not pro-life. You can say I'm anti-abortion and pro-suffering, just like my Christians."

"Why are you so sure they're your Christians?"

"Because they're so certain they're not. Their certainty makes them weak, and I feast on the weak. They're so convinced of their salvation that when they first get here, they think they're in Florida. Just so you know, God doesn't give one last vacation before going to Heaven. No one goes to Disney first."

"So, they're not being saved?"

"They're being saved, but for me."

"Is that what you meant when you told Napoleon Hill that you control ninety-eight percent of the people in the world?"[2]

"You know I don't like to talk about him."

"I'm sorry; I thought it was a point of pride."

"I'm proud of the fact I own ninety-eight out of one hundred souls, but not proud I had no choice but to share it with him. But since you brought it up, yes—it's true. Ninety-eight out of one hundred souls are mine. The two that aren't are the most uncertain. The saved are rarely convinced of their salvation. That's the thing I love most about the other ninety-eight. They spend all their time staring out their windows. They never look in a mirror."

The devil is right. Being pro-life does not equate to being anti-abortion. Any pro-lifer who dares to look in a mirror would realize that. The reflection staring them in the face would not show someone interested in all human life, but in fetuses only. If anything, conservative Republicans are pro-fetus and anti-baby; once a fetus is born, the Republican passion for life's sanctity dissipates.

Babies are the ultimate socialists after all, and we all know Republicans hate socialists. Babies are more or less equivalent to wards of the state. Take, take, take. Always taking—at the very least, until early adulthood. As babies grow up, most spend two decades with their hands out, yet never pay their parents back for room, board, education, healthcare. Even worse, once babies become adults, they oftentimes want to move back into their parents' homes after a brief stint on their own. Rent-free housing! More taking!

Fetuses, on the other hand, are the ultimate capitalists. They're happy to take what trickles down from their host, happy to occasionally divert any extra resources they can from their mothers' bodies. At first, fetuses are very happy with this arrangement. (When Republicans talk about trickle-down economics, this must be what they're referring to.) It's not until fetuses grow into their latter months that they begin to realize there's a whole other world out there; that's when they want out, and that's when the trouble begins. At birth, they morph from good capitalists to raging socialists, fully willing to demand everything while contributing nothing in return. We are all, therefore, born socialists.

Given a newborn's inability to do anything for itself, this should be expected, but the conservative Republican can't think beyond the capitalist-fetus. Sister Joan Chittister, a woman of the cloth and therefore an unlikely candidate for summing up the blatant hypocrisy of the pro-life movement, said in an interview: "I do not believe that just because you're opposed to abortion, that makes you pro-life. In fact, I think in many cases, your morality is deeply lacking if all you want is a child born but not a child fed, not a child educated, not a child housed. And why would I think that you don't? Because you don't want any tax money to go there. That's not pro-life. That's pro-birth. We need a much broader conversation on what the morality of pro-life is."[3]

Jesus couldn't have said it any better. By contrast, conservative Republicans believe life begins at conception and ends at birth, since only unborn life is considered precious. Otherwise, if they were truly pro-life, our country would have a safety net strong enough to hold Paul Ryan and the rest of us. Beyond that, our environment would be as pristine and welcoming as a healthy mother's womb. We also wouldn't have so many stand-your-ground gun laws, which are basically a license to kill. In other words, the next truly pro-life Republican will be a first, as there's no conservative out there who espouses fundamental, common-sense protections for the born.

Unfortunately, not all human life is equally sacred to these people. Why? Could it be, as the devil intimated, the pitfall lies in too many Christians having left Christ out of Christianity? Very possibly. As perplexing as it may be, Christianity has been moving away from Christ for quite some time. The religious right's embracing of a man—never mind the lawmakers of this country— who could potentially burst into sin-reckoning flames by just passing a church is a byproduct of their being conned by their own party. They've been taken in by one of the biggest proponents of abortion rights out there.

Contrary to the myths surrounding abortion, the crusade against a woman's right to choose has far less to do with *Roe v. Wade* than the casual observer might expect. If all hinged on *Roe*, the anti-abortion movement would've started immediately after the 1973 Supreme Court decision, which made it unlawful to prohibit a woman's ability to end her pregnancy. The Court determined a woman's right to privacy under the Fourteenth Amendment extended to the decision to have an abortion. The ruling was not absolute, however, because the court did allow states to prevent abortion in the third trimester of pregnancy.

Given this, one would think the anti-abortion movement started on January 23, 1973—the day after *Roe* was decided. Instead, the ruling was met with an acceptance bordering on approval by many Protestants. Baptists, in particular, applauded the decision as an appropriate articulation of the division between church and state, between personal morality and state regulation of individual behavior. "Religious liberty," wrote W. Barry Garrett of Baptist Press, "human equality, and justice are [today] advanced by the Supreme Court abortion decision."[4] Even W. A. Criswell, the Southern Baptist Convention's former president and pastor of the First Baptist Church of Dallas (and also one of the most famous fundamentalists of the twentieth century), was pleased by the *Roe* ruling. "I have always felt that it was only after a child was born and had a life separate from its mother that it became an individual person," he said, "and it has always, therefore, seemed to me that what is best for the mother and for the future should be allowed."[4]

What changed? According to Dartmouth religion professor Randall Balmer, a lot. By 1979, the megalomaniacs of the religious right were clamoring for power. In 1979, they held a conference to figure out how to gain it. Intentionally disregarding their mandate to keep "the division between church and state," they wanted a Borgia Pope dominion over the public square. They sought to inflame their parishioners by choosing an issue they could use later to control them with. Succumbing to their darker nature, the leaders of the religious right discussed which issues could divide the country. Seeking to politicize the most divisive, they choose abortion.[5]

Of course, it became so divisive because they made it so. These religious leaders needed to incite their congregants into action. Understanding that the visual medium was more effective in achieving their goals and could be easily manipulated in a way words couldn't, they turned to filmmaker Frank Schaffer. He created propaganda videos for the church. *Whatever Happened to the Human Race?* featured creepy scenes of three people in white writing on the wall, a person in a sea of dead baby dolls, a manufacturing factory where baby dolls are thrown away, and a laboratory where there is a real baby in a cage.[5]

Schaeffer's imagery still reverberates through our political discourse today. As misleading as it was, the goal was never to stop abortion. "We got middle class, white America and lower, middle class America, working class America to vote against their own economic interests by getting them very pissed off on a whole series of social issues that leaders in Washington never actually wanted to do anything about," said Schaeffer. "But they manipulated them."[5]

Religious leaders conning their flock to gain political power is nothing new. Getting used by one with such a fluid view on the very issue they staked out was. Needing a politician whom they could ride, the right-wing religious leaders turned to a governor with the most permissive stand on abortion. Without flinching, they gave him their support, further cementing a marriage of convenience that had little to do with being pro-life. Rather, it was about being pro-power. One group used the other, each convinced they would come out on top.

In 1967, six months after becoming governor, Ronald Reagan signed a law that liberalized abortion restrictions. The California Therapeutic Abortion Act liberalized abortion laws, making California the third state in the country to do so.[6] Before such laws were passed, having an abortion was a crime. Thanks to Ronald Reagan, it no longer was in California. This was six years before *Roe v. Wade*.

Of course, Ronald Reagan would claim to regret this decision. He would have regretted it even more if the religious right actually had principles. Instead, they got into bed together and unleashed the Kraken of religious intolerance and rage—one that Republicans and the religious right continue to feed and exacerbate to this day. Ironically, they picked an issue to polarize the country that isn't in the Bible. Since abortion is never mentioned in the Good Book, the devil must be onto something. Maybe, as he said in his interview, if there were more pro-life Christians instead of pro-fetus Christians, Hell would be a lot less crowded.

But he's busy for a reason. The reason Christians are willing to break with Jesus so easily is perplexing. Reagan had them at "hello." He had support from two-thirds of white evangelical voters. These so-called "family values" Republicans ignored the fact Reagan was twice-married, alienated from his children, and almost never attended church.[7] Since when did multiple marriages and not going to church make you a good Christian?

Especially when Jimmy Carter was already in the White House. When the evangelicals rejected Jimmy Carter, they were rejecting an actual Jesus-loving evangelical. I would say a *fellow*

Jesus-loving evangelical, but it's hard to love Jesus when you sell your soul for money and power. This is why it didn't bother the Christian community when Nancy Reagan hired an astrologer to protect Ronnie after his assassination attempt. Why pray to a God you can't see when you can worship a pseudoscience that studies the movements and relative positions of celestial objects?

Since Reagan was a Republican, all was forgiven. Christianity's rules only apply to those Christians want to judge. It's for windows, not mirrors. All of this makes them vulnerable to being conned. The con is best summed up by Pennsylvania Republican Representative Tim Murphy. Rather, I should say ex-Representative Tim Murphy. He resigned after having an extramarital affair. Not because of the affair, mind you. But because he *thought* the sex he had outside his marriage resulted in an out-of-wedlock pregnancy. As a staunch supporter of anti-abortion legislation, you may be thinking he resigned so he could welcome a new life into the world.

If you did, you'd be mistaken. No, Tim Murphy is an ex-Representative because he wanted his mistress to have an abortion. Reporting from *The Pittsburgh Post-Gazette* revealed text messages from his mistress confirming he asked her to abort their unborn child. When she pressed him on the hypocrisy of having one position in public and another in private, he might as well have been speaking for the Republican Party. Murphy claimed those weren't his views. He said his staff was responsible for the anti-abortion posts and rhetoric, claiming not only that he hadn't written them, but that he winced when he read them.[8]

Now, Republican "evangelical" voters don't even pretend to care about such things. Family values is nothing more than an empty slogan. If there were ever a time when Christians needed to unite in opposition to a politician's candidacy, it would have been against Donald Trump. Instead, they helped propel him into the White House. If Donald Trump had been there for Jesus' crucifixion, there is no doubt he would have proclaimed there were "very good people" on both sides of his execution. As the devil said in his interview, "Donald's my kind of people. He's like the son I never had."

God has Jesus; Satan has Donald. For a group of people always looking to label someone as the Antichrist, it's worth asking. Do Christians know what that means? Being the Antichrist means doing the opposite of what Christ would do. When President Obama passed healthcare reform, he wasn't doing the opposite of what Jesus would do. If anything, he didn't do enough. Jesus would have passed Medicare for all, not subsidies for some.

Which brings us to the cross in the room. How is it possible to determine what the Antichrist is? Perhaps we should look to the Catechism. Ever since Adam and Eve did their thing in the Garden of Eden, we have been trying to categorize and evaluate sin. Luckily, we don't have to look far. Conveniently, it's been spelled out for us. They are the seven deadly sins.

"Deadly" not only because of the virtues they oppose but because of the other vices they breed. It is safe to say they are the embodiment of what a Christian should not be. They also happen to be the personification of the individual too many Christians worship.

Speaking of worshipping false gods, it's important to point out another warning.

Biblical prophecy warns us what will happen before the end times. There will appear a mysterious figure called the Antichrist, also known as the "man of sin" and the "false prophet." His presence will bring the second coming of Christ. Let's see how the right's messiah, Donald Trump, stacks up against the seven deadly sins. Maybe the false prophet is already among us. Certainly, the man of sin is.

Pride

Only the most prideful are incapable of seeking forgiveness, for they believe they have nothing to be forgiven for. Donald Trump famously said he has never asked God for forgiveness. Seeking God's forgiveness on a daily basis is inextricably linked with being a Christian. Having an insatiable need to put your name on every building in sight is not.

Greed

Greed is the byproduct of the love of money. It's derived from the love of self. Selfishness manifests itself as self-love in its extreme. All driven by the ego. Consumed by love of self, the ego has room for no other. As such, E.G.O. stands for Edging God Out. According to Donald Trump, he had this to say about his relationship with money. "My whole life I've been greedy, greedy, greedy. I've grabbed all the money I could get. I'm so greedy." So greedy, in fact, he routinely declared bankruptcy as a way of getting more money without working for it. When he wasn't bankrupt, he wouldn't pay his bills.

One such instance was when his Chicago skyscraper ran into trouble. According to reporting from *The New York Times*, Trump handled it the Trumpian way. He defaulted on his loans, sued his lender, and got its debt forgiven—nearly $287 million worth. All while avoiding paying taxes. As Psalms 37:21 makes clear: "The wicked borrow and do not repay, but the righteous give generously." Since Donald has never been accused of giving generously, he gets extra credit for the second deadly sin.

Lust

Is it surprising the self-proclaimed "pussy-grabber" would have a lascivious heart? Is there a more lustful act than sleeping with a porn star four months after the birth of your son? Since this extramarital dalliance with Stormy Daniels was sandwiched in the middle of his ten-month affair with Karen McDougal, was Donald cheating on Melania or Karen? Even God couldn't have predicted this.

Envy

Envy is a feeling of discontented or resentful longing aroused by someone else's possessions, qualities, or luck. Is there anyone more discontented or resentful than Donald Trump? Handed everything in life, the fake billionaire can never accumulate enough possessions to convince himself he is self-made. So, he keeps trying to convince us. Forever envious of his father, Donald has a reverse

Oedipus complex. He doesn't want to kill his father so he can sleep with his mother. He wants to *be* his father so he can sleep with his daughter. Try as he might, he never seems to measure up. Not even Ivanka can fill the void envy creates.

Gluttony

Gluttony is habitual greed or excess in eating. To witness gluttony, one only needs to watch Donald Trump eat. A typical Trumpian order at McDonald's is two Big Macs, two Filet-o-Fish sandwiches, and a large chocolate shake, consisting of 2,430 calories—all in one meal.[9] He has overconsumed for so long, it is rumored his Secret Service code name is "Jabba the Trump," or JATT; aka Stay Puft the Marshmallow Man.

Wrath

Extreme anger is Donald Trump's default setting. He only seems to smile when he's around Russians. His vitriol isn't limited to just his never-ending campaign rallies. While he relishes instigating wrath in others, he prefers it when it can be up close and personal. Wrath like his knows no bounds. When Donald felt betrayed by his dead brother's son, he heartlessly took revenge on his nephew's sick child. Looking to punish him, Donald cut off health insurance coverage for his nephew's sick infant.[10] Devoid of compassion even for the innocent, Donald's thirst for vengeance is unquenchable.

Sloth

Trump's allergy to work or any type of physical exertion has been well-documented. Tales of his spending his days in a bathrobe hate-tweeting while watching television is nothing new. Until now, we didn't know the depths of his sloth. Axios news gained access to almost three months of Trump's schedules after they were leaked (reportedly by somebody in the White House). "Trump has spent around 60 percent of his scheduled time over the past three months in unstructured 'Executive Time.' He spends his mornings in the residence, watching TV, reading the papers, and responding to what he sees and reads by phoning aides, members of Congress, friends, administration officials and informal advisers," six people with direct knowledge of his schedule told Axios. Trump's first meeting of the day is usually around 11 or 11:30 a.m."[11] According to Trump's biographer, Tony Schwartz, Trump's main job seemed to be looking at fabric swatches, all while his company bled money.[12] He must be the lazy immigrant he keeps warning us about. Without a doubt, when the Trumps send their people, they're not sending their best.

Imagine how God must feel about all this. He goes to the trouble of putting a list of the seven things no one should do and all of these Christians—in name only—go out and vote for the guy that is the poster child for all of them. Maybe God should have been more specific. I wonder if it would be more obvious if He had laid things out in more detail. What if God had said this instead?

A real Christian doesn't mock the disabled. A real Christian doesn't commit sexual assault and brag about it. A real Christian doesn't covet his daughter. A real Christian seeks forgiveness. A real

Christian doesn't worship mammon. A real Christian doesn't lie breathlessly. A real Christian doesn't put children in cages and lose track of their parents' whereabouts. And most important of all, a real Christian doesn't vote for someone who does.

God would also probably want to refresh everyone's memory on John 8:44. "When he lies, he speaks his native language, for he is a liar and the father of lies." Of course, if the devil is the father of lies, then Donald Trump is the son. There hasn't been a more dishonest person in politics. He lies as he breathes: effortlessly and endlessly. A single sentence may contain a truth, a half-truth, a lie, and a contradiction. All of these Donald Trump has forgotten as soon as he moves on to the next lie.

"According to the Fact Checker database, Trump has made 7,645 'false or misleading claims' since taking office. In the month of October, he said 1,200 things that were false or misleading. There's some days where he's topped more than 100 false or misleading claims."[13] Bush may have broken the debt clock, but Trump obliterated the lie-o-meter. If you don't believe me, it's in 2 Corinthians.

Instead of quoting 2 Corinthians, Trump could have quoted Dianetics and it wouldn't have mattered. He's just another Republican using the religious right to win elections. It's been happening for decades. Republicans co-opted religion, and both pretend to walk the moral high ground while stuck in the sewer. They want to win at any and all costs. Ultimately, they want to gain power to neuter the government. They want to neuter the government because of their greatest fear. If the government works, people will want more of it.

When that happens, there's less of something they worship more than God, and that's money. Without mammonism, Corporate Stockholm Syndrome wouldn't be possible. Since the New Deal, Republicans have been trying to reverse engineer anything positive the government does. They worship at the altar of mammon. Tax cuts for the wealthy, deregulation for corporations, and slashing benefits for the poor are all done in the pursuit of more money.

But no one can worship two gods. According to Matthew 6:24, "No man can serve two masters: for either he will hate the one, and love the other; or else he will hold to the one, and despise the other. Ye cannot serve God and mammon." Mammonists are not Christians. Too many Christians are Republicans first and Christians second. Being tricked into being something you're not is no excuse. If there was one thing Jesus was not, it was a mammonist or a hypocrite.

God became man so man could become God. Yet there is nothing more human than the worship of money. In his book *Escape from Evil*, Ernest Becker states, "The early promise of Christianity was to bring about once and for all the social justice that the ancient world was crying for; Christianity never fulfilled this promise, and is as far away from it today as ever."[14] For too many on the right, their biggest concern is putting *Christ* in *Christmas*. Let's start by putting *Christ* back into *Christian*.

Men never do evil so completely and cheerfully as when they do it from a religious conviction.

—Blaise Pascal

Chapter 8: Slavery

Bloodied, battered, and bruised, America won its independence from the oppressive British regime in 1783. Over the months of June and July of 1776, the Second Continental Congress drafted a statement of independence from the Kingdom of Great Britain, with whom they had been at war since 1775. Prior to the meeting at the Pennsylvania State House in Philadelphia, America was a coalition of 13 colonies. After the ratification of the Declaration of Independence on July 4, 1776, a new nation was formed—the United States of America.

Declaring itself a nation, these new United States went on to defeat Britain and truly gain their independence. But it was not yet a true nation. It was not until June 21, 1788 that America developed the organizing principles behind which it would be governed. In doing so, the Constitution was born. It is the quintessential

American document. And being quintessentially American, it was soon up for revision.

But rather than revise the Constitution, additions were proposed. On September 25, 1789, the Bill of Rights was introduced. These amendments to the U.S. Constitution were not ratified until December 15, 1791. The formal adoption of the Bill of Rights gave the U.S. its first ten amendments to the Constitution. The purpose of these amendments was to add specific guarantees of personal freedoms and rights to the Constitution. Ironically, one of the most contentious of these amendments did just the opposite. Of course, beauty is in the eye of the beholder, and whether your rights were infringed upon rested heavily on which side of the sundial you were born.

Despite being a "nation," the United States was far from united and still was mainly a loose coalition of states. Our first president was not elected until February 4, 1789. George Washington was the unanimously elected first president of our fragile country over a decade after we declared our independence— independence for some, that is. Part of our freedom included the desire to suppress the freedom of others. This desire was the genesis of the Second Amendment to the U.S. Constitution.

Holding someone against their will poses a problem. What if one day they decide to break free from that hold? That possibility is the reason we have the Second Amendment to the Constitution. It protects the rights of slaveholders. One of the consequences of owning people is they don't want to be owned. Slaves wanted to be free and often revolted and fought for that freedom—just like the patriots that fought for American independence. Conversely, the Second Amendment enshrined the rights of states to quell such rebellions, to fight against another people's freedom. Its intention was to preserve the slave patrol militias in the southern states. These slave patrols were regulated by the state. That's why the Second Amendment deals with states' rights instead of applying to the newly formed country as a whole. The Second Amendment clearly states:

A well-regulated Militia, being necessary to the security of a free State, the right of the people to keep and bear Arms, shall not be infringed.

State-regulated slave militias were essential to the preservation of slavery. In southern states, laws were passed often requiring plantation owners to serve in the militia. This was not a suggestion. Georgia serves as a prime example of this. Laws were passed as early as 1755 that required plantation owners to be members of the Georgia Militia and to make monthly inspections of slave quarters in the state.[1] Of course, part and parcel of being a member of such conscripted service was the carrying of arms. Should there be a slave revolt or uprising, there was no better means to quash it than with the end of a musket.

The key to the Second Amendment was enshrining to the states as a right the ability to regulate—i.e., compel and dictate. Arming such militias was necessary so they could prevent slave uprisings before they occurred or end them violently once they started. With the new—yet unratified—Constitution proposing that

Congress have purview over the military under a unified government, slave-owning states feared this was a Northern Trojan horse. Relinquishing the authority to arm themselves was a pathway they did not wish to travel. Southerners felt the North would end slavery by ending the mechanism for keeping it in place: i.e., armed, state-regulated slave militias.

At the ratifying convention in Virginia in 1788, Patrick Henry made this known. "If the country be invaded, a state may go to war, but cannot suppress [slave] insurrections [under this new Constitution]. If there should happen an insurrection of slaves, the country cannot be said to be invaded. They cannot, therefore, suppress it without the interposition of Congress.... Congress, and Congress only [under this new Constitution], can call forth the militia."[1]

Clearly, Patrick Henry viewed the militia as something to be called up by the states themselves. It was never mentioned that individuals should be armed for this purpose. No one advocated for an ad hoc slave monitoring system built from disparate individuals all responsible for their property. Lest we forget, the main impetus behind all this was the southerners' insistence that their property not be confiscated from them—i.e., freed. Slavery at its heart is an issue over property rights—as distasteful as that may be.

That is why there were slave militias that were state run. The armed collective was to ensure that slavery persisted. Nowhere in the Second Amendment does it state individuals have the right to bear arms. The term "people" was explicit, as it connotes the people necessary to form a militia. There were no one-person militias in the antebellum South and therefore no reason to convey to the individual the right to bear arms. The right to bear arms was only granted in the context of the states' rights to compel armed service in the defense of slavery and to uphold the property rights of slave owners. The term "regulated" was added so the state could dictate how such service was to be carried out. With the intent and verbiage so clear, why is the Second Amendment so misinterpreted?

Historically, it hadn't been. For most of U.S. history, the meaning of the Second Amendment was exactly what it said: the right of the people of each state to maintain a well-regulated militia. Essentially, it is today's National Guard, which is state sponsored, as opposed to our military, which is government run. In case you're wondering if the founding fathers didn't know the difference between state and federal, the Tenth Amendment should clear up any confusion. The Tenth Amendment states:

The powers not delegated to the United States by the Constitution, nor prohibited by it the States, are reserved to the States respectively, or to the people.

Clearly, the authors of the Bill of Rights knew the difference between federal and state rights. They wanted to enshrine this right to the states. With their intent so clear, why is there so much obfuscation? To answer that question, look no further than to Ronald Reagan. Sitting presidents addressing the NRA had been taboo, until Ronald Reagan normalized it. When he spoke at the NRA's 112th gathering in May 1983, he promised to "never disarm any American who seeks to protect his or her family from fear and harm." In other words, he promised a right that was not found in our Constitution or Bill of Rights. But he kept his promise by ensuring the Supreme Court would become an arm of the NRA.

Before the Supreme Court majority became little more than Republicans in robes, beholden to the NRA and corporations, Republican-appointed justices cared about justice, precedent, and the Constitution. It was none other than Nixon-appointed Supreme Court Chief Justice Warren Burger who said after his retirement in 1991 that the Second Amendment "has been the subject of one of the greatest pieces of fraud—I repeat the word 'fraud'—on the American public by special interest groups that I have ever seen in my lifetime."[2]

And that was before the Heller decision. As it would turn out, he hadn't seen anything yet. That's because another fraud perpetrated on America was by a new breed of Supreme Court justice: those claiming to be originalists. An originalist believes a document like the Constitution should be interpreted by either what was meant by those who drafted and ratified it or what reasonable persons living at the time of its adoption would have understood the ordinary meaning of the text to be.

Regardless of which definition you abide by, the intent and understating of the Second Amendment was the same: to allow the state to have an armed militia and to conscript the people of the state to serve in said militia. Furthermore, the necessity for such a well-regulated militia was directly related to slavery and the need for slave patrols. That was the intent and surely the general consensus, or understanding, of all the slave owners at the time. Congruently, it was the original intent and what a reasonable person would believe at the time.

Unfortunately, reason and Reagan don't mix. He ushered in a new breed of Supreme Court Justices more interested in ideological purity and arming Americans than constitutional intent. The original intent of the Second Amendment was itself amended—by none other than Reagan-appointed Supreme Court Justice Antonin Scalia. He was one of the founding members of the originalist school of thought—which, in retrospect, was a school formed with the intent of circumventing the actual Constitution. This was in order to install a right-wing version inconsistent with our founders' *actual* intent.

Without a hint of irony, in 2008, Scalia wrote the majority Supreme Court decision in *District of Columbia et al. v. Heller*. Scalia interpreted the Second Amendment to mean something its founders did not. His decision gave rights for an individual to possess a firearm unconnected with service in a militia, including self-defense within the home. Never mentioning individuals and clearly delineating bearing arms as part of a "well-regulated militia," the Second Amendment's text was conveniently disregarded by Scalia. All with a straight face.

In doing so, not only was the intent of the Second Amendment overturned, so were hundreds of years of precedent. Never before was the Second Amendment interpreted in a fashion contrary to the founders' intent. In fact, in 1939 in *U.S. v. Miller*, the court ruled that since the possession or use of a "shotgun having a barrel of less than eighteen inches in length" had no reasonable relationship to the "preservation or efficiency of a well-regulated militia," the court could not find that the Second Amendment guaranteed "the right to keep and bear such an instrument."[2]

The fallacy of being an originalist has never been more apparent than in the *Heller* case. Unless Antonin Scalia thought so little of our founding fathers that he assumed they couldn't form complete sentences, his argument is faulty at best. Rather than justify his decision based on the Second Amendment, he should have used Reagan's speech as the basis for his decision. Scalia's "individual's right to possess a firearm ... for traditionally lawful purposes, such as self-defense within the home" sounds a lot like Reagan's promise to "never disarm any American who seeks to protect his or her family from fear and harm."

Unless the fear and harm they are frightened by is a direct result of their slaves escaping, it is not in the Second Amendment. That was by design. By constructing the Second Amendment as they did, the founders were conveying their intent. One sentence conveys one meaning, each presupposing the existence of the other to form an interconnected whole. If there was one thing the founders knew how to do, it was to write a sentence with specific intent. Of the 55 framers of the Constitution, 32 were lawyers.

Even if you were able to twist their words into an individual's right to bear arms, you would have to concede it was a right that was to be regulated by the states. In other words, states could restrict or expand such a right as it sees fit. As an originalist, you would also have to concede that this right pertained to what was considered an arm at the time. To the founders, an automatic weapon was a pre-loaded musket. If a shortened shotgun had no reasonable relationship to the "preservation or efficiency of a well-regulated militia," how does an AR-15?

It doesn't, but it didn't matter. By 2008, all of the Republican-appointed justices that comprised the 5-4 majority in the *Heller* case were bought and paid for by the NRA. Just like the Republicans who appointed them. When Antonin Scalia delivered his decision, he must have based it on the original intent of the gun lobby. Since the NRA is one of the founding fathers of today's GOP (along with ALEC, lobbyists, the Koch brothers, etc.), it's the only rationale that makes sense. Because the NRA's original intent is to get a gun in every home and scare the shit out of as many people as possible in the process, that must be the basis for his decision.

Or it could be much simpler. Perhaps it was just a way to justify making his ideology law—ideology rather than law being the driving force behind the Republican Supreme Court's decisions. This is an ideology that has upended our legal system. By ignoring precedent—a cornerstone of our democracy—these five Justices also discarded a fundamental facet of how American law operates.

Without precedent, our laws become opaque. Precedent forms the foundation on which other laws are formed. They are the building blocks of our legal system. Ignoring them implies legal decisions have no basis or standing. The doctrine of *stare decisis* means that prior decisions should be maintained—even if the current court would otherwise rule differently. It also states lower courts must abide by the prior decisions of higher courts. Instead of using prior cases and legal reasoning to reach a conclusion, Republican justices would rather reach a conclusion and create legal reasons to justify it—undermining our legal foundation.

The concept behind *stare decisis* is the belief that government needs to be relatively stable and predictable. Overturning precedent upends both and destabilizes the judiciary *and* society. Valuing ideology over law, the right-wing activists on the Supreme Court disregard precedent when it contradicts their ideology. They use their lifetime appointments to bend the law so it conforms to their worldview—a worldview devoid of the constructs that made America a country our forefathers fought to form and protect.

Part of this is an artifact from our past that should have died long ago—another relic from the days when people owned people is the Electoral College. The Electoral College is as antiquated as the Second Amendment. Just as there is no need for well-regulated and armed slave militias, there is no need to have an electoral system predicated on counting blacks as part human. That was the genesis behind the Three-Fifths Compromise that led to the formation of the Electoral College.

Slavery elected Donald Trump in 2016. While James Comey and Vladimir Putin had a hand in installing him in the White House, their influence would not have been enough for him to win an election he lost by 3,000,000 votes. At least not without the Electoral College. It is one of the most undemocratic parts of our supposed democracy. In actuality, we are the only major "democratic" nation that does not elect its president based on the supposition that the person with the most votes wins.

This anomaly is a direct result of our slaveholding past. It is the stain that continues to tarnish our nation. Sadistically, slavery was responsible for putting the most overtly racist person into the White House. Sadly, so many of the African American voices that could have stopped it were silenced. Stifled by this outdated relic of slavery. Our forefathers saw to that, as did their forebearers.

Slavery's repercussions are still being felt. Without slavery, there wouldn't have been the Three-Fifths Compromise. Without the Three-Fifths Compromise, there would be no Electoral College. Without the Electoral College, there would be no Donald Trump. The racist-in-chief would not be anywhere near the White House. The White House is aptly named, especially considering how he got there. With his sole mission erasing the legacy of our first and only black president, slavery will not die.

When it comes to slavery, compromise seems to be an oxymoron. If you're a slave, everything is compromised. If you're a slave owner, nothing is. But in a new nation comprised of free states and slave states, legislative representation depended on whether slaves were counted as people. The stakes were high. Counting slaves as people would dilute the voting power of the predominately free Northern states, while negating their population would adversely affect the slave-owning Southern states. Hence the need for a compromise.

Unlike today's winner-take-all Republicans in Congress who view compromise as un-American, in 1787 our forefathers knew it was an essential part of the fabric of our country. Only compromise could hold our fragile democracy together. Born out of the desire for country to triumph over party was the Three-Fifths Compromise. Considering the diametrically opposed viewpoints of slaveholding versus non-slaveholding states, a compromise was the only path forward.

The Three-Fifths Compromise determined how slaves would be counted when determining a state's total population. This population number was used to calculate the number of seats each state would have in the United States House of Representatives. The "compromise" part of this solution was to count slaves and freed blacks in the slave states as three-fifths of a white person. According to George C. Edwards III, the Winant Professor of American Government at Oxford University, "A direct election for president did not sit well with most delegates from the slave states, which had large populations but far fewer eligible voters."[3]

They gravitated toward the Electoral College as a compromise because it was based on *total* population. This compromise gave Southern states a disproportionate representation in the House of Representatives and undue influence over presidential elections—the latter of which remains with us to this day.

Even the abolition of slavery was not enough to abolish this slave relic. Proposed on January 31, 1865 and ratified on December 6, 1865, the 13th Amendment abolished slavery in the United States. The amendment states that: "Neither slavery nor involuntary servitude, except as a punishment for crime whereof the party shall have been duly convicted, shall exist within the United States, or any place subject to their jurisdiction."

Despite this amendment, the Electoral College was allowed to persist. With it lives the remnants of slavery. To this day, the Electoral College serves as a reminder of America's slaveholding past and continues to undermine our democracy. The idea of one person, one vote will never be realized until we finally break the chains of slavery.

But not everyone wants those shackles removed. In fact, the legacy of slavery lives on. Mitch McConnell, the Republican Senate Majority Leader from Kentucky, must have been channeling his inner plantation owner when he looked to the Three-Fifths Compromise and decided our first black president would only be allowed three-fifths of his constitutionally appointed powers. When Mitch McConnell prevented President Barack Obama from executing his powers as president, it was as though the 806,787 predominantly white Kentuckian votes he received outweighed their black counterparts.

Perhaps Mitch thought President Obama was three-fifths of a person and should therefore be three-fifths of a president as well. By not allowing President Obama's Supreme Court nominee Merrick Garland to receive a hearing, he usurped the powers of the president. In doing so, he suppressed the will of the people and silenced the voices of 65,915,795 Americans. Millions of black votes became null and void. If Supreme Court Justice Clarence Thomas considered his appointment hearing to be a "modern-day lynching," how could he sit silently by as his Republican counterpart performed a modern-day castration?

Because first and foremost, Clarence Thomas is a Republican. Regardless of skin color, slavery will not die and Republicans will keep trying to suppress black voices and black votes. Voter suppression is a key component of the Republican Party's quest for power at all costs. Until recently, there were safeguards against taking away the minority's right to vote. "The Voting Rights Act of 1965, signed into law by President Lyndon B. Johnson, aimed to overcome legal barriers at the state and local levels that prevented African Americans from exercising their right to vote as guaranteed under the 15th Amendment to the U.S. Constitution."[4]

Despite the passage of the 15th Amendment, legal barriers were erected at the state and local levels preventing African Americans from exercising their right to vote. As described on History.com, "Blacks attempting to vote often were told by election officials that they had gotten the date, time or polling place wrong, that they possessed insufficient literacy skills or that they had filled out an application incorrectly. Blacks, whose population suffered a high rate of illiteracy due to centuries of oppression and poverty, often would be forced to take literacy tests, which they sometimes failed."[4]

"President Johnson also told Congress that voting officials, primarily in Southern states, had been known to force black voters to 'recite the entire Constitution or explain the most complex provisions of state laws,' a task most white voters would have been hard-pressed to accomplish. In some cases, even blacks with college degrees were turned away from the polls."[4] The Voting Rights Act righted this wrong, making it illegal to suppress minority voting rights. Southern states' disfranchisement of African Americans' constitutional right to vote was the impetus behind the Voting Rights Act. It was the law of the land—until America became a post-racial country.

According to the five Republicans on the Supreme Court, America had in 2013 conquered racism. Using the election of Barack Obama as a cynical pretext for dismantling the very protections that African Americans needed under the Act, all five Republican justices struck down key parts of the Voting Rights Act. Ironically, without the Voting Rights Act, we may not have had our first black president. The fact that minorities *were not* disenfranchised helped propel Barack Obama to the presidency. Had there not been voting protections in place, large swaths of African American voters would have been prevented from exercising their right to vote.

Thanks to *Shelby County v. Holder*, these protections have been dealt a crippling blow. Prior to this ruling, states with a history of racial discrimination could not make changes affecting the ability of citizens to vote without prior consent. This was in addition to a nationwide prohibition against literacy tests. According to the Department of Justice's History of Federal Voting Rights Laws, "The Act contained special enforcement provisions targeted at those areas of the country where Congress believed the potential for discrimination to be the greatest. Under Section 5, jurisdictions covered by these special provisions could not implement any change affecting voting until the Attorney General or the United States

District Court for the District of Columbia determined that the change did not have a discriminatory purpose and would not have a discriminatory effect."[5]

While Section 5 of the Voting Rights Act constitutionality was maintained, it was effectively neutered. This was because Chief Justice Roberts, writing for the 5-4 Republican majority, ruled Section 4 unconstitutional. Without Section 4, Section 5 becomes essentially irrelevant. Section 4 provided the formula for determining which states violated voting rights. Absent a way to determine which states were disenfranchising voters based on race, it is nearly impossible to make them get pre-clearance for changes to voting.

This is exactly the outcome Republicans had hoped for. Immediately afterward, states with a history of voter suppression began to pass laws legalizing voter suppression. Freed from the confines of the protections afforded by the Voting Rights Act, they began implementing voter ID laws—cutting voting hours, purging voter rolls, or ending same-day registration. The objective was to disenfranchise low-income voters, young people, and minorities.

The intention was to sway elections. The years 2016 and 2018 are prime examples of how this has already eroded our democracy. According to the Pew Research Center, "In 2016, the black voter turnout rate declined for the first time in 20 years in a presidential election, falling to 59.6% in 2016 after reaching a record-high 66.6% in 2012."[6] This drop translated into nearly two million fewer African Americans votes being cast in the 2016 election than in 2012.[7] Even with Hillary winning by three million votes, she needed an extra 79,316 to win. Thanks to the racist Electoral College, Hillary lost an election she won. Thanks to racist Republicans who want to keep blacks as three-fifths of a person, the two million votes they suppressed would have swung the election.

Faults and all, a five-million-vote-win total should have been enough. While Hillary may have been a flawed candidate, she wasn't *that* flawed. Even without Barack Obama galvanizing the ticket, a 20-year low in voter turnout among African Americans in a year of record turnout is not a coincidence. It is due in large part to Republican efforts at voter suppression. As stated by former chairman James Greer of Florida's Republican Party when asked about the GOP's concern over voter fraud, which is the basis of their voter ID laws, Greer said, "They never came in to see me and tell me we had a fraud issue. It's all a marketing ploy."[8]

Ask Stacey Abrams how it feels to be on the receiving end of such an un-American tactic. In November of 2018, Stacey Abrams, a female, black Democratic gubernatorial candidate in Georgia went to cast her vote—presumably for herself. When she arrived at her polling place, a poll worker claimed she had already filed for an absentee ballot.[8] While she was able to rectify the mistake, how many voters didn't or couldn't? Not all black voters are running for governor.

Maybe they need to be. In Georgia alone, Stacey Abrams watched as 500,000 people were purged from the voting rolls in 2017 and an additional 700,000 in 2018.[9] The purge was overseen by Secretary of State Brian Kemp—who happened to be her Republican opponent. Considering she lost by only 54,723 votes, it's safe to say

Brian Kemp stole the election. Had he not disenfranchised 1.2 million voters, she would be governor of Georgia.

With very few voters left to purge, a funny thing happened in Georgia in 2020. Joe Biden turned the state blue—with a huge assist from Stacey Abrams. In 2018, she founded Fair Fight Action, an organization to address voter suppression. She's been working to make sure African American voices are heard—creating another bit of irony. Thanks to Abrams trying to restore democracy to Georgia, neither Republican Senate candidate got over 50% of the vote. Consequently, Georgia has to have a runoff for both of their Senate seats in January. What did both Republicans do? They accused the Republican Secretary of State of allowing too many people to vote and demanded he resign.

As did their fellow Republicans. Georgia Secretary of State Brad Raffensperger told *The Washington Post* that he has come under increasing pressure in recent days from fellow Republicans, including Sen. Lindsey O. Graham (S.C.), to find a way to toss legally cast ballots. Refusing to do so, he also informed *The Washington Post* that he and his wife have received death threats. One was a text message that read: "You better not botch this recount. Your life depends on it."

Such is democracy under Republican rule. Republicans want to keep as much of slavery alive as they can. Voter suppression and voter ID laws are nothing more than a thinly veiled attempt to keep blacks as three-fifths of a person. It strips away their constitutional rights under the guise that it protects election integrity. While

Republicans claim there is widespread voter fraud, they can't seem to find any.

Other than Republican fraud, that is. The only in-person cases of voter fraud in 2016 on record were for Donald Trump. Vann R. Newkirk II, reporting for *The Atlantic*, wrote, "A woman in Iowa, Terri Lynn Rote, voted twice. Rote decided to try to vote twice in Des Moines and got caught. She voted for Trump. A man in Texas, Phillip Cook, was arrested on Election Day after voting twice. He claimed to be an employee of Trump's campaign who was testing the security of the electoral system. He wasn't an employee of the campaign—and the polling location's security worked perfectly well, it seems. Finally, Audrey Cook, a Republican election judge in Illinois, cast a ballot on behalf of her dead husband."[10]

It seems that if voter fraud is a problem, it's a Republican one. Conversely, voter suppression is a solution looking for a problem. Even these egregious examples do not refute the fact that voter fraud is almost nonexistent. Study after study proves this truism. In fact, a study of the 12-year period between 2000 and 2012 found exactly ten cases of voter impersonation out of 146 million registered voters and two thousand cases of total election fraud.[11] That is .0000001%, which is not only statistically insignificant, it essentially rounds to zero. Compare that with the numbers of those disenfranchised and you'll see where the *real* problem lies.

Pennsylvania alone has 758,000 voters lacking the proper identification needed to vote.[12] Again, this is by design. Pennsylvania State House Majority Leader Mike Turzai (R) bragged about it being one of his accomplishments before the 2012 elections, convinced that implementing voter ID laws would allow Governor Romney to win the state. He didn't bother mentioning election integrity because that would be an oxymoron. Undermining rather than bolstering the integrity of our electoral process was his goal.

While 2012 didn't turn out as he planned, time was not on democracy's side. Republican-controlled states enacted the kind of voter suppression laws that cost Hillary the election. Wisconsin is a textbook example of the GOP playbook when it comes to the reason Republicans suppress voting rights. Even the thought of disenfranchisement had Republicans in Wisconsin rabid. Former government officials testified that behind closed doors, Republicans pushing for the voter ID laws were "politically frothing at the mouth" over the prospect that it would make it more difficult for people to cast ballots for Democrats.

Being one of the infected, Wisconsin's (then) Republican Governor Scott Walker signed a voter ID law in 2011 that was so restrictive, a federal court held that the law unconstitutionally burdened low-income people of color. But that didn't stop the Republican Supreme Court from trampling minority rights and allowing the law to go into effect for the 2016 election. Considering up to 300,000 people didn't have the intentionally discriminatory ID to cast a ballot, they were stripped of their constitutional rights to vote. With the 2016 presential election decided by 30,000 votes in Wisconsin, you can also consider that decisive.

It's decisively undemocratic—which happens to be the goal. Republicans are not interested in electoral integrity; they are only concerned with winning at all costs and by any means necessary.

Each time Republicans eliminate same-day voter registration or cut early voting or bar voters from casting a ballot outside their home precincts or scrap straight-ticket voting or get rid of programs to pre-register high school students, they are attempting to take away voting rights. As Newt Gingrich intimated, it's because they can't win any other way.

Speaking of which, can you imagine anywhere else this system would be allowed to exist? From the time we are young, we're taught the winner wins, the loser loses. Get the most points, get the trophy. Not—get fewer points but somehow win based on some archaic formula involving slavery and adjusted populations.

Think about what would happen if sports were run this way. Imagine the Super Bowl with New England playing North Carolina. Before the game, the referees come out and announce some rule changes based on the adjusted slave population from 1787. After behind-the-scenes calculations and accounting for black residents being counted as three-fifths of a person, the following will be implemented. New England would get two downs every time they had the ball. In order to get a first down, they would need 35 yards. They would receive no timeouts and no challenges. North Carolina, on the other hand, would only need to gain three yards for a first down. They would get six downs to do so, also receiving six timeouts per half and eight challenges.

Let's say, despite the overwhelming odds against winning, New England manages to be down by five points in the fourth quarter. There's five seconds left and they're at the Carolina six-yard line. Time for one last play. The ball is hiked; Cam Newton drops back and hits Julian Edelman in the back corner of the end zone for a touchdown.

But wait. The referees called him out of bounds. Game over? Not so fast. Even though New England can't challenge the play—since all their challenges were taken away because of slavery—there is hope. One rule still exists in their favor. Any score with under two minutes remaining in the game automatically goes to the replay booth for review.

With the replay being shown on TV, it's obvious Julian Edelman was in bounds. Both toes were dragging across the green grass safely away from the out-of-bounds marker. Then, former official and current NFL rules analyst Mike Pereira declared, "He was in bounds. It's obvious. This play will be overturned. New England wins."

New England sees the jumbotron too. They've started celebrating. It's not official yet, though. The play is still being reviewed. Watching the referees huddle on the field, it's obvious the decision has been made. The head referee trots to midfield to make the announcement. "The Supreme Review Court, which has five members from North Carolina and four from New England, have made a 5-4 ruling. The review of the play on the field has been stopped. The play stands. North Carolina wins."

That's the Republican Super Bowl. If Republicans were interested at all in the right to vote, they would be expanding access and availability to voting, not curtailing it. Non-existent voter fraud is the propaganda they use the maintain the roots of slavery. They use it to perpetuate a lie that allows them to steal elections they are not capable of winning. Malfeasance often hides under the cover of feigned integrity.

It's what fascists do. By possessing the former, they con the public into believing they stand for the latter. That's why the only voter fraud is coming from the Republican Party. As long as we allow it to persist, their cult will only grow stronger and more emboldened. Lacking substance, chicanery is the only way for the cult to survive.

And they know it.

Chapter 9: Her Majesty

Dog whistles inevitably turn into bullhorns. For years, the Republican Party has used dog whistles to rile up their base. They're very convenient. It's easy to put them in your pocket when you don't need them. That way, you can claim you're not racist when you say and do racist things. Bullhorns are harder to hide and much harder to ignore, which makes it more difficult to hide behind being a "compassionate conservative."

That was a nice cover story considering Republicans' long history with racism—a history that goes back to the 1960s. That was when the South was lost. According to legend, after he signed the 1964 Civil Rights Act, Democratic President Lyndon B. Johnson told an aide, "We have lost the South for a generation." Signing the Voting Rights Act a year later probably required amending that statement by another generation or two. President Johnson knew Republicans would use racism to their advantage, especially because it would divide the country.

Republican opposition to "big government" was always a metaphor for opposition to the 1964 Civil Rights Act and the 1965 Voting Rights Act. Fostering and inflaming that government hatred was something Ronald Reagan would turn into an art form. He used race as a means to an end. Richard Nixon, on the other hand, was more interested in inflaming racial resentments. That was the key to his "Southern Strategy."

Piggybacking off the recent civil rights victory was an equally uncivil resistance to it. Those were the voters Nixon courted. The Southern Strategy was a race-based appeal to white voters. Nixon used racial animus to garner white votes in the 1968 and 1972 presidential elections. Knowing they couldn't run an overtly racist campaign, they ran on "law and order" and "states' rights," both of which translated into anti-civil rights. That was the beginning of dog-whistle politics.

A dog whistle is used to train dogs. These whistles emit a sound in the ultrasonic range, which people cannot hear. But dogs can. The same goes for racists. The Southern Strategy was predicated on the fact certain people (white racists) would hear the true meaning of what Republicans were saying while the rest of the population wouldn't. They understood every word—being well-trained *and* obedient.

And it was all without being held accountable. Dog whistles also provided plausible deniability. "I'm not racist, I'm just for states' rights!" *wink-wink*, says the politician as he feigns injury from such an outlandish accusation. This is the dance. Republicans say and do racist things, then pretend to get offended when they're called racist. Wash, rinse, repeat. Since this has been going on for decades, we should let one of the architects of Nixon's Southern Strategy explain what Republicans were trying to accomplish.

In a 1981 interview, Lee Atwater famously explained the maturation of Republicans' racist appeal:

You start out in 1954 by saying, "[N-word], [N-word], [N-word]." By 1968 you can't say "[N-word]"—that hurts you, backfires. So you say stuff like, uh, forced busing, states' rights, and all that stuff, and you're getting so abstract. Now, you're talking about cutting taxes, and all these things you're talking about are totally economic things and a byproduct of them is, blacks get hurt worse than whites... "We want to cut this," is much more abstract than even the busing thing, uh, and a hell of a lot more abstract than "[N-word], [N-word]."[1]

Essentially, the Southern Strategy was a way to racialize and radicalize the economic policies of the Republican Party. By tying welfare with black and brown people, it became a way to politicize the safety net as well. It was a twofer, using race *and* welfare to divide the country—which is what two professors from Princeton found out. Tali Mendelberg and Martin Gilens have studied how terms like "welfare" influence people's political opinions. "They have discovered that the use of the term 'welfare' leads to a priming of white racial bias. In other words, the mere use of 'welfare,' and presumably also 'food stamps,' as well as some other expressions referencing social spending programs, primes racial bias against Blacks."[1]

And no one knew how to prime racial animus more than Ronald Reagan. You can say his 1976 attempt to gain the GOP nomination—against sitting Republican president Gerald Ford—was a dry run. That's when Reagan unveiled the mythical "welfare queen" in his speeches.

If this sounds familiar, it should. It has been GOP orthodoxy for decades. Welfare is little more than an entitlement program for the unentitled—the unentitled being people of color. To justify how wasteful welfare is, Reagan insisted recipients were buying T-bone steaks with food stamps. Living the life of Riley in housing projects with 11-foot ceilings and a swimming pool. All this was unsubstantiated, of course.

Unsubstantiated but effective. Reagan was priming the white racial bias he would need to get elected. It was his warm-up for the main act: the welfare queen. Infamously, Reagan told the story of a woman from Chicago (of course) who used 80 names, 30 addresses, and had 15 telephone numbers.[2] All this was done to collect food stamps, Social Security, and veterans' benefits for four nonexistent deceased veteran husbands, as well as welfare.

Then he explained how well she was living off of white taxpayers. Reagan claimed, "Her tax-free cash income alone has been running at $150,000 a year."[2] From that moment forward, she was known as the welfare queen. Not just any queen, but a black one. Just using the term "queen" for a black woman connotes theft since most Americans think of queens in the Elizabethan (white) sense. Gillian Brockell writes in *The Washington Post*, "The term was designed to conjure racist stereotypes of a single black mother living large on the taxpayers' largesse, collecting government checks while bedecked in diamonds and driving a Cadillac."[2]

The problem was, she wasn't black. Even knowing that, it's hard not to close your eyes and envision Reagan's black welfare queen. This was what Reagan wanted: an indelible image of a black woman stealing white people's money. In reality, Reagan's welfare queen was based on a real-life person. Her name was Linda Taylor. "Born Martha Miller, she was listed as white in the 1930 Census, just like everyone else in her family. But she had darker skin and darker hair,"[3] Gene Demby points out on NPR.com.

The problem wasn't just that she *wasn't black*. When it came to welfare, whites were just as likely to receive benefits as blacks. "There was never a point at which blacks accounted for a majority of recipients. The typical AFDC (Aid to Families with Dependent Children) recipient, even in Reagan's day, was white."[4]

But had Reagan talked about the "trailer king" in lieu of the welfare queen, it wouldn't have fit his narrative. Describing Billy Bob stumbling out of a welfare trailer wouldn't have gotten whites to resent welfare. Telling West Virginians that "you can take the trash out of the trailer, but you can't take the trailer out of the trash" wasn't going to get him many votes. Building a coalition against welfare and people of color would. Doing so required white voters to resent handouts to "those people." Explaining how welfare benefitted all people regardless of color wasn't something that interested him. Facts rarely did.

Besides, Reagan didn't want to point out the obvious. Government handouts don't know race. Black and white alike lean on government for support. By making welfare a black issue, Republicans could work to dismantle it—even though, and especially because, they were hurting the very same white voters who relied on it. Hence the Republican paradox. Hurting people with your economic policies and getting them to vote for you anyway.

This issue circles back to slavery. The South still hasn't gotten over the fact something was taken from them: real wealth. Freeing slaves and ending slavery erased some $4 billion from slaveholder's fortunes.[5] They haven't forgotten. That's why linking welfare or any other government program to blacks is so effective at ginning up opposition to it. In the Southerner's mind, the government is once again taking *their* money and handing it over to *them*. They already feel like they've paid reparations.

Exacerbating this tension was something Reagan encouraged and fed on. For Reagan, mixing racism with politics was an ongoing affair. According to Matthew Yglesias of *The Atlantic*, "Reagan opposed the Civil Rights Act of 1964, opposed the Voting Rights Act of 1965 (calling it 'humiliating to the South'), and ran for governor of California in 1966 promising to wipe the Fair Housing Act off the books. 'If an individual wants to discriminate against Negroes or others in selling or renting his house,' he said, 'he has a right to do so.'"[6]

That's what he said in public. It should come as no surprise that when he thought no one was listening Reagan felt free to say how he really felt. Unfortunately for Reagan, he felt a little too comfortable with the wrong person—a fellow racist with a penchant for taping conversations. During one such conversation with Richard Nixon, Reagan let loose his inner white supremacist. Frustrated over African Nations helping China get recognition with the United Nations, he said "To see those, those monkeys from those African countries—damn them, they're still uncomfortable wearing shoes!"[7]

Of course, if Reagan were alive today, I'm certain he would have said something about defending states' rights. Rather than admit being racist, he would have fallen back on typical GOP talking points. Today, calling African countries "shitholes" and declaring white nationalists "good people" doesn't count as racist in the Republican Party. This is why I'm nostalgic for the days when Nixon was running the GOP.

Having the Republican Party be more like Nixon would be refreshing. With today's GOP, you get all of Nixon's racism and corruption without the environmental protections or the ability to balance a checkbook. Nixon may have been racist and corrupt, but at least he had basic math and environmental skills.

Dealing with corrupt racists while facing bankruptcy and environmental Armageddon is nearly impossible. When Nixon proposed an economic budget in 1971 with an $11.6 billion deficit, it wasn't to give tax cuts to the wealthy. The gap was to get the country out of a recession. The economy had stalled, and Nixon was following basic Keynesian economic principles to get the economy moving again. John Maynard Keynes, a British economist, was one of the most influential economists of the twentieth century. Keynes advocated for increasing government spending to battle recessions. In other words, Keynes knew that when consumer spending fell in a recession, government spending needed to take its place. Unlike today's GOP, Nixon knew Keynes was right.

Unfortunately, today's Republicans have taken all of the bad and none of the good from the Nixon years. In the process, they've dismissed things like basic facts, science, and knowledge. Perhaps Trump can honor this dichotomy with his next campaign slogan (in 2024), maybe with one that is a little more honest. Let's say "Trump—all the racism of Nixon with none of the brains." It may not fit on a hat, but with a winning message like that, he just might get elected for real next time. At least he wouldn't be accused of dishonesty for once.

Then again, honesty and Donald Trump mix as well as churches and Donald Trump. One inevitable will burst into flames— and it isn't the flame retardant one who catches fire. In fact, he seems to bathe in truth repellent—not unlike his party. Republicans want you to believe that somehow welfare is the root of America's economic problems. Reagan famously started a war on the poor when his administration began slashing the budget for those most in need. Heartlessly, he went after the most vulnerable: low-income pregnant women and children. After his cuts, Women, Infants, and Children (WIC) could only serve a third of those eligible for help.[8]

WIC assists low-income pregnant women and children up to age 5 who are found to be at nutritional risk. In other words, poor mothers and their children who don't have enough to eat. WIC helps by providing nutritious foods to supplement their diets. Considering how critical diet is in cognitive health, especially in a child's formative years, his ruthlessness practically guaranteed that the two-thirds of eligible children left out the program would be little more than future wards of the state.

The state is not much interested in caring for them, as evidenced by his cuts to Medicaid and food stamps. This has become a GOP staple. Not wanting to let his cruelty only affect the most innocent, Reagan heaved his budget-cutting axe across a wide swath of programs. Working his way up the age bracket, Reagan did his best to take away from those with the least. A million kids lost reduced-price school lunches, 600,000 people were kicked off Medicaid, and a million lost food stamps.[8]

All in the name of tax cuts for the wealthy. That's where Republican fealty and fiscal responsibility start and end. Spending to help the poor is irresponsible. Deficits to help the rich laudable. Give more to those who have. Take away from those who don't. Somehow, it's justified under the guise of morality. Those that don't have don't deserve to have.

Deserve is a funny thing though. Who deserves what depends on whose hand is out. Never has this been clearer than with Medicaid. Under President Obama, Medicaid was expanded to help cover the working poor. The working poor make too much money to qualify for Medicaid and not enough to qualify for healthcare subsidies. Medicaid expansion was designed to close that coverage gap and encourage the working poor to keep working. This was a bridge too far for the GOP.

After the Affordable Care Act was passed into law, Republicans immediately sued to have the democratically passed legislation overturned. Their reasoning was that the mandate was unconstitutional. Rather than declaring the Act null and void, Supreme Court Chief Justice Roberts said that Congress has the right to tax its citizens. Roberts viewed the mandate as a tax for not buying insurance and that it is therefore constitutional. In his words, "The Affordable Care Act's requirement that certain individuals pay a financial penalty for not obtaining health insurance may reasonably be characterized as a tax. Because the Constitution permits such a tax, it is not our role to forbid it, or to pass upon its wisdom or fairness." The four other Republican justices disagreed, wanting to take-down the ACA.

While the law was upheld, he and the other Republicans on the Supreme Court damaged its impact. Medicaid expansion, which had been mandatory at the state level, was now voluntary. Not surprisingly, most Republican-controlled states decided to refuse government money to help their own citizens. In the name of...? It couldn't be cost. Twenty-two states didn't expand Medicaid eligibility after Obamacare was passed and their healthcare costs to the poor soared, rising twice as fast as states that extended benefits to more low-income residents.[9]

Was it cruelty, then? As the GOP fiscal façade crumbles, all that's left is animus for those in need. Disdain for the losers in life who've been dealt all the wrong cards in a perpetual game of Pond Scum. A game that plays out across lifetimes. Perhaps it's not the game, but the ability *to* game.

When it comes to Medicaid, it's not the poor who are gaming the system—it's the wealthy. One of the quirks of Medicare is that nursing home care and assisted living are not provided for. Anyone needing such care will come to realize it is expensive and asset depleting. Paying for your own medical care is expensive. What can someone who would rather leave his assets to his children than pay his own way possibly do to preserve his wealth?

Turn to the government for a handout—what else? Medicaid, which pays for nursing home care and assisted living, is only for the indigent. In 2019, an individual could only earn $2,313 a month and have assets not exceeding $2,000 to qualify. In other words, it's for the poor. Which is why there is a cottage industry of attorneys and other professionals that help families qualify for a government handout so they can avoid paying their own way. It's euphemistically referred to as "Medicaid planning."

Planning is a key component. Not everyone plans, and that could be a problem. Medicaid has a look-back period. It turns out a lot of wealthy people who found themselves needing long-term care were looking for a way to get someone else to pay for it. That someone else is you and me. By giving away their fortune, they could qualify for Medicaid. The taxpayer paid their bills and their family received an inheritance.

Never intended to be a wealth replacement vehicle, Medicaid was forced to make some changes in the way it determined eligibility. Enter the look-back period. Now, Medicaid looks back five years (except in California where it is 30 months) to determine whether a Medicaid applicant is truly indigent. Assets given away during the look-back period could undermine or delay eligibility for free nursing home care.

Of course, it's only free because taxpayers are paying for it. And not planning ahead can be expensive. Sometimes things like dementia creep up on someone. Initially, when a loved one begins to deteriorate cognitively, the reaction is for the spouse to care for them. Until they can't. Without advance planning, who will pay? For creative types, there is still a way to force you and me to pay *their* expenses.

Not long after the 2016 election, I was at a party and couldn't help but overhear someone talking about just that type of situation. His mother-in-law had Alzheimer's and it progressed to the point where she needed nursing home care. Since his in-laws had resources, but they were "modest," he quickly found out that no one was going to help foot the bill. I then heard him brag about how he helped his in-laws hide money in a safety deposit box so his mother-in-law could qualify for Medicaid. Apparently, he had experience in this area since this is how he helped them qualify for subsidized housing in a 55 plus community. Courtesy of the taxpayer.

I'm not sure what shocked me more, bragging about a felony or being a Trump supporter. When I heard him announce he voted for Trump because "at least he might cut my taxes," the circle was complete. If you're not going to hold yourself to a moral standard, why would morality matter in whom you vote for? Cut my taxes while I steal from the government programs that my lowered taxes won't be high enough to support.

Typical Republican morality. Vote for someone you think will reduce your taxes so they can take money away from the program you're stealing from. By denigrating welfare receipts as "welfare queens" and tying welfare to race, it's easy to see how this can play out. Stealing from the government turns into "getting mine before they get theirs." Besides, when the government is also the enemy, is it really stealing? If the objective is to avoid paying your fair share, then no.

This was why the T.E.A. Party was formed. Not in 2009 as an antitax protest, but back in 2002. After Bush broke the debt clock, being taxed enough already became an oxymoron. It's impossible to have been taxed enough already when you've run up over a ten-trillion-dollar national debt. In fact, the only movement that should have started was the W.A.T.H. Party. As in why aren't taxes higher? Or the "who's going to pay the credit card bill" movement?

The T.E.A. Party was created because of the fear some had about having to pay their fair share. It wasn't a grassroots uprising, but rather a well-thought-out billionaire insurgency. It was the brainchild of wealthy industrialists whose objective was to avoid taxes and regulations. Groups tied to the tobacco industry and the billionaire Koch brothers founded the T.E.A. Party in 2002.[10] It was nearly a decade before it assailed our country.

For the Koch brothers, there was a reason to wait. Since their fortune rests on fossil fuels, they've been able to amass billions of dollars by avoiding paying their taxes and their expenses. That's what drives their anti-tax and anti-regulatory zeal: greed. They are mammonists through and through, which is why they got into bed with the tobacco company. The Kochs hired many of the same anti-science operatives who defended cigarette companies in order to avoid paying for the looming climate disaster caused by their products.[10]

And the climate in which they did it couldn't have been better. With an anti-tax, pro-pollution president in the White House in 2002, what would have been the point of launching an anti-tax "grassroots" movement? It would have been redundant. The first thing W. did was squander the Clinton surpluses with tax cuts for the wealthy. Anyone earning over $1 million saw their tax bill go down by over $100,000 on average.

Seven years later, things were different. By then, the deficit and national debt had exploded and the country was teetering on the brink of a second Great Depression. Even better, a black man was elected president. What better way to exacerbate the nation's racial wounds than to pin the mess the white guy made on our first black president? *Now* the T.E.A. Party could be launched. With Bush bankrupting the country, the only thing able to save the economy from a depression was an infusion of government cash. It was the perfect time for the billionaire-funded T.E.A. Party to make its debut.

With our first black president writing the checks, the racial animus ginned itself up. Lost in it all was the fact that George Bush was responsible for The Emergency Economic Stabilization Act of 2008, which created the $700 billion Troubled Asset Relief Program. The purpose of the fund was to purchase the toxic assets from banks that created the economic disaster to begin with. While $700 billion sounds like a lot, it's quite quaint. It is estimated that the total cost of the government bailout is as much as $29 trillion.[11]

Now that would be something to protest. Instead, we got a billionaire-backed fake grassroots movement that the media couldn't get enough of. Railing against taxes and deficits did the Kochs' bidding, all while making it seem like the average taxpayer had had enough. Where is the T.E.A Party now when there are trillion-dollar annual deficits that are only projected to accelerate? Nowhere to be found. The Kochs got their tax cut and the polluter-in-chief is ensuring they don't pay a penny for the damage their products do to the environment.

By the time that bill comes due, it will be too late—unless we form a real movement. Not a Why Aren't Taxes Higher? movement. We're beyond that. We need a Why Aren't *Their* Taxes Higher!? movement. The prospect that enough Americans would come to that realization is the reason the Kochs formed the T.E.A. Party to begin with. Its genesis was to prevent a real grassroots movement from forming. It's hard to have a real tax conversation when a bunch of racists are dressing up as teapots and holding muskets.

That was the point all along. Feigning outrage at deficits obscures the fact the wealthy are the real welfare queens. Who got bailed out again? It wasn't homeless Joe living out of a shopping cart. Or the average underwater homeowner. Besides, what kind of queen lives on $200 a month? That's the amount a single person can receive from welfare, with an average family of four pulling in a whopping $900 monthly.[12] Not quite enough to build a castle.

But $29 trillion? That can buy a lot of yachts. It's Pond Scum playing out right in front of us. Like in Pond Scum, the plutocrats take all our best cards. Then they use those cards to consolidate power. With that power, they are able to rig the game so that all of the money flows to an ever-smaller group of people. Not the one-percenters, but rather the point-centers. It's the .01 or .001% that make the game unwinnable for the rest of us.

Take the Koch brothers, for example. Their nearly $100 billion net worth primarily comes from fossil fuels. In order to increase profits, they lobby to get regulations dismantled. They're trying to avoid paying for the pollution and environmental damage associated with their products. By enlisting the same anti-science operatives who defended cigarette companies to spread the lie that global warming is not real (just like how cigarettes didn't cause cancer), they're attempting to shirk their liability for the devolving climate—the one we are seeing deteriorate before our very eyes. Somebody's going to have to pay and try to save the planet, and it won't be them. They've found a way to transfer their current and future expenses onto the rest of us.

It's all to further their own well-being. Basic economics states that reducing expenses increases profits. Crapitalism as practiced by people like the Kochs states that having someone else pay your expenses will have the same effect. But these welfare queens aren't just satisfied with us paying their expenses. No, they also want to be subsidized for the privilege. In Pond Scum, they take our best cards. In crapitalism, they take our money.

In accounting, there are two ledgers when computing a profit or loss: the income ledger and the expense ledger. Not satisfied to get a handout on just the expense side of things, we're also subsidizing the income ledger. Whereas expenses that are borne by someone else become phantom expenses and aren't accounted for, subsidies show up. For the fossil fuel industry, this is to the tune of some $20 billion a year.[13]

In other words, we're giving some of the most profitable companies handouts so they can use that money to continue denying the calamity their products create. All while not paying their fair share of the tax burden. One of the defining characteristics of crapitalism is expense and tax avoidance. It's one of the easiest ways to maximize profits. Since capitalism morphed into crapitalism, the prevailing wisdom is that a company's only responsibility is to shareholders. Not all of its stakeholders, mind you, just the ones who own stock. As you can see from the following chart, those with the most pay the least.

These are the 30 most profitable companies that paid no federal income taxes in 2018. In many cases, the companies also received tax rebates that could be used to reduce their tax burdens in other years.[14]

None of them paid taxes on profits in the billions. In fact, Amazon's profit exceeded $10 billion. Not only did they not pay any taxes, they received a rebate.

Her Majesty

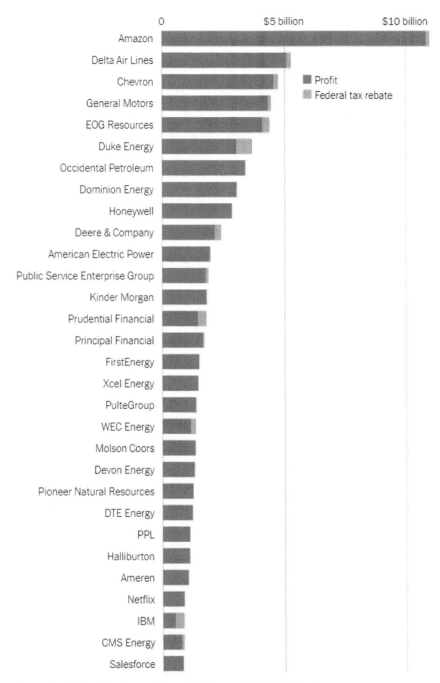

	0	$5 billion	$10 billion

Amazon
Delta Air Lines
Chevron
General Motors
EOG Resources
Duke Energy
Occidental Petroleum
Dominion Energy
Honeywell
Deere & Company
American Electric Power
Public Service Enterprise Group
Kinder Morgan
Prudential Financial
Principal Financial
FirstEnergy
Xcel Energy
PulteGroup
WEC Energy
Molson Coors
Devon Energy
Pioneer Natural Resources
DTE Energy
PPL
Halliburton
Ameren
Netflix
IBM
CMS Energy
Salesforce

■ Profit
▨ Federal tax rebate

Source: Institute on Taxation and Economic Policy · By Scott Reinhard

Quickly glancing at the list, over half of the most profitable companies not paying taxes are energy companies. Why are we subsidizing them again? It's not as though they aren't earning a profit. To the contrary, these companies made the list because they are both enormously profitable and aren't paying any taxes. Can you imagine earning over $10 billion and getting a tax rebate?

Talk about welfare queens. Not even grateful welfare queens. Corporations have taken their handouts, tax cuts, and subsidies and done the opposite of what is good for the economy. Being beholden only to their shareholders, they have given this windfall back to stockholders in the form of dividends and buybacks. The only things trickling down are stock dividends into the goblets of the point-centers.

Investing in new plants, equipment, and employees would create a virtuous cycle—a self-reinforcing cycle that would increase economic output. Increased economic output leads to higher wages. These higher wages lead to increased demand for products. Higher product demand allows companies to charge higher prices. Higher prices lead to inflation. Inflation leads the Fed to increase interest rates so that the economy doesn't overheat—which also helps savers and retirees who rely on fixed-income investments.

Instead, the opposite has happened. Besides leading to lower economic output, gusher-up economics leads to lower interest rates. Paradoxically, this leads to even more borrowing and buybacks. Prior to Reagan's election, lower interest rates encouraged companies to borrow in order to invest in their business. This started the virtuous economic cycle listed above. Companies borrowed to improve their companies. Now, they borrow to improve the lives of their shareholders.

In the past, there was an understanding. Taxes are public assets. So are subsidies. Lowering taxes and giving out subsidies takes public assets and makes them private. In return, private companies are supposed to turn around and invest those assets to benefit the public. Same thing with lower interest rates. The Fed lowers interest rates—which hurts savers, i.e., the public—to encourage companies to borrow and invest. In a way, the Fed is transferring money from public to private hands.

Increased borrowing used to lead to increased investing, benefiting the overall economy. Our stagnating economy reflects how those ties have broken. They weakened in the 80s and 90s as companies focused on increasing returns to shareholders.[15] Now it's their sole focus. It also shows the hypocrisy of trickle-down economics. With subsidies, tax cuts, and near-zero interest rates, the economy should be flying at warp speed. Instead, it's mired in mediocrity. Nothing can trickle when the spigot is upside down.

Thus, the unvirtuous cycle persists. The only thing tax cuts grow is our deficit, which we are responsible for. The investment boom never materialized. Instead, tax cuts led to record stock buybacks. In 2019, the prior year's record is expected to be eclipsed with $1 trillion in buybacks. This leads to increasing wealth concentration, high inequality, and low investment.[15] As if all these handouts weren't enough, these companies get to write off the interest on the money they borrow. They keep taking and we keep giving.

To the point-centers, that is. Our entire system seems designed for wealth concentration. Progressive taxation is a myth. For the first time, the 400 wealthiest Americans last year paid a lower tax rate than any other group.[16] This regressive trend has been on the rise since Reagan's election in 1980. Starting it may have been the reason he got into politics to begin with. Reagan ran for president because he didn't want to pay taxes. Meaning it should come as no surprise who one of the biggest beneficiaries of his tax cut were: Ronald Reagan.

Margaret O'Mara of *The New York Times* points out, "When Ronald Reagan released his 1982 taxes, they revealed not only that this great advocate of voluntary giving had made rather paltry charitable donations himself, but that he had shaved over $90,000 off his tax bill thanks to economic legislation he signed after becoming president in 1980."[17] Trump was even worse. *The New York Times* reported Trump paid no taxes in 11 of the 18 years between 2000 and 2017. Then, in his welfare queen impression, he paid only $750 both in 2016 and 2017. Recent decades have seen the incomes of the top one percent, the top 0.1 percent, and the top 0.01 percent roughly doubled, tripled, and quadrupled.[18] Yet somehow their taxes have fallen.

No trend has been in the average worker's favor since Reagan took office. Since 1978, CEO compensation has grown 940% while the average worker saw a 12% increase in pay.[19] This is despite surging worker productivity. Between 1973 and 2014, American workers' productivity grew more than 72 percent.[20] Six times their increase in wages. In other words, the more productive we are, the less we get paid. The only thing increasing is wealth inequality. Just like in Pond Scum, getting better cards doesn't mean you can keep them.

Allowing anything to trickle down is the last thing on the plutocrat's mind. The share of national income going to business profits is at its highest level since World War II while total worker compensation is at its lowest level since the 1940s.[21] With the gig economy, things can only get worse. Part of the rationale behind guns for hire is that they cost less. Gig or contract workers don't get benefits—nor do they receive worker protections. Without having to pay either, profits increase at the expense of the working man. That's why Uber is fighting so hard to be able to classify their drivers as contract workers.

As if these obstacles weren't enough, there's more. On the off chance the point-centers might owe taxes, paying is pretty much optional thanks to the nearly non-existent chance of an audit. This is the one thing the working poor have in common with the wealthy. Because it's easier and cheaper to audit the poor, the wealthiest 1% and the working poor are audited at about the same rate.[22] Once again, thanks to the Republican Party.

Wealthier taxpayers have more complex returns. Auditing them requires experienced auditors and an extensive amount of time. This requires manpower and resources, both of which Republicans have savaged. Republicans have slashed the IRS's enforcement budget to the bone—leaving barely enough meat for agents to do their jobs. By design. Since 2011, they have cut the IRS budget to the point where it is (adjusted for inflation) a quarter lower than it was in 2010.[22]

Not for cost savings, mind you. If the IRS were an investment, it would have hedge fund-like returns. The Treasury could have collected $34.3 billion more in tax revenue with an additional $13.7 billion in resources. [23] Another way of saying this is that your investment would have returned 150%. Not bad for a bunch of bureaucrats. Unfortunately, Republicans are more interested in what's good for their donors and not for our country. What really scares them is the thought of the IRS doing its job and collecting the taxes we are owed.

Which brings us back to Lee Atwater. Using race to distract our country enables Republicans to enact policies that benefit the few at the expense of the many—under the guise that it hurts blacks more than whites. Distraction leads to disaster. While we've been looking away, they've been using the government as a siphon to transfer more and more assets to the wealthiest Americans. Starving the beast only to protect the protected. If we're not careful, soon they will have all the cards. Then we won't even be able to pretend we have a shot at winning the game.

We'll all be Pond Scum. Or welfare queens.

Chapter 10: Alpha of the Omega

Propaganda. Its uses are varied, but its intent is the same: convincing someone to believe something they shouldn't, then getting them to act on it. Throughout history, it has been a very useful tool. Especially in wartime.

Getting a human being to kill another human being willfully is not an easy thing to do. It goes against our nature. It's the reason the trauma of war is so stark and the reason our boys spend their lives battling PTSD. War is irrational. It goes against the very fabric of our being. It wounds our souls.

That's why propaganda is a necessary evil. When there are existential threats, propaganda is used to mollify and justify the unjustifiable. Creating and dehumanizing an enemy makes killing them easier. During World War II, we weren't fighting fellow human beings; we were battling "krauts" and "japs." Justifiably so, based on Hitler's atrocities and the horrors of Pearl Harbor.

While it may be a necessary tactic, it leaves a lasting legacy. It was forever seared in my father's memories. Being the proud son of immigrants, my father signed up to fight in World War II at age 17. At such a tender age, he needed his parents' permission to do so— which he got. He then found himself on a PT boat in the middle of the Pacific Ocean.

After the war, he learned what his last mission would have been had we not dropped the atomic bomb. Without the A-bomb, he and his crew had orders to go to the coast of Japan. Once off the coastline, their objective was to draw enemy fire. That would allow the larger battleships and destroyers to locate Japan's land artillery. Knowing the location of their artillery was critical. Taking out Japan's big guns would make it safe for a land invasion. Euphemistically, his mission could be called a sacrifice for the greater good. America's version of the kamikaze. In other words, a suicide mission.

Like most of my father's war experience, he rarely spoke of it. For the most part, the greatest generation kept things to themselves—other than a few light-hearted stories. Like the time my father was on a Pacific Island, turned a corner, and found himself face-to-face with a Japanese soldier. Both unarmed, they turned and ran. Or the time he was swimming about 100 yards from his PT boat when he looked back and saw his fellow sailors waving frantically to him.

When he looked behind where he was swimming, he saw fins. Even before *Jaws*, he knew what that meant. Morphing into Michael Phelps, he was in a life-or-death race to get back to his ship—which he did. Safely on board, he felt his lungs bursting with saltwater, his body wracked with fatigue. And nicotine. After prodigiously vomiting on the deck, he realized his fellow sailors were uproarious with laughter. The fins weren't shark; they were dolphin. His fellow sailors thought it would be funny to let him think otherwise.

It was war, after all, and anything that eased the mind—even for a moment—was a welcome distraction. Unfortunately, some things aren't so easily dismissed. I saw this firsthand years later. As the grip my father's Alzheimer's had on his brain tightened, it became increasingly difficult to know what was happening to him behind the scenes. What version of his life was he living at any given moment?

Then one day at lunch, he pounded his fists on the table. An anger overtook him and he yelled, "Those damn Japs!" He was back in the war, face-to-face with his enemy once again. For him, it was as if time had collapsed. The steady diet of dehumanization he was fed may have been compartmentalized, but it was never forgotten. Unable to keep it at bay, it was front and center once again. That's the power of propaganda 50 years later—unabated and unstoppable.

Perhaps for a noble cause, this can be forgiven. Fighting fascism during World War II would certainly come to mind when discussing righteous uses of propaganda. What happens, however, when the cause is less altruistic? When it's more means to an end? Using propaganda to justify atrocities rather than fight them—what then? Whitewash history, perhaps?

This is what happened with the founding of America. Literally and figuratively. Folklore would have us believe the New World was a vast, uninhabited world just waiting for us. The reality of the situation was far different. When the settlers came to America, it turns out it was already settled. The New World was actually old to the people living here. They were Native Americans, after all.

Justifying the stealing of native lands becoming more challenging. Without propaganda, that is. Suddenly, Native Americans were no longer peaceful hunters and gathers. They were savages. Wiping them out became necessary. From the moment our settlers arrived on their soil, it was preordained. The fact these indigenous tribes did not go quietly only reinforced the narrative, turning it into a self-fulfilling prophecy. Everything from infecting them with smallpox to driving them off their property was justified. We weren't stealing their land; we were relocating savages. Is there anything not okay to do to a *savage*?

I'd say yes, there's plenty. Starting with calling Americans "savages." Unfortunately, our history followed our founding. It's littered with instances of Americans being used to turn on their fellow Americans—a recurring theme of our brief history as a country. Settlers turned on Native Americans. The North turned on the South. Now we have Red turning on Blue. Or more accurately, turned.

There's disturbing rhetoric being championed on the right: talk of a Second Civil War. A war they've been arming themselves to fight for decades, full of anticipation and hope. While Republicans may be erstwhile for the 1860s, they need to take a closer look at 1980. That's when their coveted Second Civil War started. Another in a long line of Americans turning on their fellow American.

It was started by Ronald Reagan and perfected by Newt Gingrich. At the time, neither was able to call it what it truly was: a war on America. So, they called it something else: The Reagan Revolution—smelling just as sweet as a rose by another name. The other name was the start of the Second American Civil War. For that's what their self-professed revolution was and continues to be: a way to divide America until it breaks in half.

While Reagan may have laid the foundation for America's Second Civil War, Newt Gingrich made it possible. Reagan was a bit of a one-trick pony. He convinced people to hate government. Part of his schtick was to accuse anyone who wanted the government to do good of being a socialist. Don't get me wrong; his act has held the test of time. He's the Lenny Bruce of his day. The socialism thing still kills, and Republicans are still using it to pit us against each other. But Newt knew something Reagan didn't. You can't just hate government. You had to hate people.

That was the impetus behind the Gingrich Doctrine: to divide and conquer. Newt was very clear about his intentions. When he said, "One of the great problems we have in the Republican Party is that we don't encourage you to be nasty," he planned on using politics to divide our country. His memo, titled "Language: A Key

Mechanism of Control," implored Republicans to describe Democrats as: sick, pathetic, lie, anti-flag, traitors, radical, corrupt.[1] In other words, to dehumanize his enemies.

Newt's dilemma was that he needed his propaganda to infect the masses. It had to be broadcast so he could render his real problem null and void. That is, facts were the enemy of propaganda and Republican orthodoxy. If he could tackle his first problem, the second he could render moot. He knew with a big enough megaphone, propaganda could drown out even the most salient facts, making them irrelevant. Much like today. As a student of history, Newt was well aware of the power of propaganda. The problem was, he needed a delivery system much bigger than his big mouth.

Turning Americans against one another would not be as easy as turning his caucus. Propaganda is the most effective when it galvanizes one group against another. Then when it is called out for what it is, the cries fall on deaf ears. Without a legitimate platform of ideas, the GOP had no other option but to tear the country in two. Hence their dilemma and the reason for their decades-long assault on facts, reason, and science. Rather than alter the way they approached the world, they began to alter the world itself. Revisiting our economic numbers from earlier, it is obvious they could not subsist in a reality-based world. Facts are never the friend of the fascist.

Especially 64 years of facts. That was the time period professor Mark Watson and Alan Blinder, Ph.D., both of the Economics Department and Woodrow Wilson School of Public and

International Affairs at Princeton University, studied.[2] They went back to the beginning of the Truman presidency to discover a fact that is rarely talked about. Democrats are better for the economy and the stock market. The following data from their study underscores that in dramatic fashion.

GDP Average Growth Rates/Recession Quarters on Average by Party

	Democratic	Republican	Difference
GDP Growth Rate	4.33%	2.54%	1.79%
Quarters in Recession	1.14%	4.56%	-3.41%

Source: *American Economic Review*, April 2014, "Presidents and the U.S. Economy: An Econometric Exploration"

Stock Returns and Corporate Profits—Average Values by Party of President

	Democratic	Republican	Difference
Returns S&P 500 Index	8.35%	2.70%	5.65%
Corporate Profits share of gross domestic investment (GDI)	5.61%	4.71%	0.87%

Source: *American Economic Review*, April 2014, "Presidents and the U.S. Economy: An Econometric Exploration"

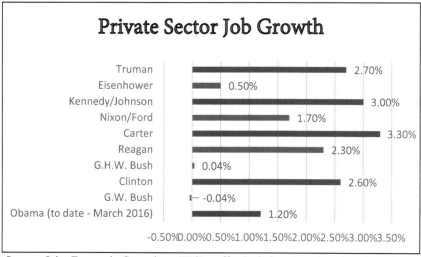

Source: Joint Economic Committee (JEC) staff calculations based on data from the Bureau of Economic Analysis, updated through May 2016 jobs report, released June 2016.

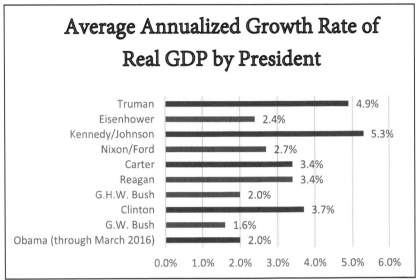

Average Annualized Growth Rate of Real GDP by President

Truman	4.9%
Eisenhower	2.4%
Kennedy/Johnson	5.3%
Nixon/Ford	2.7%
Carter	3.4%
Reagan	3.4%
G.H.W. Bush	2.0%
Clinton	3.7%
G.W. Bush	1.6%
Obama (through March 2016)	2.0%

Source: Joint Economic Committee (JEC) staff calculations based on data from the Bureau of Economic Analysis, updated through Q1 2016, second estimate, released May 2016.

Analyzing 64 years of economic data, two things become clear. The first is—no wonder Republicans don't want to talk about facts. How could they? The second is, they're horrible economic stewards—simultaneously wrecking the economy *and* underperforming in the stock market. All while being unable to perform the simple task of balancing a checkbook. Keeping in mind the fact that since Reagan, Republican presidents have been running up huge deficits without benefitting the economy or the stock market.

Speaking of which, shouldn't the wealthy be livid about such a huge economic disparity? Democrats are crushing it compared to their crimson brethren across the aisle. Which begs the question, why did Republicans choose red as the color to represent their party?

Was it because of all the deficits they run up? Or was it their inability to perform as well as Democrats? They're in the red for a reason. Maybe green would have been more appropriate. After all, with Democratic stock markets outperforming Republicans' by 5.65%, how could you not be green with envy?

Even hedge fund managers don't generate that level of outperformance (alpha)—let alone year in and year out. With increased stock returns of 5.65% a year, increased GDP growth of 1.79% a year, less time spent in recessions, and more jobs created, aren't we all better off with a Democrat in charge?

It depends on who "we" is. One thing to keep in mind when it comes to the economy and the stock market is Republicans only care to the extent they don't want to make things bad enough to lose elections. Knowing the economy and stock market underperform when they are in charge is irrelevant. Especially because they'll claim the opposite. But what they really care about are their donors—more precisely, what their donors care about.

Life for the point-centers isn't like life for you and me. Little things like GDP growth, recessions, and stock market returns are quaint to them. We worry about our jobs and 401(k) statements while they worry about the important things in life. Like maximizing the graft and corruption they feel their political contributions entitle them to. If they're going to hold all the best cards in Pond Scum, they might as well use them, shouldn't they? That's where the real money is. It's the gift crapitalism keeps on giving.

One such gift is one of the hallmarks of crapitalism. Having someone else, preferably the public, pay your expenses—all while

216

running an extremely profitable, taxpayer-subsidized company that pays little to no taxes. The apex predator of this handout is the fossil fuel industry. They notoriously avoid paying the costs of running their businesses. Air pollution kills people and makes them sick. Society bears these costs. Global warming will make the planet uninhabitable and racks up costs the fossil fuel industry has no intention of assuming. Paying their own way is antithetical to their business model.

This is all by necessity and by design. They're what Paul Krugman calls "zombie firms." Like zombie ideas (i.e., trickle-down economics), they will not die. Unlike ideas—which are harder to kill—zombie firms exist not in the mind but rather because of our actions. The biggest of these are huge infusions of cash into their businesses—which, according to the International Monetary Fund, equate to subsidies at more than $600 billion or roughly $3 million for each worker in the industry.[3] Wouldn't we be better off paying each worker a fraction of that giveaway? Then use the balance to try and save our planet? Especially considering the market value of their production was less than $300 billion in 2017?[3]

In other words, aren't we better off not giving an industry $600 billion so they can turn it into $300 billion? Before answering, it's important to calculate the total giveaway. The true cost we're giving to the fossil fuel industry dwarfs the $600 billion in direct subsidies they receive. To capture our cost accurately, we have to factor in not just direct subsidies but indirect ones as well. Indirect costs are expenses businesses do not bear directly. However, they are costs resulting from their business activity. In the case of the fossil fuel industry, these costs are enormous.

Taken together, they are roughly $5.2 trillion a year. According to the International Monetary Fund's recent working paper, "The vast majority of the IMF's subsidy tally comes from failing to price greenhouse gas emissions, a.k.a. 'post-tax subsidies.' In essence, the world's carbon polluters are dumping their waste into the atmosphere for free. About 87 percent of greenhouse gas emissions don't face any kind of carbon price at all."[4]

Another way of looking at this is: why are we giving an industry $600 billion a year so they can turn it into $300 billion? All while leaving us with a $4.6 trillion bill for the expenses they aren't paying? Wouldn't we better off with that $5.2 trillion? Again, it depends on your definition of "we." When "we" the taxpayers are paying for the "we" of the plutocrats, then the answer is no. They're better off when we give them $600 billion so they can turn it into $300 billion and leave us with a $4.6 trillion tab. Don't forget, their "we" is roughly 80, and our "we" is in the billions. Thinking about it from their perspective makes it completely reasonable for them to expect us to foot the bill to create their wealth.

What's not reasonable is that you rarely hear the media talk about this—until you find out why. It hearkens back to a time when reporting on the truth was not a partisan issue. Even reporters on the right were out to find a verifiable, objective set of facts to report to America. In 1967, the conservative columnist Irving Kristol wrote, "To keep his judgment out of a story is to guarantee that the truth will be emasculated."[5] In 1967, Kristol felt a journalist's job was to root out the truth—until he realized what that meant for conservatives.

Then Watergate happened. Once the media had done its job and uncovered the corruption in the Nixon presidency, he changed his tune. Apparently, Kristol's penchant for truth telling was short-lived. Conservatives no longer believed in a truth that would ferret out corruption, nor one that would contradict their worldview. Facts should present the world as they see it rather than as it actually is. By 1975, with Watergate in the rearview mirror, facts and journalistic integrity no longer held the same allure for those on the right. Kristol was insisting that "most journalists today … are 'liberals,' and the conservative attack on the press was off and running."[5]

It was off and running largely thanks to Ronald Reagan. Reagan's second war was launched against facts. Being notoriously inconvenient for Republicans, he sought to eliminate facts from the public discourse. This is something that had been a fear of the FCC since 1949. After watching propaganda spread into the hearts of minds of Nazi Germany, the danger that propaganda posed was unquestionable.

Preempting the same thing happening here, the Federal Communications Commission (FCC) created the Fairness Doctrine. This was the policy of the United States FCC starting in 1949. It required holders of broadcast licenses to present fair and balanced coverage of controversial issues that were in the public interest, including equal airtime to opposing points of view that were honest, equitable, and balanced.

Whenever a Republican complains about the media, this is their fear: being forced to present an honest counterpoint to their propaganda. They wanted a media ecosystem that was free to use government airwaves to be dishonest, inequitable, and unbalanced. Propaganda withers on the vine of truth. In order for Republicans to spread disinformation on the airwaves, the Fairness Doctrine needed to be done away with.

Having little regard for Supreme Court precedent, Republicans were unconcerned that the Court upheld its constitutionality. The Fairness Doctrine was in their crosshairs. On August 5, 1987, the FCC abolished the doctrine by a 4-0 vote. The commissioners were all Republican. Three were nominated by Ronald Reagan and one by Richard Nixon. With one major impediment removed, there was still a problem. Major newscasters and reporters were loath to spread propaganda. Back then, they viewed news as news, facts as facts.

Less than a decade after the Fairness Doctrine was dismantled, things were about to change. There happened to be a media tycoon whose business model fit perfectly with the Gingrich Doctrine. The timing of their mutual ascension was fortuitous. In 1995, Newt Gingrich became Speaker of the House of Representatives. A year earlier, an immigrant was planning the demise of the United States. He had his blueprint—one that succeeded in his native Australia and then Britain.

Formulaically, it was genius in its simplicity. Grab the attention of middle-class men by objectifying women. In England, that included topless models. In America, the blonder the better.

Once he had your undivided attention, Rupert Murdock could begin to use that attention to get what he was really after, convincing you to hurt yourself economically. Monetizing your fear and anger with the ultimate goal of enriching himself.

This is easier than it sounds. Propaganda spreads without the countervailing force of facts. Change the narrative from facts to feelings, and there is nothing standing in its way. Remember, no one was talking about the good economic ideas Adolph Hitler had in *Mein Kampf.* Hitler was evil and needed to be stopped. The conversation stopped before it started. Change the conversation and you can change reality.

Blair Levin, who was the chief of staff at the FCC, said "Fox's great insight wasn't necessarily that there was a great desire for a more conservative point of view. The genius was seeing that there's an attraction to fear-based, anger-based politics that has to do with class and race."[6] In his quest to turn fear and anger into profits, Murdock turned to the political operative Roger Ailes. Levin contends that Ailes's programming "confirmed all your worst instincts—Fox News' fundamental business model is driving fear."[6]

Fear leads to ignorance. It's rumored that prolonged exposure to Fox News causes the brain to atrophy, self-cannibalizing as a defense mechanism to an overwhelmed amygdala. It often results in a catatonic state called a Foxbotomy, rendering the critical neurons of the brain useless. Even after a prolonged Fox detox, the amygdala is so engorged, a fear-based relapse is almost a foregone conclusion.

Addiction to fear is a powerful opioid. In fact, it's even more addictive than opioids, because Fox isn't just making people afraid. They're telling them what to do with that fear. As an ex-Guantánamo guard Steve Wood put it, his political views were "whatever Fox News told us."[7] Which is why Republicans fought to do away with the Fairness Doctrine. They didn't want news that allowed people to think. They wanted to do the thinking for them.

This is why calling Fox "news" is a bit spurious. So was their "Fair and Balanced" canard. It's almost like Murdock was mocking the Fairness Doctrine with his laughable tagline. Unless there is a hidden meaning. Maybe "Fair and Balanced" is a condensed version of their real motto. "At Fox, we pledge that our propagandists will be *fair*-skinned without ever being fair. Fox will *balance* its opinion between the right and the far right. As for news, at Fox we are committed to never deliver 'news' that contradicts our worldview."

Now I see why they went with "Fair and Balanced." Because Fox is a propaganda machine whose sole mission is to poison the well of public discourse, it is even more critical that the real media do its job. Sadly, they haven't. Instead, they have become are an arm of the right-wing propaganda machine, spreading Republican myths and lies. Both through obfuscation and an obsession with false equivalencies. Social media has only made things worse.

If legacy media helped start the fire burning down our democracy, social media has added accelerant. Social media is nothing more than a digital version of Fox—beholden to little more than money. Meaning, they too, monetize (or at least profit from): fear, anger, propaganda, and division. All in the name of honoring the First Amendment. To clarify, the First Amendment gives individuals the right to freedom of speech free from *government* interference or regulation.

No one has First Amendment rights on *private* property. As a private company, Facebook can regulate or censor speech any way they want. The First Amendment doesn't mean you can send a batshit letter to the editor and force them to print it. You have the right to send it, but that's where your rights end. On the back end, they have the right to put it in the trash. The same goes for the online world. Ask anyone who's had a review taken down for violating the terms and conditions of the *private* company posting it.

Facebook knows this; they just hide behind the First Amendment because it offers them a shield from criticism. They use it as a prop, not for their love of country but rather for their love of money. Facebook knows what Fox and Blair Levine know. As Blair Levine said, "There's an attraction to fear-based, anger-based politics that has to do with class and race." The attraction is money. Right-wing propaganda and misinformation drives both their profit machines, which is why the dance between Republicans and Facebook is so laughable.

Their dance is a delicate one where neither side speaks the truth. When Republican politicians accuse social media companies of censorship, it's really a threat. The threat is that they'll take away Section 230. Section 230 is a provision of the 1996 Communications Decency Act. It says that companies that operate online forums cannot be considered the publisher of the posts other people put on their sites. Since they are not the publisher, they can't be held liable for the content of those posts, even if those posts break a law.

In essence, it is a liability shield—which is why Facebook and others have a catch-22 when it comes to dealing with congressional Republicans. Tearing down Section 230 (revoking their liability shield) would be equivalent to enacting a digital Fairness Doctrine. If they were liable for the content of the posts on their site, it would be devastating to Republicans. Their biggest fear is not being able to lie with impunity. Facing actual consequences for the damages caused by their product—and not being able to hide behind an amendment that doesn't apply to them—companies like Facebook would *have* to start censoring their content.

The bulk of that censorship would fall on the right. So, the dance continues. Republicans accuse Facebook and others of censorship, knowing they can censor whoever and whatever they want. But more importantly, they know that if they do, it will hurt their profits. Republicans threaten and bully because they know companies like Facebook value one thing above all others: money. It was the playbook they used with legacy media.

The right calls the mainstream media the "lamestream media," but not for the reason you might think. The right knows they have bullied the media into being their surrogates. Right-wing politicians and media talking heads have come to terms with the fact the best way to spread disinformation and propaganda is by bullying the mainstream media into doing their bidding.

It's the reason the media propagates the myth that Republicans are good for the economy. Surely, with any research, they would know what we do. With a Democrat as president, we had increased stock returns of 5.65% a year, increased GDP growth of 1.79% a year, and had less time spent in recessions. Yet the Republicans are the businessmen that should be running our country?

Economically, Republicans are more like Ricardo Montalbán than any real economist. Even Tattoo knows they can't add—or subtract. That's why they run up such huge deficits. Yet the media continues to portray Republicans as fiscally conservative, spreading their propaganda for them. Republicans spend money like drunken sailors on shore leave and the media talks about how fiscally disciplined they are.

They're constantly blowing their entire paycheck. Wondering who's going to pay for everything they put on the government credit card—which the media allows them to get away with. They call Democrats the party of tax and spend but never mention how Republicans are the party of spend and borrow. One party pays its bills; the other doesn't. If the media looked, they would find ample evidence to report the facts.

Starting with an inconvenient truth. The only president to have a fiscal surplus in the last 40 years was a Democrat: Bill Clinton. This was immediately turned into a deficit by George Bush, who then proceeded to wreck the economy. He left an unprecedented fiscal mess that President Obama cleaned up. Miraculously while lowering our budget deficits. And Republicans quickly undid this, saddling us with trillion-dollar annual deficits and an exploding national debt.

This is a debt Republicans ran up and are patiently waiting to pay. When they do, don't be surprised. They told us how they'd do it: with drastic cuts to our Social Security and Medicare benefits. Yet somehow, Republicans are continually portrayed as serious people with real economic ideas. In the face of all evidence to the contrary, the media perpetuates the myth of the fiscally responsible Republican. When they're not helping Republicans undermine what's good for our country, that is.

If there's one thing Republicans know how to do, it's to scare the shit out of people. If there's one thing the media knows, scaring the shit out of people is good for business. Just by adding "death" in front of something, the media starts frothing at the mouth. Scary propaganda turns newsworthy. Take a kernel of truth, mix in fearmongering, and it turns it into a delectable lie pie. One so delicious, the media can't help but gorge on it.

Take death taxes. There's no such thing. For 99.9% of us, when we die, there is no tax. We have a "no tax on death." How is that possible when the media loves to talk about the death tax? Because Republicans wanted them to. Only the very, very, very rich pay the estate tax. Republicans know getting everyone to believe there is a death tax was the best way to eliminate it. Not being able to eliminate it, it's now barely a point-center problem. Only individuals with more than $11.58 million pay any estate taxes. If an individual leaves his or her $11.58 million to their spouse, then there's no tax until the spouse dies. Even for the wealthy, no tax on death. Then the spouse can leave $23.16 million tax-free to their heirs.

It's safe to say paying a tax on over $23.16 million is a point point-center problem. It's not one for you or me. An even bigger point-center problem is the government taxing the wealthy so some of us might have access to—or better—health insurance. If you want a Republican to shit *their* pants, talk about expanding health insurance—or, God forbid, Medicare.

Luckily for them, they have the media on their side. Expanding healthcare was frightening until Republicans remembered who they are: the ones spreading fear, not succumbing to it. Thanks to the media pushing the falsehood of the death panel, public support for healthcare reform among Republican voters turned into fanatical opposition. Ironically, the very people so opposed to the Affordable Care Act were the ones it helps the most. Poor Republicans.

By lying about death panels, Republicans were able to oppose the Affordable Care Act and prevent it from becoming more affordable and more comprehensive. Republicans took end-of-life planning and contorted it into another lie. Being able to consult with your doctor about palliative care as a humane way to deal with terminal illness turned into a bureaucrat executing your grandmother. A lie with a purpose, as long as it benefits the wealthy, is business as usual for the GOP.

But don't call them on it. They're very sensitive. When HBO warned us that "Winter Is Coming," they were 30 years too late. The first snowflakes started falling all over Fox Studios in the 90s. Not only did Fox usher in the age of rage, they simultaneously trained their audience to be hypersensitive to real and perceived slights.

They're mostly perceived—or manufactured—by the right. Much of their programming is geared toward making their viewers feel belittled.

Then the right-wing media and politicians can use those hurt feelings to claim that the elites on the coasts were always belittling the "Real America." On cue, the mainstream media jumped on the bruised-ego bandwagon the right was cultivating. Suddenly, there was a real America full of real Americans. Per Fox's dictum, they lived in the heartland, i.e., red states. That's why the media spends so much time in diners interviewing elderly white people. To get the pulse of real Americans.

But if they wanted to get the pulse of real Americans, shouldn't the media be talking with the ones with family values? When it comes to those, Republicans are more Addams Family than Joseph and Mary. Republican family values are just another empty slogan and media canard. Despite constantly claiming to be morally superior to everyone else, these Bible-thumpers could learn a thing or two on how to run a family from coastal elites.

When it comes to family values, there seems to be a gap between reality and rhetoric. The top 10 states with the highest divorce rates are: Oklahoma, Nevada, Wyoming, Texas, Idaho, Arkansas, Alaska, Florida, West Virginia, and Alabama.[8] As for teen pregnancies, the top 10 states are: Arkansas, Mississippi, Oklahoma, Louisiana, Kentucky, New Mexico, Texas, West Virginia, Alabama, and Tennessee.[9] Real America.

What's so elite about staying married and teaching your children not to have children? Aren't those the family values

228

Republicans are always whining about? Someone needs to inform the media that traditional family values start with an intact marriage. That and teaching your children not to have children. Maybe the media should spend some time in blue state bodegas with intact families the next time they want to talk to "real Americans."

Even if Republicans acknowledged the facts behind their high divorce and teen pregnancy rates, they'd surely put the GOP spin on it. No doubt, they'd argue red states have the right to run their families like a brothel if they want to. After all, Republicans are for states' rights, aren't they? Not really. Unless, of course, the states are exercising their rights in accordance with Republican ideology. Bringing up another perpetuated media myth—that Republicans are the champions of a state's rights. Not to be trampled by the overbearing government.

Unless they're *doing* the trampling. Like the rest of the Republican platform, it doesn't conform to a set of beliefs. They believe in states' rights as long as it benefits their party. They have a broken moral compass. It only points in one direction—at their amoral ideology. That's why there is no consistency in their beliefs. They aren't against small government, just small government for the poor and middle class. They aren't against deficits, except when deficits are run for any reason other than to give tax cuts to the wealthy.

Being consistently inconsistent *is* their ideology. Never more so than with states' rights. States' rights are little more than a dog whistle Republicans use to get their base to vote. However, when it comes to actually defending a state's rights, those whistles grow silent or are swallowed. Like they were in 2000 when Republicans notoriously became advocates of government interference in a state's right to choose who it wanted for president.

Florida was a disaster. There were hanging chads everywhere, most of which were invalidated. In order to make sure every vote counted, Florida initiated a recount—which Republicans tried to stop. They sent protesters to Florida to physically try to intimidate the officials conducting the recount—a precursor of things to come. Then they turned to their friends on the Supreme Court. The Republicans in robes delivered as they knew they would. In a 5-4 party line vote, the Republican Supreme Court prevented Florida from conducting its constitutional duty to count its votes. There would be no states' rights for you, Florida. Big-government Republicans made sure of it.

This all was done so that the loser of the popular vote—and soon-to-be loser of the Electoral College—could be handed the presidency. What did our illegitimate Supreme Court-appointed president do after being handed the Oval Office? Act like he won in a landslide, of course. It was Christmas in July, and Santa Bush was busy giving presents to all his wealthy friends and donors. There were deficit-busting tax cuts, surplus squelching, and more. Under the tree was an even bigger gift—the one that keeps on giving. Deregulation!

Or rather, self-regulation. One of the GOP's favorite ways to give back to their donors is by reducing their expenses. According to Alec MacGillis of *The New Yorker*, "In 2005, embracing the deregulatory agenda promoted by the Bush Administration and the

Republicans in Congress, the F.A.A. (The Federal Aviation Administration) changed to a model called Organization Designation Authorization. Manufacturers would now select and supervise the safety monitors. If the monitors saw something amiss, they would raise the issue with their managers rather than with the F.A.A."[10]

In other words, the government agency responsible for keeping us safe in the sky was out of the loop. The F.A.A. was no longer keeping the public safe. You could say things at the F.A.A. were "unsafe at any speed," which is also the title of the well-known consumer safety advocate Ralph Nader's book, published in 1965. Ralph Nader may be single-handedly responsible for forcing automobile manufacturers to begin implementing safety features in their cars. Ironically, he may also be single-handedly responsible for reversing the ones in the air.

That's because the Republican Supreme Court never should have had a chance to elect George W. Bush. Even without a recount, Bush only received 537 more votes than Al Gore in Florida. In that same election, Ralph Nader received 97,488. Without Nader on the ballot, sufficient evidence points out that Gore would have won a majority of his votes, winning Florida handily.[11] Forgetting Florida—wouldn't it be nice—adding Nader's four percent New Hampshire vote to Gore's total would have given him an extra four Electoral College votes. That would've given him a 270-to-267 victory in the Electoral College in addition to winning the popular vote.

Ralph Nader had no chance of winning the presidency. His run was a pure vanity play. Losing was predetermined. Tragically, Nader's run for office ended in not just defeat but death. One of the airlines that was self-regulating thanks to the Bush Administration was Boeing. The Boeing 737 Max had a faulty sensor that increased the likelihood pilots would lose control of the airline under certain circumstances.

Two of their planes crashed, killing everyone on board. Lion Air Flight 610 plunged into the sea 11 minutes after takeoff, hitting the water with such force that some metal fixtures on the aircraft disintegrated. All 189 people on board were killed. Ethiopian Airlines Flight 302 suffered the same fate, killing 157 passengers. In a cruel twist of fate, one of the passengers on the Lion Air flight was someone's niece. Ralph Nader's.

Donald Rumsfeld famously said, "There are known knowns. These are things we know that we know. There are known unknowns. That is to say, there are things that we know we don't know. But there are also unknown unknowns. There are things we don't know we don't know."

With Rumsfeld's parlance in mind, it is safe to say there is a known known with voting for Republicans. What we do know is that pulling the lever for Republicans puts us at risk. That's the known. The unknown is what that risk will be. It's known that 9/11 happened because George Bush ignored warnings of an imminent attack on America. The Great Recession was because of his deregulatory zeal. Now, our planet is being pushed to the point of no return—in the middle of a pandemic. All while our financial coffers are being drained to support the wealthy.

That's why vanity politics and vanity voting is so dangerous. Pulling that lever is not just a vote. You never know when you or your loved one may be flying on a self-regulating plane. Unless things change soon, we won't need to know. We'll all be on board. Spiraling downward on a bankrupt plane heading toward what's left of our planet—with some of us wearing masks. Maybe the next time the media wants a story with death in it, they could mention that one.

Chapter 11: The Omega

Karl Marx said religion is the opiate of the masses. He was close. Religion is just one of the delivery systems. The true opiate is the worship of mammon. Worshipping money is the reason Christians have abandoned Christ. It's the reason capitalists have abandoned capitalism. It's the reason Republicans have abandoned conservativism. The worship of mammon is the truest expression of conserve-yourself-ism.

There is a chicken-and-egg conundrum when it comes to Republicans and money. Do Republicans hate democracy because of their love of money? Or did their love of money lead them to hate democracy? Either way, we're left with a world where they have one and we don't have the other.

We know Republicans have been trying to get rid of democracy since they invented the Hastert Rule. Was it because democracy was standing in the way of implementing their point-center agenda? Was craving money a by-product of their dismantling of democracy or the cause? Possibly their love of money and hatred of democracy hatched at the same time. Like two chickens climbing out of the same egg. Regardless of how many GOP chickens are clucking around, it's clear where their allegiances lie.

Not with voters. There is a perfect illustration of that dichotomy and Republicans' true fidelity. It isn't with the people who voted for them, but rather with the people who bought them. This provides yet another example of media bias. They pretend all politicians are bought and paid for. Turns out that distinction falls clearly on one side of the aisle. One party is for democracy—it's in their name. The other is not—it's in their DNA. And they govern accordingly.

For a simple reason. Democracy is inherently incompatible with Republican values. Democracy can best be summed up as the greatest good for the greatest number. Republicanism can best be summed up as the greatest good for the fewest possible. In other words, crapitalism. Republican capitalism and democracy cannot coexist. They are mutually exclusive. It is not possible to pursue the greatest good for the most and least simultaneously.

That's why Republicans choose to do what's best for the least. It's where the money is. According to *The Economist*,

Republican senators vote with their rich constituents 86% of the time compared with only 35% for Democrats.[1]

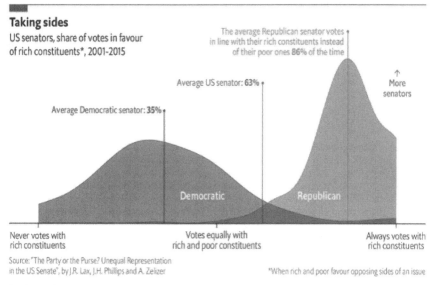

Taking sides

US senators, share of votes in favour
of rich constituents*, 2001-2015

The average Republican senator votes
in line with their rich constituents instead
of their poor ones **86%** of the time

Average US senator: **63%**

↑
More
senators

Average Democratic senator: **35%**

Democratic

Republican

Never votes with
rich constituents

Votes equally with
rich and poor constituents

Always votes with
rich constituents

Source: "The Party or the Purse? Unequal Representation
in the US Senate", by J.R. Lax, J.H. Phillips and A. Zelizer

*When rich and poor favour opposing sides of an issue

The Economist

Investing in Republicans is good business. Getting someone to vote in favor of your economic interests 86% of the time is a no-brainer. If you can afford it, that is. But if you're an oil conglomerate or a point-center, can you afford not to? And what are your investment choices, anyway? Unlike the rest of us who are limited to our 401(k)s and their myriad investment options, for the plutocracy, there is only one real choice.

There's one choice if all you care about are your own narrow economic self-interests, that is. Which begs the question, how much does it cost to buy a Republican? A lot less than you get back. Looking back to the fossil fuel industry crystalizes this fact. It's the perfect industry to analyze for multiple reasons. First is the gap between their contributions to each political party. Over time, it has become a rather one-sided affair.[2]

Party Split, 1990-2020

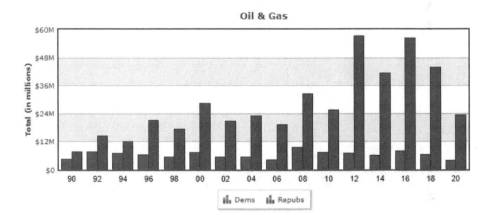

Top Contributors, 2019-2020

Contributor		Amount
Koch Industries		$6,212,852
Marathon Petroleum		$2,596,328
Chevron Corp		$2,573,715
Midland Energy		$1,802,121
Parman Capital Group		$1,782,054
Energy Transfer Partners		$1,624,805
ConocoPhillips		$1,472,904
Samson Energy		$1,154,552
Walter Oil & Gas		$1,143,235
Energy Transfer Equity		$1,100,000
Hunt Companies		$1,079,137
Exxon Mobil		$983,098
Red Apple Group		$870,686
Valero Services		$785,351
Otis Eastern		$739,980
Valero Energy		$663,391
Occidental Petroleum		$651,295
Berexco Inc		$558,655
Hilcorp Energy		$505,865
CI Machinery Co		$500,000
Petroplex Energy		$500,000

Contributions to:
Democrats
Republicans
Liberal Groups
Conservative Groups
Nonpartisan

Even as far back as 1990, there was a significant gap between political contributions to Democrats and Republicans. It was almost double, even then. Over time, it has only widened. Now, nearly all political contributions from the fossil fuel industry flow through the GOP—directly or indirectly. That brings us back to the question: how much does it cost to buy a Republican? The answer is about $30 million. At least that's what the top political contributors spent.

It's not a bad investment considering the fossil fuel industry got about $5.2 trillion back. They also get a political party that will do everything in its power to spread and defend the myth that climate change has nothing to do with them. In other words, they successfully bought and paid for one of our political parties. For their rather paltry investment, the GOP spreads lies about climate change and its economic and environmental impacts. All while undermining the legitimacy of science, facts, and reason.

They may be undermining, but they're not eliminating. One of the problems for Republicans was they needed a bigger bullhorn. Democracy was still working. After Barack Obama was elected, they realized they had a problem. Even with their propaganda machine and neutered mainstream media, the people still voted for a Democrat. Apparently, there's only so much stupidity money can buy. If there's one thing Republican donors fear, it's sunlight. With a Democrat in the White House, the collateral damage caused by companies like the fossil fuel industry wouldn't stand. Democrats are capitalists and expect businesses to pay their own way.

Imagine the horror across corporate boardrooms when they thought of having to pay that $5.2 trillion themselves. Something needed to be done. That something was to turn to the right-wing Supreme Court for help. Luckily for them, the Court agreed with their fellow Republicans. Democracy only works when money is polluting politics. To drown out facts, it takes a geyser of cash.

If the birth of the death of democracy was November 4, 1980, the rest of its tombstone would read "until January 21, 2010." That was the day democracy died. It had been on life support for years. Then the decision to pull the plug was finally made. Five people made the decision, in fact. Five people on behalf of over 300 million Americans. Backed by the United Corporations of America, the Supreme Court declared that corporations were people.

This begs the question: if corporations are people, why aren't any of them in jail? Probably because they have too much money to go to prison. They know something the Supreme Court doesn't. Money buys a lot of things, including free speech. That's the conclusion we can draw from the right-wing Supreme Court's decision in 2010 in *Citizens United v. Federal Election Commission*.

It was another 5-4 vote, with Republicans passing the decision that our democracy may never recover from. They asserted that the First Amendment allowed unlimited expenditures for political communications by corporations, including nonprofit corporations, labor unions, and other associations. All under the guise of free speech.

What the Court failed to take into account was how money can affect everyone else's free speech. If you don't believe me, I have a question for you. How much would it cost to change your mind? Or even better, when was the last time your senator returned your phone call? How about your house representative? Can you even get your mayor to return your call? How about the dog catcher?

If Bill Maher couldn't get through to President Barack Obama, what chance do you or I have? Famously, Bill Maher pledged $1 million to a Super PAC supporting President Obama's reelection effort in 2012. This was another by-product of the *Citizens United* decision, the Super PAC. Super PACs pooled all these unlimited corporate and individual contributions to better coordinate their ad spending. But even that wasn't enough to coax President Obama on his show.

To summarize: even if you have your own show on HBO, are famous, and donate a million dollars to the president, that's still not enough money to buy access. How much does it take? Apparently, $122 million should do it. That's what Sheldon Adelson and his wife, Miriam, contributed to support Republican candidates in 2018, up from a previous high of $7.5 million from Robert and Doylene Perry in 2010—also in support of Republican candidates.[4] They get their phone calls returned.

And then some. Incredibly, Timothy Egan, a *New York Times* contributing opinion writer, asserts that "an 85-year-old casino magnate, Sheldon Adelson, now has more influence on American foreign policy than even the secretary of state, the Koch [Brothers] tool Mike Pompeo."[5] At the same time, he revealed the influence of another Republican mega-donor, the Koch brothers. It's almost like Republicans are letting our country be run by their billionaire donors.

Not "almost"—they are. I'm just surprised they only get their way 86% of the time. Saying money doesn't influence speech is like saying money doesn't influence your ability to pay your mortgage. If money didn't alter other people's behavior, which is the ultimate expression of speech, why is Google's market cap over $1 trillion while Facebook's isn't far behind? Their entire business model is to get us to buy things and believe things we wouldn't otherwise buy or believe. They turn needs into wants. Money is used to influence us and enrich themselves.

In other words, advertising. It's the same with politics. Whereas a few dominant players rule adverting, a few wealthy families rule politics. The richest one percent of Americans contribute more to politics than the bottom 75 percent combined, with 158 families responsible for half of the initial phase of the 2016 presidential election.[6] It's safe to say their speech is more valuable and valued than ours. Perhaps not as much as the Koch brothers, though. Their network of mega-donors would spend nearly $1 billion promoting their interests.[6]

Now that buys a lot of bullhorns—which they use to drown out anything that threatens *their* free speech. Most notably, my speech and your speech. Evidently, it's not as free as we are led to believe. From the plutocrat's perspective, the loudest voice wins, and they have the money to drown out any voice they don't want to hear. More importantly, any voice they don't want you to hear. Drowning out the masses enables them to enrich themselves. If it's in the public interest, it's probably not in theirs.

Take public transportation, for example. Its benefits are multifaceted. For starters, it takes cars off the roads. Anyone living near a metropolitan area can attest to how awful congestion is. Rush hour can be *hours* spent in a car—by yourself, idling between stop and go. As opposed to public transportation, which shepherds dozens or more people at the same time, reducing congestion and fuel consumption. The latter is essential in reducing global warming.

Which also reduces something else: profits. Profits from burning fossil fuels and profits from repairing roadways and automobiles. Less congestion may be better for our mental well-being, but it's bad for roads and the cars driving on them in the sense that they'll need less work to repair them. If that's your business, less congestion means less profits.

It just so happens one of the mainstay companies of Koch Industries is a major producer of gasoline, asphalt, and other automobile parts.[7] They're the kinds of products that rely on heavy automobile usage. Preferably without the use of HOV lanes. Alone in their cars on congested roads heading nowhere slowly. Guess who benefits from that scenario? The same people opposing public transportation.

These people are the Koch brothers and their network of greedy, climate-change-denying donors. Hiroko Tabuchi reports in *The New York Times*, "In cities and countries across the country—including Little Rock, Ark.; Phoenix Ariz.; southeast Michigan; central Utah; and in Tennessee—the Koch brothers are fueling a fight against public transit."[7] And they're winning. Even with overwhelming support, the public transit plan in Nashville was killed.

The Kochs' $5.4 billion opposition plan defeated it in a landslide despite the public transit plan's support from a popular mayor and a coalition of businesses.[7] Also defeated, once again, were the losers of Pond Scum. Not only does public transportation help reduce global warming and congestion, it helps those who have the least. What gives the Kochs their fortune is also what compels the poor to need the very thing people like the Kochs oppose: inequality. As gentrification places home affordability out of the reach of more and more Americans, they are pushed further and further from their jobs—jobs they have to find a way to get to.

Lattes still need to be frothed, and it doesn't matter how far someone has to travel to do the frothing. Increasingly, that is the life many Americans live—forced to travel a far distance in public transportation to perform menial service jobs. For welfare wages. Often without benefits. Not only has the American Dream of home ownership faded from view, so has the financial wherewithal to purchase a car. Hence the reliance on public transportation.

If you're wondering how the Koch brothers could impose their will on cities across the country, it's because they're good at it and they've been doing it a long time. One of the things about the Koch brothers is they've been working to undermine our democracy to prop up their profits for decades. When they manufactured the T.E.A. Party, it was a logical manifestation of the groundwork they had laid from years earlier.

Creating fake parties to promote their interests was something they had experience with. Much to my surprise, I learned they were behind the Libertarian Party. Contrary to my belief, it wasn't an offshoot of the GOP, born out of their hostility to government and taxes. It was their inspiration. In fact, the platform for the Libertarian Party was underwritten by the billionaire brothers Charles and David Koch in 1980.[8] Not surprisingly, it coincided with Ronald Reagan's election and his embrace of ALEC.

Ever since, the Koch brothers have worked tirelessly to deceive Americans and strip them of their free speech. They're doing so because they have the money needed to amplify their voices and drown out ours. Creating the Libertarian Party, the Kochs knew anything was possible. All to further their own agenda. They laid out a road map that would destroy anything in their way. And the Libertarian Party called for the abolition of almost every federal agency, including the FDA (The United States Food and Drug Administration).[8] They didn't even want our food to be safe if it stood in the way of their profits.

For the winners, making life more bearable for everyone else is not part of crapitalism. Forget allowing it; they actively oppose it— spending whatever it takes in the process. Doing otherwise may actually be an admission that the game is rigged. Not to mention the fact there is a definite sense of urgency on one side of the aisle. The mammonists know time is running out. Despite their protestations to the contrary, the monied elite on the right are well aware that global warming is real and their livelihood depends on saying otherwise. They just don't want to get stuck with the bill.

Let's not forget the economic damage their products do to the rest of us. Down the road, $5.2 trillion will look quaint. In retrospect, we might ask ourselves, "Back when we could have done something about it, it would have only cost $5.2 trillion in lost profits from companies set on destroying our planet?" In light of the future cost, it would be a bargain. Without significant action, global damages from climate change are estimated to be as high as $100 trillion per year by 2100—more than the global GDP today.[9]

By then, it will be too late. Polluting politics with money is nothing new. Republicans have been using money in one form or another to influence policy on behalf of their donors for decades. The gravest threats are the ones they want to obfuscate the most. It's the reason we don't have any sensible gun legislation.

When it comes to reasoning, there are two important points to keep in mind. The first is, "It is difficult to get a man to understand something when his salary depends upon his not understanding it?" It explains Republicans' lack of basic math and science skills. They're paid not to have them. A corollary to that is, "It's important to make a man not understand something when *your* salary depends upon his not understanding it."

Or even better, believing it's opposite. Both hold true for global warming and guns. It's why so much money is poured into denying that global warming exists and that gun ownership increases safety. Neither is true. Whereas the NRA would lead you to believe that guns in the home are the only way to protect your family, it's only because they've silenced opposing voices. Specifically, the government.

With money. What we don't know hurts us. What we do know hurts the NRA. That's why the NRA doesn't want gun violence to be studied. When it is, they don't like the results. A landmark study from 1993 showed that bringing a gun into the home puts everyone at risk.[10] Rather than advocating for a way to mitigate this danger, the NRA sought to conceal it—like the guns they promote.

The NRA pushed Congress to stop the CDC from researching gun violence. This was thanks to Republican House of Representative member Jay Dickey from Arkansas. His amendment stated that "none of the funds made available for injury prevention and control at the Centers for Disease Control and Prevention may be used to advocate or promote gun control." From that day forward, the CDC was unable to research gun fatalities, why they happen, and how they can be mitigated. We all know where that has led.

It's gone down a road of carnage paved by the NRA's financial interests. Bodies and blood on their hands. Sacrifices at the altar of mammon. Mass shootings now occurring on what seems like a daily basis. Without any facts to counteract the NRA's rhetoric, all we are left with is their propaganda and a lot of dead Americans. Even the children couldn't change anything. That's how powerful the monied voices are compared to the moneyless masses. Free speech doesn't mean much if you're an NRA casualty.

Ironically, by 2100, with the planet expected to barely be inhabitable, the one thing we'll all need will be guns. And gas for our dune buggies. Which means one thing. Well after their deaths, we'll still be filling the Koch brothers' coffers. All so they can keep buying our free speech. From the grave.

Mad Max would be so proud.

Chapter 12: Tyranny

Tyranny is often thought of as the majority inflicting its will on the minority. Clearly, it's easy to see how the minority can be persecuted. Sheer numbers enable one group to dominate another. Our country was founded on the fight against just that type of tyranny—the oppressive rule by a foreign country an ocean away from our shores. Clearly outnumbered, England was in the majority and we were the subjugated minority. Not for long. Heroically, we fought for our freedom, breaking our bonds and ultimately forming a new nation.

History, however, is not always so neat. It is littered not with valorous uprisings against oppressive majorities but rather with authoritarian rises of the minority. No example is starker than Nazi Germany in World War II. The Nazis were a minority party who only began to win elections by attacking the current government.

Even then, they only won 37% of parliamentary seats. It was July of 1932 when they captured 230 out of the 608 seats in the German parliament, which was known as the "Reichstag."[1]

Campaigning on fear and hate, Hitler was appointed German chancellor in January 1933. Within 100 days, Germany was transformed. It was swift and complete. On day four, they came for the press. The press was censored if they showed any "contempt" for government.[2] (Ironically, Hitler's contempt for government propelled him to power.) From there, civil liberties were taken away under the guise of law and order. Demonization of the Jews happened on day 61 when Jewish businesses were boycotted and Jews purged from civil service.[2]

Under Nazi rule, all other political parties were banned and political prisoners were housed in the Nazis' first concentration camp—in Dachau, Germany.[1] Without any opposition in the form of a free press or opposition political party, the Nazi takeover of Germany was finalized. The minority party ruled with ferocity and without mercy. They sought to simultaneously eliminate the Jews and rule the world—subjugating their conquests along the way.

Subjugation is an apt description of what another infamous minority did. This time, the minority was defined numerically and racially. For in this case, the minority subjugated the minority. Under the banner of apartheid, legal apparatuses were put in place to separate whites from people of color. Physically and economically, these barriers created a white upper class and a black lower class.

A series of Land Acts set aside more than 80 percent of the country's land for the white minority and from 1961 to 1994, more than 3.5 million people were forcibly removed from their homes.[3] Landless, separate, and hopeless, they plunged into poverty and despair. To this day, many South Africans of color live in ghettos. Even with the end of apartheid, the economic damage has not abated. Economic despair still haunts black South Africans, as my visit to the ghettos showed me firsthand. This proved that political power without economic power is as irrelevant as a democracy without the right to vote.

Conversely, feelings of racial superiority may be borne out of economic necessity. Economic dominance requires obtaining political control. For the minority to rule, it requires vilification. To have a superior race, it necessitates having an inferior one. Being worthy of economic abundance means someone else deserves poverty. Essential for any minority takeover is the idea of the deserving and the undeserving. The right and the wrong. The good and the bad.

The problem is, once the minority takes power, it becomes increasingly difficult to wrest it from them. Power begets the desire for more power. The deserving become even more entrenched in their belief that they have an exalted status. Scapegoats become enemies. Justifications become ideology—no more so than with today's Republican Party.

The cult posing as a political party pursues power as a means to an end. Ronald Reagan got into politics because he didn't want to pay taxes during a war. Why should he pay extra taxes just because his country was at war? So, he stopped working. His love of money was greater than that of country. It was so great, it led to his hatred of government. It's been a cumulative disease afflicting his party ever since. Mammonism and hatred form an easily spread pandemic for anyone hoisting an "R" next to their name.

There is none more contaminated than Newt Gingrich. Newt showed it wasn't enough to hate government; you had to hate the people who represented government. Government by itself was too abstract. Besides, Americans were only receptive to anti-government rhetoric because of Republicans. We entered the Vietnam conflict under Republican president Dwight Eisenhower. We lost our first war under Richard Nixon, the president who lied about bombing Cambodia—a country we weren't at war with—on his way to losing the Vietnam War. Then, Richard Nixon forever sullied the presidency with the Watergate break-in and subsequent cover-up, leaving office in disgrace. With a Republican pardon. All this corruption tore at our national fabric and provided an opening for an anti-government zealot.

Hypocritically, it was the Republican Party that exploited the distrust *they* created. Then, they exasperated it for their own personal gain. As has become customary, Republicans create problems they then exploit for political purposes. Against all credulity, again and again. Only because they have followed the minority playbook. Or more specifically, the Gingrich Doctrine of divide and conquer.

When Republicans launched the Second Civil War, they called it the Reagan Revolution. Unlike in Nazi Germany, their takeover was gradual and deliberate. Dividing Americans and destroying democracy would take more than 100 days. Censoring the press and eliminating political opposition were pipe dreams at the time. It took years for Fox to use propaganda to emasculate the press and change facts into optionable bits of opinion. All while subjugating democracy in the name of a belief.

That belief was the legitimacy of one party. Slowly, this belief took hold of the GOP, starting with Reagan's commandment to never speak ill of a fellow Republican. This continued to Newt Gingrich's scorched-earth policy of attacking all Democrats as socialist and un-American. Eventually, it yielded to a more formalized concept of one-party rule.

When Republicans made up the Hastert Rule, they proverbially "jumped the shark." Officially, democracy was under attack. After the fiasco of Reagan's trickle-down economic policy, Republicans knew they couldn't win political arguments on merit. Rather than abandon broken ideas, they abandoned democracy. The Hastert Rule was their opening salvo in the war against voters. By only voting on legislation that could pass exclusively with a majority of Republicans, they negated the will of the people. Essentially, they laid the groundwork for acting as if elections were meaningless and creating barriers to ensure they were.

Once the House of Representatives started acting like democratic votes didn't matter, it wasn't long before they turned their sights from congressional races to the presidency. When Bill Clinton was elected president in 1992, Republicans tried to delegitimize him from day one. From Whitewater in 1992 to Travelgate in 1993, Republicans used their power to undermine a duly elected president. They even tried to pin Vince Foster's suicide on the Clintons. The vast right-wing conspiracy was in motion. And unstoppable.

Without a legitimate way to take down a president, they found what would turn out to be the only way. Infamously, Bill Clinton's philandering was as unrelenting as the Republicans' desire to remove him from office. Those two forces met in the Oval Office. Under a desk. What came next (infidelity) should have been between a husband and a wife. Instead, it was the opening Republicans had been searching for. Bill Clinton lied about receiving oral sex. The floodgates were open.

Of all the egregious things that happened during this sorrowful episode, Clinton's blow job was last on the list. Rather, it was the way Republicans prostrated themselves to justify impeachment on grounds not in the Constitution. They existed only in the minds of Republicans. This dichotomy is even worse when looked at from present day. Especially in light of their moral *and* constitutional ignorance to all things Trump.

Consider Lindsey Graham, the Republican then-Representative from South Carolina, as perhaps the most flagrant example of this. During the Clinton impeachment proceedings, he said, "If this body [Congress] determines that your conduct as a public official is clearly out of bounds in your role . . . because impeachment is not about punishment. Impeachment is about cleansing the office. Impeachment is about restoring honor and integrity to the office." According to Lindsey, if you were a bad boy, that was enough to remove you from office.

Compare that to what he said about Donald Trump, perhaps the most bath-needy person on the planet. He has so sullied "the office," it should make even Lindsey Graham clutch his pearls and shudder. If a blow job requires a cleansing of the office, shouldn't banging a porn star require the same thing? Especially when your recently pregnant wife is around the corner with your four-month-old son. Wouldn't that fall under "cleanse-worthy?"

Maybe if Monica Lewinsky had been an adult performer, Lindsey would have let it slide. You know, "Boys will be boys." Confoundingly, the now-senator from South Carolina went even further perfecting his impression of a pretzel. While the Constitution specifically names bribery as an impeachable offense, Lindsey said it was very appropriate for the president to pressure a foreign leader for dirt on a political opponent, and that impeaching any president over a phone call is just insane. More insane than a blow job?

Watching Lindsey Graham hysterically go after Bill Clinton, then enervate himself trying to defend the indefensible leaves us to draw one of two conclusions. Perhaps Lindsey's farcical performances are because Putin has a Lindsey "pee tape." Maybe with the perpetually single man in a dress? Which leads to another possibility. What if Lindsey doesn't care about the cleanliness of the office at all? Is it possible Lindsey's hysteria over Bill Clinton had more to do with jealousy than the rule of law? Maybe he wanted the blue dress to be *his*?

Those are the only two logical explanations. Otherwise, Lindsey is just another member of the Republican cult, worshipping little else than each other. Which seems likely, since after Bill

Clinton's impeachment trial, things only got worse. Republicans weaponized their power to investigate and were all too ready to impeach the baseless and defend the guilty—depending on which party was in power. Measuring Democrats by one yardstick and Republicans by another became entrenched in the GOP playbook. Never more so than after 9/11.

Look no further to the contrast between Democratic behavior after 9/11 and Republicans after Benghazi. To this day, Democrats have not politized 9/11. In fact, they rallied around George Bush on that sullen day and continued to do so—proving Democrats put country above party. Contrast that to what Republicans did after Benghazi. Jumping at the chance, they politicized the tragic deaths and went after Hillary Clinton, launching investigation after investigation. Ten investigations were conducted into the 2012 Benghazi attack, costing taxpayers millions of dollars.

They did this all without spending a single dollar investigating who was actually responsible for the deaths in Benghazi: Republicans. Waving their fiscal axe around haphazardly looking for ways to cut taxes for the wealthy, they slashed security. Security that could have prevented the attacks in Benghazi or at least the deaths resulting from them. Instead, mindless budget-slashing led House Republicans to deprioritize the security forces protecting State Department personnel around the world. Benghazi happened because of them.

In 2011, Republicans cut $128 million from Obama's request for embassy security, and in 2012, House Republicans drained off even more funds—cutting back on the department's request by $331 million.[4] This left Americans more vulnerable than ever. If there's blood on anyone's hands, it's with the GOP. But that would be assuming the party of personal responsibility could be held accountable for their actions. Instead, when blood is spilled, it's never their fault—as 9/11 proved.

Once the dust settled, the real culprit behind 9/11 began to emerge: government negligence. This should come as no surprise. When you hate something, you can't be good at it. If there's one thing Republicans hate, it's government. Expecting them to be good at government is not only an oxymoron, it hurts their brand. Being bad at government insulates them with their base while proving their point. Government is the problem and when it's not, they'll make sure it is. They're going to prove it.

Partly because it's in their DNA. More importantly because they never pay a penalty. Defunding the State Department led to a tragedy they created and then exploited for political purposes. The same could be said of 9/11. George Bush ignored a memo titled "Bin Laden to attack the U.S." Even worse, two months before the suicide hijackings, the FBI warned that Middle Eastern men were taking flight classes in the U.S. They were alarmed because they wanted to learn how to fly commercial jets but not to land them.

To say 9/11 could have been prevented is an understatement. While we will never know for sure what would have happened if President Gore had been allowed to take office, we know he would not have ignored a memo titled "Bin Laden to attack the U.S." Or an FBI warning that Middle Eastern men were in U.S. flight schools with no interest in landing planes. Imagine if President Gore had arrested every last Arab flight school trainee. President Gore would have been prevented 9/11. But if even one of those planes were not grounded by the Gore Administration, Republicans would still be relentlessly attacking Democrats for not keeping us safe. Probably starting on 9/12. There would be no unified, non-political response. Republicans would follow the Gingrich Doctrine to its logical conclusion. Divide. Conquer. Look no further than what they did to Hillary Clinton over Benghazi for proof. Faux patriots using tragedy for political gain.

Somehow, Republicans use their incompetence to prove they are the party to protect us. Ignoring threats leading to the biggest American tragedy outside of Pearl Harbor makes us safe? In Republiclandia, it does. It was a running joke that Rudy Giuliani couldn't form a sentence without saying 9/11 in it. Tragically, it was Mayor Giuliani who overrode the New York Police Department's opposition to locate its emergency command center at the World Trade Center. The Giuliani Administration insisted otherwise. When the World Trade Center collapsed, it was on top of that very command center. Following in the footsteps of George Bush, Giuliani somehow capitalized on a tragedy he made worse.

Shamelessly, Republicans seek to exploit and divide, and 9/11 provided them with the perfect platform to do just that. When George Bush said, "You are either with us, or with the terrorists," what choice did we have? Republicans pounced on any dissent or questioning on everything from the Patriot Act to the War in Iraq.

Just the name "Patriot Act" was an act of defiance. Meaning "I dare you to defy what I want to do by opposing the 'Patriot' Act."

As if the Gingrich Doctrine wasn't bad enough, here came the neocons of the Bush Administration. Hyper-partisanship masking as patriotism became Orwellian. Republicans were already primed to slander Democrats as unpatriotic and socialists as it was. Not falling in line after an attack on our sovereignty opened anyone up to claims of palling around with terrorists. If Republicans can turn their 9/11 and Benghazi incompetence into an advantage, imagine what they would do if a Democrat offered some nuance to their neocon, authoritarian agenda.

This was the intended effect. While opposing political parties may not have been outlawed, opposing viewpoints were stymied. From Democrats and the media. Laying down the gauntlet, no one wanted to be attacked as being "with the terrorists." You were either with us or against us—meaning with the Bush agenda or with the terrorists' agenda. In hindsight, it became a Faustian bargain, and it was one most took.

For it became clear that the president who ignored a mortal threat would be the same one who would create one where none existed. Creating a false reality while ignoring what is in front of you is the Republican modus operandi. None more operandi than Iraq. Failing to protect us from the actual threat of 9/11, Bush wanted to attack an old foe—regardless of their culpability.

Following the Gingrich Doctrine, Bush knew a nebulous enemy like "terrorists" would not rally Americans indefinitely. Terrorists can come from any country. Just like Newt Gingrich knew hating government wasn't sufficient when Republicans launched the Second Civil War, Bush knew hating terrorists wasn't enough in his War on Terror.

Selling the American public on a war was what the Bush Administration needed to do. What better way than trotting out a retired four-star general? Adding gravitas and legitimacy to their case against Saddam Hussein was all they needed. Handing him faulty information, Secretary of State Colin L. Powell gave a speech in 2003 to the United Nations. He made his case for war, claiming Iraq had weapons of mass destruction.

Powell gave a detailed description of the Iraqi weapons program. The problem is, it didn't exist. Despite combing the country for any sign of a weapons program, there weren't any WMDs to be found. Anywhere. It's just like searching for voter fraud. Both are nonexistent, but Republicans keep insisting they're there. Even worse, they keep searching. While Powell acknowledges how "painful" this revelation was for him personally and how it's a permanent "blot" on his record, what is really painful is what the aftermath of Bush's deception wrought.

Going to war with the wrong country had consequences. The first was that Iraq's defeat led to the emergence of ISIS. Saddam Hussein kept terrorists in check. Once he was gone, ISIS was unleashed. Now Iraq is more unstable than ever. After nearly 20 years, the death toll continues to mount, with over 36,000 U.S. servicemen and servicewomen killed or wounded. Over one million Iraqis were killed or injured—at a running cost of over two trillion dollars. Consider that the next time Republicans claim we can't provide medical care for Americans.

With the death and financial toll of going to war under false pretenses, some might wonder if a war crime had been committed. Or at the very least, an impeachable offense. Especially when you add wrecking the global economy on top of all the other incompetence. It would be for a Democrat. But for Republicans, there is a different set of rules. Whereas Bush's lies cost us trillions of dollars and countless lives, Bill Clinton's cost him little more than an $18 dry-cleaning bill. Yet somehow Republicans claim to care about the rule of law.

Until it applies to someone from their own party. Then the rules change. Never more so than with Donald Trump. Litigating his impeachable offenses has been done thoroughly enough to know he sought the help of foreigners to help him win an election. Then he committed obstruction of justice trying to deny it. First with Russia, then with Ukraine.

Trump said, "Russia, if you're listening, I hope you're able to find the thirty thousand emails that are missing. I think you will probably be rewarded mightily by our press." The same day, July 27, 2016, he asked Russia for help, they delivered. Russian hackers made their first attempt to infiltrate the computer servers in Clinton's personal offices.[5] So yes, Russia was listening. And most likely coordinating, too, as an email dump occurred on the same day Trump's "pussy grabbing" video came out. On cue, the media rewarded them, too.

The media was all too happy to pretend nondescript emails were newsworthy while ignoring the fact a crime had been committed in obtaining them. Mainly a cyber-Watergate. It involved breaking into a campaign office and stealing documents by a foreign adversary intent on influencing a U.S. election. Worse than Watergate. At least that criminal worked with Americans to undermine an election. But if you're going to outsource the manufacturing of your ties, you might as well outsource your espionage.

Given the Trump family's competency level, one can see why. Don Jr. was forced to release damning emails that proved he was more than eager to have help from a foreign adversary. After receiving an email stating, "This is obviously very high level and sensitive information but is part of Russia and its government's support for Mr. Trump," he replied, "If it's what you say, I love it, especially later in the summer." How is asking for the release of damning information from a foreign adversary *not* coordination?

Then there was his infamous meeting with the Russians at Trump Tower, all of which paints a pretty obvious picture. Trump was asking for help and getting it. Trump Jr. was offered help and was enthusiastically embracing it. All from the Russian government. Not "Little Russia" in Brighton Beach, but the foreign one where Siberia's located. From the outside looking in, this was a nice package of collusion. Add in Trump's admission he fired James Comey over the Russia investigation, and you can add a bow of obstruction.

All we needed was a no-nonsense G-man to get the job done. As if carved from our collective imaginations, in walked Robert Mueller. Straight out of central casting. Serious and stern. Always in a suit. He looked the part. Confidence was rising that Mueller would come through in our national time of crisis. We could only imagine what he would uncover. The open admissions by Trump alone proved his case. Collusion and obstruction of justice were no-brainers. Just the things Trump said in public would result in an indictment. It was like having a bank robber on tape bragging about all the banks he robbed. Open. Shut. The only question left was what else Robert Mueller would find.

Apparently, what Robert Mueller uncovered was that Robert Mueller was a Republican above all else. America needed Jack McCoy from *Law and Order*. Instead, we got Fredo from *The Godfather*. Robert Mueller shrank so far from his role, he would not even read his own report. When asked in testimony to read from his finding out loud, Mueller refused. "I would be happy to have you read it out loud," a smiling Mueller told Rep. Jamie Raskin (D-Md.) when asked if he could read one passage. He was smiling because Mueller is, at the end of the day, a Republican. And he did what they all do: fall in line. Despite the fact he uncovered extensive evidence that Trump had repeatedly committed the crime of obstruction of justice.[6]

Our savior turned into another toady. He was obsequious even after being emasculated by Attorney General William Barr. Barr lied when he summarized Mueller's report, falsely claiming there's no collusion and no findings of obstruction of justice. In fact, Judge Reggie B. Walton said Mr. Barr could not be trusted, and he cited "inconsistencies" between his statements about the report when it was secret and its actual contents, which turned out to be more damaging to President Trump.[7]

Yet Mueller was still kowtowed—so much so, he never filed any charges against Don Jr. In non-legal terms, Mueller decided he was too stupid to know what he was doing was potentially illegal. The same held true for Paul Manafort and Jared Kushner. Can you name one person of color who avoided prosecution for being too stupid to know they were committing a crime? Or is stupidity a white thing?

With Mueller in line, impeachment offered no hope. Republicans would acquiesce as they always do. Free of any repercussions for asking one foreign country for help in an election, he moved to another. When Trump threatened/bribed/extorted Ukraine President Volodymyr Zelenskyy, he committed an impeachable offense. Trump told President Zelenskyy that funds for Ukraine would be withheld until they gave him dirt on Joe Biden.

Republicans insisted there was no quid pro quo—until the transcript of Trump's Ukraine call was released. Then they claimed it couldn't be a quid pro quo because nothing of value was given. Based on their pretzelian logic, it couldn't be because it was asked for but not received. When that theory was debunked, they just argued it was okay to coerce a foreign power to help interfere in an election. Not based on the Constitution they pretend to love, honor, and defend:

SECTION 4. The President, Vice President and all civil Officers of the United States, shall be removed from Office on

Impeachment for, and Conviction of, Treason, Bribery, or other high Crimes and Misdemeanors.

As they show time after time, government isn't the problem; it's Republicans in government that is the problem. When Reagan said the nine most terrifying words are "I'm from the government and I'm here to help," he missed a word or two. He abridged the original, more accurate statement. "I'm *a Republican* from the government and I'm here to help."

That is what is truly terrifying, as we are all witnessing firsthand. You always find out what Republicans have been doing behind our backs during a crisis. How they've hobbled government or ignored experts. From 9/11 to Hurricane Katrina, to the Iraq War to the Global Recession to Hurricane Maria to self-regulating planes to bankruptcy-inducing tax cuts. We don't know how they'll make us unsafe; we just know they will.

Never more so than with the Trump pandemic. Ignorance and mindless budgetary cuts are on full display, which only got worse as more information came to light. As the pandemic was raging, our medical community faced a shortage of ventilators and other personal protective equipment. In response, Donald Trump bragged about the U.S. stockpile of ventilators, many of which were defective.

In true Trumpian fashion, 2,109 lifesaving ventilators didn't work because he allowed their servicing contracts to lapse late last summer after a contracting dispute.[8] Think about that as you're slowly suffocating to death. Your defective ventilator helped Trump shave a few dollars off of his deficit. Rest easy knowing your suffering is not in vain, though. Your defective ventilator served a higher purpose. You helped pay for the trillion-dollar tax cut for the wealthy. Without you, a plutocrat may not be breathing quite so freely in their summer mansion, away from the rest of us—the ones who will bear the brunt of COVID-19.

While the damage done by our most recent illegitimate president may be irreversible, we need to understand how we got here in the first place. Once we see how our first misbegotten president was elected, everything starts to fall into place. Going back to 2000 shows why the GOP is so adamant about voter suppression. Without it, George Bush never would have been in *a position* to be elected by the Supreme Court.

His narrow 537-vote lead would have been overwhelmed by votes for Al Gore—except racism won and democracy lost. Again. Because those votes were never allowed to be cast. Under the guise of voter integrity, Florida sent its county election supervisors a list of 58,000 "alleged" felons to purge from the voting rolls.[9] Or as they are more accurately called by Republicans: black voters.

As is common with voter purges nationwide, they are littered with errors. These errors end up disenfranchising voters—by design. If you're poor and black, when you show up at a polling place and find your name has been purged, your options are almost nonexistent. Best-case scenario? You try to fix a problem that doesn't exist and hope to do so before *the next* election. Assuming you have the means and wherewithal to fight to begin with.

Remember, not every person of color is running for governor of Georgia.

Republicans are counting on that. After the NAACP sued Florida for violating the Voting Rights Act, it became evident why Republicans want to suppress the vote. It's how they win elections—a fact confirmed by Florida's settlement. As part of that settlement, the company in charge of the voter purge—Database Technologies (DBT)—ran the names on their purge list using stricter criteria and found 12,000 voters who shouldn't have been labeled felons.[9]

While it's safe to say 12,000 is greater than 537, further analysis was needed to see how many of those purged votes would have gone to Al Gore. According to Edward Hailes of the U.S. Civil Rights Commission, it was enough to swing the election. Through his analysis of the racial makeup of the purge combined with voting data, he concluded 4,752 black Gore voters were stripped of their right to vote.[9] This is almost nine times Bush's margin of victory.

Lesson learned. It was time to start disenfranchising voters everywhere they could. During the 1990s, Republicans disenfranchised voters by ignoring them. That's what the Hastert Rule did. It was a voter purge that relied on Republicans getting enough votes in the House of Representatives *to be able* to ignore voters they didn't like. They still had to win elections, though. Or did they?

The real lesson from 2000 was they didn't. By preventing blacks from voting, they could steal elections. Forget about getting more votes. That is so 1776. It was easier to get fewer votes and win. Just make sure the votes you don't like don't count. Or if you can, prevent them from ever being cast to begin with. Keep them as three-fifths of a person. That's the lesson that current Supreme Court Chief Justice John Roberts learned firsthand.

In 2000, he was a lawyer hired by Bush to work on the 2000 Florida recount. "Work on the recount" is a euphemism for preventing it from happening. It's better known as taking away an American's right to vote. Specifically, an African American's right to vote. Given Roberts's history, he was the right man for the job. Under Ronald Reagan, John Roberts led the charge against reauthorizing the Voting Rights Act in 1982.[9] This is the Voting Rights Act he would later gut.

Failing to do so under Reagan, he was undeterred. He succeeded in getting Bush elected without winning the election. His reward was a seat on the United States Supreme Court. Now he's the Chief Justice—further delegitimizing today's right-wing Court. Especially because his disdain for the rights of minorities did not dissipate with his failure to end the Voting Rights Act under Reagan. It burned so bright, he finally got his wish. First, he helped disenfranchise all voters in Florida. Then he neutered the Voting Rights Act so thoroughly, it ushered in a wave of voter suppression efforts across the South and spread to Republican states nationwide.

Keep them from voting and keep power. That's what voter purges are all about. Any inconsistency can place you in their crosshairs. A missing middle initial or your name being "Steve" here and "Steven" there and voilà, you lose your right to vote. Effective as that may be, it is only one front on Republicans' war against democracy. The other is a modern-day poll tax, otherwise known as voter ID laws.

Republicans know the people they don't want to vote are the ones most likely not to have a government ID. Students, minorities, and the poor are disproportionately affected by voter ID laws. In other words, Democratic voters. As an example, John Pawasarat, an analyst and researcher, sought to quantify the disenfranchising effects voter ID laws had on people of color. In Wisconsin alone, he found that only 53 percent of black adults and 52 percent of Hispanic adults had driver's licenses, compared with 85 percent of whites.[10]

Those are election-altering numbers. Further proof that these ID laws are poorly disguised poll taxes came from his other finding. Pawasarat found that 60 percent of blacks and Hispanics lost their licenses for things like failure to pay fines unrelated to driving—like loitering or jaywalking.[10] Losing your right to vote by crossing the street at the wrong time. Does it get any more undemocratic than that?

Actually, it does. Republicans realized that voter purges and voter ID laws may wound democracy but not kill it. After all, their policies are so abhorrent that a lot of white voters and middle-class people of color will still go to the polls and vote them out. They're the ones who have the ways and means to ensure their votes are counted. Or should I say *cast*?

Republicans know they can't take away *everyone's* right to vote, so they did the next best thing: make it irrelevant. One person, one vote is for democracies. Not plutocracies. In Pond Scum, the objective is not only to get the best cards that life deals. You need to *keep* getting them. Republicans already have a structural advantage because of the racist Electoral College. No inherent advantage is great enough for them, however. There's a reason they've won the popular vote once in the last 30 years. They're not popular and neither are their policies.

Rather than look for ways to become more popular, they have sought ways to cement their partisan electoral advantage. Given their reliance on low-population rural areas, Republicans have sought to increase their already over-weighted vote count. In a cruel twist of fate, this has been done through prison gerrymandering. Republicans have spent decades filling prisons with people of color who unknowingly have helped them retain power. This is a power they use to incarcerate and disenfranchise people of color even further.

Prison gerrymandering is the process of counting prisoners toward overall population. Think about it as today's Three-Fifths Compromise. Under the Three-Fifths Compromise, slaves were counted as three-fifths of a person so Southern states would have a larger say in elections. Today, prisoners give rural areas a larger say in elections because without them there wouldn't be enough people to justify state representation. In Pennsylvania alone, there are eight state legislative districts that have too few non-incarcerated residents to be state legislative districts without counting the mostly urban prisoners.[11]

It doesn't take much of an intellectual leap to see how this self-fulfilling prophecy works. If I want to have a representative, I need to have prisoners because no one wants to live in my barely inhabited community. The more prisoners I have, the greater my vote becomes. With greater voting clout and an increasing prison population, the fewer people I need to attract to my rural area. Voting Republican helps fill the jails with urban people of color. These are people who help my vote count more than theirs, and they're kept behind bars. I keep voting so I can have my rights and strip them of theirs.

And the war keeps raging. With minorities stripped of their rights or incarcerated, Republicans moved on to the next front: gerrymandering. Gerrymandering is basically when politicians pick their voters. Historically, Democrats and Republicans worked together to carve out safe districts. This gives certain politicians a high chance of reelection while the overall state balance between Democrats and Republicans reflected actual voter preferences. Back then, Republicans still somewhat respected the voters' will. This respect stopped after they developed the nuclear gerrymander.

Unlike a regular gerrymander, the nuclear gerrymander eliminates voters and Democrats almost entirely. No longer do voters' intentions or wishes matter. With the nuclear gerrymander, Republicans have gained a distorted electoral advantage despite voters' wishes to the contrary. Republicans have drawn congressional maps so twisted that these distortions are nearly insurmountable. Democrats are packed into districts with no rhyme or reason other than locking in Republican majorities.

Republican mapmakers readily admit this. In North Carolina, the Republican in charge of the redistricting effort in the statehouse, Rep. David Lewis, justified the current drawing of the map, saying: "I think electing Republicans is better than electing Democrats. So, I drew this map to help foster what I think is better for the country."

Not what's best for North Carolina or what North Carolinians want, but rather what a Republican politician representing the minority wants. This is why in North Carolina in 2012, Democrats won 50.6 percent of the vote and only captured four of 13 seats.[12] That means that over 50% of North Carolinians wanted Democratic representation and ended up with 30%. In other words, they voted for democracy and got fascism.

Republican state after Republican state has followed the same blueprint. The 2010 census and GOP takeover in statehouses ushered in an era of right-wing vote rigging, culminating in the 2012 elections. During those elections, Democratic House candidates won 1.4 million more votes nationally than Republicans, but the GOP won 33 more seats.[13] Welcome to Moscow!

Democracy as we know it may be on life support. According to former Attorney General Eric Holder, the prognosis does not look good. He emphasized the problem thusly. "Unregulated dark money combined with these voter-ID laws combined with gerrymandering is inconsistent with how our nation's system is supposed to be set up. American citizens ought to be concerned about the state of our democracy. We could end up with a system where a well-financed minority that has views inconsistent with the vast majority of the American people runs this country."[13]

I would counter we're already there. On top of every other method Republicans use to end democracy, they find new ways to push our country even further toward fascism. Against all odds, Democrats have managed to win some statehouses. Unlike with congressional races, Republicans cannot gerrymander their way to a governorship. Stripping voting rights still leaves enough voters around to see to it that some semblance of democracy is restored.

Until Republican fascism rears its ugly head. Even when a governor manages to get elected, it may not mean much. After losing the governorship in North Carolina in 2016 and Wisconsin in 2018, Republicans went post-nuclear. They used lame duck legislative sessions to enact bills stripping the incoming Democratic governors of power.[13] These were gerrymandered non-representative legislatures, it should be noted. Furthering their assault on voters, in North Carolina, Republican legislators held a surprise vote on 9/11 to overturn Democratic Governor Roy Cooper's budget veto.[14] They did so after telling Democrats no vote would be held on such a solemn day of remembrance.

Another way of saying this is *we* should never forget. Never forget how Republicans shamelessly continue to exploit a tragedy of their own making. All while being subsidized by the same Americans they call enemies. An oft-overlooked component of the GOP's Second Civil War is the fact it's being funded by the states they're at war with. High-tax blue states pay a disproportionate share of taxes relative to their red state brethren. We're paying for their war. For nearly 80 years, poorer, low-tax states—where anti-government ideology and hostility to Washington, D.C. have generally flourished—have benefitted disproportionately from federal spending.[15]

As an example of this largesse, take welfare queen South Carolina. Despite its long history of opposition to the federal government, South Carolina takes in nearly $4 in federal benefits for every dollar its citizens pay in federal taxes.[15] If they were a hedge fund, they would be legends. Instead, they're one in a long line of moochers—red states that are stealing money and votes from blue states.

This monetary and electoral imbalance is reaching its breaking point. How much longer will blue states send money to these welfare queens while they steal their votes? As the causalities from the Republican war on democracy grow, so does the fallout. The elections of this past decade show how far the pendulum has swung from the voices of the many to those of the few. The consequences of the Republican war on democracy is about to result in actual lives lost.

Wisconsin's electoral tragedy may turn into a real one. In the middle of the Trump pandemic, their governor tried to postpone the Wisconsin primary. The illegitimate Republican legislature refused. Democratic Governor Tony Evers sought the postponement after the Republican legislature rejected his call to cancel in-person voting and extend the time to return absentee ballots into late May. Republicans want people risking their lives in the hope it will prevent them from voting. Add pandemic disenfranchisement to the long list of ways Republicans will deny your constitutional right to one person, one vote. Especially when one person turns into many people.

Because when the thought of people voting by mail came up, Republicans in unison nearly goose-stepped their way off of a cliff as

276

their heads exploded. Keeping Americans safe in the middle of a pandemic necessitates keeping them away from large public gatherings—like polling places. It's the only way to keep poll workers *and* voters safe. The problem is, not everyone's safe when people vote by mail. Like the people who want to disenfranchise voters.

None other than Donald Trump said out loud what Republicans have been saying in private for decades. Facing the prospect of saving American lives in the fall with mail-in ballots nationwide, he said with such an increase in voter turnout, "You'd never have a Republican elected in this country again." This caps modern-day Republicans' pledge to put party before country. Republicans would rather steal a blood-stained election than risk losing one legitimately. That brings Reagan's religion to its logical conclusion: the dissolution of democracy.

Think of all the lives and money that would have been saved if American votes actually counted. From 9/11 to the Trump pandemic, people died because democracy died. Lives were lost because we lost our way. We are like the proverbial frog in the pot. When Reagan turned on the burner, it felt warm and cozy. Like getting a hug from a loved one, and drifting off to sleep. Then awakening because we sense the flames scorching the sides of the pot. Waking as the water surrounding us comes to a full boil. Cooking us and our democracy.

In hindsight, maybe getting into the pot was a bad idea. It prevented us from seeing what Republicans were doing to our country. Lulled into complacency by faux patriotism, it never occurred to us they were destroying the foundation of our country. They were pulling their party ever closer to fascism and away from a country that is center left. Ruling further and further from the right, Republican governance long ago stopped representing the will of the people. As the following chart shows, they have more in common with the Alternative for Germany Party than the United States, or even the party of Reagan.[16]

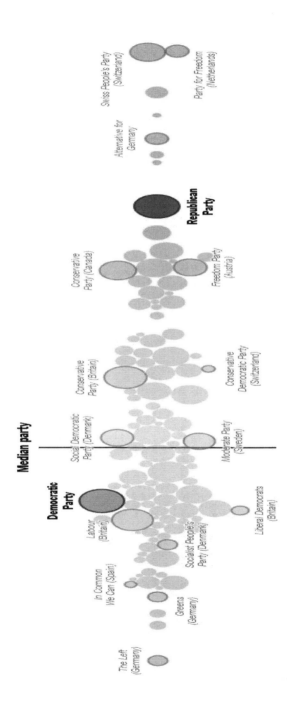

Median party

The Left (Germany)

In Common We Can (Spain)

Greens (Germany)

Democratic Party

Labour (Britain)

Socialist People's Party (Denmark)

Liberal Democrats (Britain)

Social Democratic Party (Denmark)

Moderate Party (Sweden)

Conservative Party (Britain)

Conservative Democratic Party (Switzerland)

Republican Party

Conservative Party (Canada)

Freedom Party (Austria)

Alternative for Germany

Swiss People's Party (Switzerland)

Party for Freedom (Netherlands)

The tyranny of the minority is only going to escalate. A man who received three million fewer votes than his opponent just put his third justice on the Supreme Court in a confirmation process run by a Senate unrepresentative of America. Democratic senators have only 47 seats yet represent nearly 169 million people while Republicans hold 53 seats representing only 158 million people.[17] In other words, Democrats represent 52% of the country and hold only 47% of the Senate—a discrepancy that has held. Since 2014, the Senate has been controlled by Republicans cumulatively representing less than half of the country, and in 61 of the past 100 years, Republicans have held more of the Senate than it represents in the population.[18]

Thus, the will of the minority is thrust onto the majority, cementing it with a Supreme Court comprised of justices the people did not approve. Adding Bush's two Supreme Court justices, five of the nine justices are from presidents the people rejected. If past is prologue, the Court will be voting against the interests of those very people. They are the majority of Americans who used their vote to prevent these justices from getting on the Court to begin with. Unwanted justices rule on everything from environmental regulations to our personal freedoms for generations. Possibly even anointing another Republican president the people rejected. Forced onto a country against our will.

With Republicans jamming Amy Coney Barrett through the nomination process, it is no longer conjecture. She was confirmed to the Supreme Court a week before the election, cementing the 6-3 arch-conservative majority for decades. This is in violation of the

McConnell rule, which prohibits Supreme Court vacancies to be filled in an election year. It was violated by none other than Mitch McConnell. Proving yet again the vacuity of the Republican Party. Refusing to follow rules even of their own making. Acting as little more than placeholders for their wealthy donors. It's a party devoid of all integrity. Lacking in even the basic respect for tradition, the will of the people, and the Constitution. Standing for little else than what their mammonist overlords tell them to.

When Ronald Reagan was elected president, he drew the battle lines that his Republican Party is fighting behind. His nine words let everyone know the government was the enemy. His cavalry was formed with his eleventh commandment, with Republicans walking in lockstep ever since. Every step they took was a step toward ending our democracy.

Each step was launching a trial balloon. When Newt Gingrich dehumanized and delegitimized his "enemies," not only did he not receive pushback, he was rewarded when Republicans took over the House of Representatives. His objective of turning the United States of America into the Divided States of America was a winning one—for Republicans. When Dennis Hastert and his fellow Republicans decided Democratic voters' votes didn't count and that their representatives' voices in the House should be silenced, there were no repercussions. Treating Democratic victories as illegitimate became another reinforcing stone on the pathway to one-party rule.

This culminated in the heist of the 2000 election, when they prevented the votes from being counted that would have allowed Al Gore to be president—having the Republican Supreme Court elect

George Bush instead. Lessons learned? Suppress votes while stacking the judiciary in their favor. This is why Mitch McConnell negated 66 million votes when he blocked President Obama's nominees and prevented his Supreme Court pick from even having a hearing. All while trying to push the U.S. economy into a recession. Because he could. Because it was good for him. Because it was good for his party. Because it was bad for democracy and the country.

All of this is why we have not been living in a democracy for some 30 years. Our system of government is Democratic Fascism. Thirty years ago, we had a capital D and a lowercase f. Now, the letters are reversed, with the lowercase d in our democracy in tatters and on the verge of collapse. We are potentially crossing the Rubicon where voting no longer matters—landing us in purely authoritarian lands.

With Republicans stealing and invalidating elections for decades, it was only a matter of time before they tried to overturn one. The only question is whether this is another trial balloon—or will they be successful in their first foray into despotism? For despite the resounding victory President-Elect Joe Biden received, Republicans are either actively trying to undermine election results or sitting idly by while their counterparts do. Acting or enabling, the end result is the same: sabotaging what's left of our democratic norms.

This is a year that is truly historic. With unrivaled turnout and Joe Biden receiving more votes than any other presidential candidate in history, he is on pace to beat Donald Trump by five to seven million votes while achieving over 300 Electoral College votes.

When adding Joe Biden's popular vote margin with Hillary Clinton's, Donald Trump will make history by being the only person to lose the popular vote by close to 10,000,000 ballots.

Further amplifying Donald Trump's historic accomplishments is the fact he is the only president to keep his approval rating below 50% for four years.[19] Never before had a president managed to have a majority of Americans disapprove of their performance in our 244-year history. Further gaining him notoriety is that he is one of only ten sitting presidents not to get reelected, capping off his agonizingly long four years as one of only three presidents to be impeached. With the distinction as the *only* president to get impeached while losing the popular vote twice.

Despite this, or perhaps because of it, Donald Trump is trying to overturn the election. He is claiming voter fraud without providing a single piece of evidence. In Republican-run states that saw Republicans get elected down ballot while the up ballot went to Joe Biden. Meaning the criminal masterminds in the Democratic Party launched a sinister plot to steal the presidency, lose seats in the House of Representatives, and leave the Senate in Republican hands. All this is ensuring that they won't be able to enact their agenda. And Mitch McConnell is saying he may not even approve any of Joe Biden's cabinet picks. Purely diabolical.

But not on the part of Democrats. What we need to understand is that Donald Trump has initiated a coup. The Trump crime family is trying to strong-arm Republican legislators to not certify their election results—in the process, acknowledging the elections they ran were fraudulent. Their express purpose is to deny either candidate the possibility of receiving the 270 electoral college votes needed for the presidency, forcing the election to be decided in the House of Representatives, where each state gets one vote. With Republicans holding more statehouses, the coup would be complete. Are there enough patriotic Republicans to stop him? If there are, it needs to be clearly stated: if the bullet doesn't assassinate our morbid democracy this time, it will the next.

The next time, there won't be anything left between the GOP and official one-party rule. When elections no longer matter, we'll still be able to vote; it's just that Republicans will claim voter fraud and overturn elections they don't like. Without voters to worry about, they'll be able to realize their goal of shredding what's left of our safety net. Disenfranchising the less fortunate before working their way up to slaying their white whale—Social Security and Medicare. Finally achieving their long sought-after dream of a fascist plutocratic nirvana.

As the above scenario unfolds, it will become crystal clear why Republicans have been lying to the American public since 1980, when Ronald Reagan said he wanted a gun in every home. It was in preparation for this day. A day Republicans knew would come— when they could overthrow the government. The enemy they created. The enemy they defiled. The enemy they crippled from within. The enemy they ultimately took down. A day they prepared for.

They knew protestors would hit the streets and that they would be no match against the military and armed domestic terrorists. Ironically, these militias would finally be an accurate representation of what the Second Amendment's true intention was. The only difference is that instead of putting down slave rebellions, they would be putting down all Americans—any member of the wrong party regardless of skin color. If you don't think it can happen here, it has been. Step by step, we have inched closer to that day. We have been traveling down the path toward totalitarianism—one few democracies recover from. Only one in five democracies that start down this path is able to reverse the damage before succumbing to full-blown autocracy.[20]

With that in mind, it's worth remembering that Hitler turned Germany fascist with only 37% support. In the United States, Republicans have the support of over 45% of the population. Forty-five percent of Americans who forgot what our country fought for and against. Something I will *never* forget.

My Italian grandfather fought against fascism in the First World War. He was an Italian who volunteered for the allies and was given a boat pass to America because he survived. His reward was being told America didn't want "dirty Italians" in their country. Growing up in a country that didn't want him, my father was spit on and ridiculed as a child because of who he was. Despite it all, my father loved his country—the one he was born in. So much so, he forced his parents to write a letter of consent so he could fight in World War II against the tyranny and fascism of Germany and Japan.

I never imagined one day I, too, would be called upon to fight that same threat. Not from abroad, but at home. The same home my forefathers fought to save from tyranny, so that such tyranny would never reach our shores. They never expected that one day our borders would be breached from within. Trying to prevent a cold coup, I feel like a modern-day Paul Revere, not galloping down cobblestone streets warning, "The British are coming, the British are coming," but alone on a rooftop, yelling, "The fascists are here! The fascists are here!" I only have one question.

Can anyone hear me?

When Fascism comes to America it will be wrapped in the flag and carrying a cross.
—Sinclair Lewis

Chapter 13: Handmaidens in High Castles

That's how we got here.

If Donald Trump is Frankenstein's monster, Doctor Frankenstein is surely Ronald Reagan. According to legend, there is only one way to kill Frankenstein's monster. We must storm the gates. Pitchforks raised high, torches lighting our way. Unfortunately, when we get there, we find out we're not alone. The entire Republican Party and its media ecosystem are waiting for us, waving their pitchforks and tiki torches. Not to take down Frankenstein's monster. They're there to protect him.

When Ronald Reagan told Mikhail Gorbachev "to tear down this wall," did he know what his fellow Republicans would do with the rubble? To rebuild it as a sanctuary for Vladimir Putin and his Russian enablers. Maybe they misunderstood him. Because there's little doubt the GOP has become the party of Russia. Once a superpower, Russia finds itself in a position of gaining strength only by stripping it from others. The biggest feather in its cap is taking down the United States.

More specifically, taking down American democracy. Vladimir Putin has had us in his sight since he was with the KGB decades ago. Showing the world that democracy doesn't work props up his autocracy. His tactics were on full display in 2016 as Russia launched attacks through social media designed to alienate and fracture our country. The attacks were also designed to turn American against American and sow doubt in the legitimacy of our institutions and government.

Coincidentally, this is what Newt Gingrich was trying to do. It was the platform Vladimir Putin emulated: the Gingrich Doctrine. Delegitimize government and turn Americans against one another. Of course, the Russians wouldn't have been successful without Gingrich and the Reagan blueprint. The one that demonized government and labeled anything Republicans didn't like as socialism.

Putin took their game plan and used it to alter our election, helping him pave the way to his lifetime appointment as Russian president. All 85 regional governments in Russia approved a measure to allow President Vladimir Putin to remain in office until

2036. This is a precursor to what our elections will look like. Without a functioning democracy, we no longer stand as a beacon of hope for the rest of the world. Instead, we are just as dysfunctional as Russia. If democracy doesn't work here, why would it work there?

Essentially, Vladimir Putin helped elect someone who received three million fewer votes than his opponent. Is there any greater indictment of democracy than that? Especially when Republicans were in on it. They knew Vladimir Putin was influencing our election to help Donald Trump. In fact, "Moscow" Mitch McConnell knew about Russian interference and threatened to tear the country apart if President Obama ever brought it up.

James Comey knew, too. While he launched a public investigation into Hillary's email server (in which she was found innocent of any malintent), he never breathed a word about the FBI's investigation of Donald Trump. The FBI was investigating his campaign's possible collusion with a communist superpower. One was a crime, the other bad judgment. James Comey thought the public needed to know about a private email server but not treason?

Not that anyone on the right was the least bit concerned about having a Russian-installed dictator wannabe as president. In 2016, House Majority Leader Kevin McCarthy (R-CA) told then-Speaker of the House Paul Ryan (R-WI) and his fellow Republican colleagues that he thought Donald Trump was being paid by President Vladimir Putin. They denied it until they found out *The Washington Post* had a tape of the conversation. The following is a quote from *The Washington Post*'s reporting—coming directly from the recording:[1]

"I'll guarantee you that's what it is...The Russians hacked the DNC and got the opp [opposition] research that they had on Trump," McCarthy said with a laugh.

Ryan asked who the Russians "delivered" the opposition research to.

"There's... there's two people, I think, Putin pays: Rohrabacher and Trump," McCarthy said, drawing some laughter. "Swear to God," McCarthy added.

Kevin McCarthy also says, "I think Putin pays Trump."

"This is an off the record," Ryan said.

Not anymore, it's not. Neither is the fact the GOP sold us out to the Russians. Having Donald Trump on the Russian payroll is one thing, but the rest of the GOP? It's no secret that after multiple bankruptcies, Donald Trump couldn't get an American bank to loan him a wooden nickel. "Bankrupt Boy," as he was being called, would find a way to weasel out of that debt, too. With nowhere else to go, he turned overseas. Far overseas.

That's why he won't release his tax returns. Sure, his wealth is nowhere near what he claims, and he doesn't pay any taxes, but the real fear is divulging the reason he has any wealth at all. Rumor has it he's in hock to Russian gangsters and oligarchs. And if you owe them, Putin *owns* you. It's "kompromat," which is Russian for compromising material. It's what Vladimir Putin relies on when he's searching for a useful idiot. Someone he can groom for later. Like now.

Putin's kompromat isn't the loans. That's just what got him in the door. Once inside, the money bought him access to Donald Trump. Then, he used familiar KGB tactics to gain his trust. Once Donald trusted Vlad, he dropped his guard. That's when you're susceptible to giving away compromising material. Especially when you're put into compromising positions in a country full of secret video cameras.

Just ask James Comey. There's an infamous report by an ex-spy from Britain known as the "Steele dossier." In it is a claim that the Russians possess a "pee tape." For the uninitiated, it's a tape purporting to show multiple interactions between Donald Trump and Russian prostitutes in which they were allegedly paid to pee on a bed that President Obama slept in or perhaps on each other. Maybe even on Donald himself in what is known as a "golden shower." Who knows what, if anything, happened? Vlad's been silent about the whole thing, which is a critical component of the whole blackmail—I mean kompromat thing.

Not being so quiet is Donald Trump. After James Comey told him about the tape, he said Donald brought it up frequently. Apparently, he was obsessed about it. So much so, James Comey believes the "pee tape" might be real. It must be his experience investigating criminals that brought him to that conclusion. Guilty people tend to act a certain way.

Like wanting to know who said they had the "pee tape" and what was on it. Wanting those types of details tends to be less for the inquisitive and more for the culpable. In particular, this applies when they refute parts of the story—the one they purportedly had no part of. When someone clarifies details of an event they claim never happened, it makes one wonder. James Comey found himself in just that situation. After prodding by Donald Trump, James Comey began explaining the contents of the tape to him. Before he could finish detailing the allegations, Trump interrupted him. Donald Trump wanted to clarify part of the story. He wanted to make sure Comey understood an important point of the story (the one that wasn't true). Comey recalled, Donald "interjected: 'There were no prostitutes; there were never prostitutes'."[2]

Clarifying such a point would seem to indicate Donald Trump was more concerned about James Comey knowing that he didn't need to *pay* for women. More so than the fact he *needed* to have women peeing on each other in front of him. And there may be a tape to prove it. Would there be anything more compromising than that? Allegedly being in debt to Russian mobsters whose kingpin had a tape of you with your pants around your ankles. Grabbing yourself as Russian prostitutes pissed all over you? Or each other? Or Obama's bed?

You know that Vlad probably paid for the "girls" anyway, like all Russian mobsters do for their KGB stoolies. By the way, it should be noted, if someone else pays for *your* prostitute, she's still a prostitute. Only time will tell if we ever find out the truth. Maybe one day Vlad will no longer have any use for Donald and we'll find out what really happened. In the meantime, it's safe to say if anything from the loans to the "pee tape" are real, that means Vladimir Putin has Donald Trump on a short leash. And it's one he seems to yank with great frequency.

If he does, it should come as no surprise. Neither should Republican fealty to Russia. Whether they're allowing and welcoming election interference because they worship power or money, the results are the same: a divided, undemocratic nation headed toward fascism. Patriots would never allow a communist foreign power to infiltrate our elections. Welcoming such interference sounds like treason, doesn't it? I'm sure it would to our founding fathers. But when it comes to patriotism, the only sovereign nation Republicans care about protecting is the one made of gold.

Perhaps Karl Marx was right after all. When he said religion is the opiate of the masses, maybe he just got the religion wrong. Worshipping God isn't the problem. Republicans' real religion is money. This Marxian love of mammon is the reason Republicans launched the Second Civil War. In a cruel twist of fate, Republicans fought the first to end slavery and launched the second to end democracy, fighting with the relics of our slaveholding past.

In the name of mammon. Neither Civil War would have been fought were it not for the love of money. And indirectly, a European sweet tooth. For profits and sugar cane, both helping drive the slave trade. As the luxury ingredient sugar dropped in price, it became available to the masses. No longer a bourgeois product, sugar made its way into countless goods for the commoner. More goods equaled more demand, presenting a problem similar to today.

Harvesting sugar cane is labor intensive. Furthermore, few people wanted to work long hours in malaria-infested sugar fields wilting under an oppressive sun.[3] Getting them to do so would be cost prohibitive. Just like energy companies today, sugar plantation owners didn't want to pay their own way. Doing so then, as it would now, would make their product too expensive or their profits too low. As Yuval Noah Harari explains in his book *Sapiens,* "Sensitive to market forces, and greedy for profits and economic growth, European plantation owners switched to slaves."[3]

Slavery is synonymous with assumptions of racial superiority. These are presuppositions that continue to stain our country to this very day. Unbelievably, the party of Lincoln has been using race as a cudgel to divide us for decades. From Nixon's Southern Strategy to Reagan's welfare queen to Trump's white supremacy, Republicans have been using racial animus to their political advantage. They do this knowing they are ripping open festering wounds, yet somehow claiming not to be racist.

Donald Trump even went so far as to say, "I don't have a racist bone in my body," which may be true. But we're not worried about the bones. It's the racist heart pumping the racist blood to the racist brain. Perhaps less of a brain than a resting place for random thoughts—racist ones, usually. Like the ones that get him to put kids in cages because they didn't come from non-shithole—read, *white*—countries.

It's like we're living in a horror show version of *The Wizard of Oz.* Instead of searching for his missing brain and heart, the tinfoil hat man runs around proudly heartless and brainless, without a care in the world. No care besides trying to convince everyone how much of a stable genius he is and surrounding him with people who do just that.

Because they are doing what has always been done for Donald Trump: enabling him. Lax bankruptcy laws allowed him to cause economic destruction and pass it off to someone else. Threats of litigation allowed him to stiff people who worked for him, creating the sense of entitlement and lack of personal responsibility he carries with him to this day. Fostered, of course, by the media he loathes.

This is the one that helped put him in the White House. Without the free advertising Trump received, he would not have become president. Losing by over three million votes but winning where it mattered: free, unceasing airtime. Studies show that Trump received the equivalent of more than $5 billion in free advertising.[4] As Leslie Moonves said about Donald Trump: "It May Not Be Good for America, but It's Damn Good for CBS."

Is it still, Les? Or how about you, Mark Burnett? Without *The Apprentice*, Donald Trump would just be another floundering D-lister roaming the streets of New York. But as luck would have it, Donald Trump found an even bigger con man than himself. Amazingly, Mark Burnett managed to convince the viewing public that Donald Trump was not a bankrupt loser with no business acumen (other than an unconquerable ego). Even more surprisingly, he conned them into believing someone with a low IQ and no attention span was actually a business tycoon.

As becomes increasingly more apparent by the day, the real apprentice on that show was Donald Trump. He watched Mark Burnett transform a broke loser into a reality television star. He gained wealth only because everyone bought into the con. Trump must have been thinking, *If America will buy this, they'll buy anything*. And they did. Except for those who knew better.

Like the producers of *The Apprentice*. They knew better. Jonathan Braun, a producer on the show, said, "Most of us knew he was a fake. He had gone through I don't know how many bankruptcies. But we made him out to be the most important person in the world. It was like making the court jester the king."[5] With a disintegrating kingdom, they had their work cut out for them.

Another producer, Bill Pruitt, said, "We walked through the offices and saw a crumbling empire at every turn. Our job was to make it seem otherwise."[5] They also had to deal with someone who wasn't even up to the task of being a reality television star. Part of being a reality television star is having the mental acuity to understand it's not real. Following the teleprompter helps the script work, so the audience believes what the creators want them to believe.

Part of this means being able to fire the right person. Being the entire point of the show, it would be considered a critical task. Not for Donald Trump. At least not one he could handle. Trump was frequently unprepared for the boardroom sessions and would fire the wrong person, which meant the episode had to be reverse engineered.[5] This created more work for the production team. Now they had to find video to support firing a contestant who, by reasonable measures, should have been moving on to the next week.

Sort of like his staff does for him today. Because if there's a recurring theme with Trump, it's his own incompetence. The list of Trump enablers is exhaustive. What we can ascertain is that the media invention of Donald Trump mirrors what has happened to the entire Republican Party. It's the creation of an alternate reality bearing little to no resemblance to the world we actually live in.

Just as Donald Trump is little more than a failed trust fund brat, Republicans are little more than a cult posing as a political party. Whereas the cult of Donald Trump was born out of the media's thirst for short-term profits, the cult of Republicanism has a thirst not so easily quenched. They've patiently been playing the long game executing the long con.

For they know satisfying their thirst is only possible at the altar of mammon. They deceive themselves and their country along the way. Worship of mammon has caused them to abandon all their principles. Everything they once held dear was sold to the highest bidder. Empty rhetoric has allowed them to persevere. They're getting away with not only hijacking our language, but everything that is fundamentally American.

It allows them to claim they're Christian while they worship the Antichrist. Wave the flag as they desecrate the Constitution. Stand behind free-market capitalism as they ensure information and wealth only flow to the elite. Allow the foreign infiltration of our elections while pretending to be patriots. Call themselves conservatives as they deplete our financial and natural resources. Immorally take resources from the poor and give them to the rich. Falsely claim government is the problem rather than their greed.

For Republicans, there is an inverse relationship between money and government. The more they worship money, the more they hate government. Critically for us, it also why they work so hard to tear it down. Because a functioning government stands in the way of what they really are, and that is neoliberals. The thing they claim to hate is the thing they actually are. Neoliberals want everything privatized, deregulated, and globalized under the banner of free trade. All while inflicting austerity on the masses and crippling government.

Unfortunately, government is like plumbing. It takes your shit and moves it out of the house. All behind the scenes (or walls). No one ever praises plumbing. Imagine saying, "Wow, honey, can you believe how well our plumbing works? I haven't stepped in shit or piss for weeks." Praising plumbing never happens because you take it for granted. Maybe like your spouse. Until there's a problem.

This is why Republicans can't be trusted with our plumbing. They're constantly ripping out pipes and hoping you don't notice. And we don't until there's shit on the floor. What kind of moron rips out the plumbing to prevent it from working too well? The kind who doesn't care if we get shit on our shoes. In other words, the Republican kind. Republicans are going to republic. It's what they do. Now we're all covered in shit.

Covered because the following warning from the Department of Health and Human Services was ignored:

The outbreak of the respiratory virus began in China and was quickly spread around the world by air travelers, who ran high fevers. In the United States, it was first detected in Chicago, and 47 days later, the World Health Organization declared a pandemic. By then it was too late: 110 million Americans were expected to become ill, leading to 7.7 million hospitalized and 586,000 dead.[6]

If it sounds like a warning given to the Trump Administration in early January, you'd be wrong. It's not an analysis of the coronavirus; it's a prescient warning about what would happen if such a virus were to become a pandemic. And how unprepared we would be. Unprepared because the Trump Administration dismissed it.

Under the code name "Crimson Contagion," the Department of Health and Human Services imagined an influenza pandemic and simulated outcomes in a series of exercises that ran from last January to August. Crimson Contagion concluded that the federal government was woefully underfunded, underprepared, and uncoordinated for a life-or-death battle with a virus for which no treatment existed.[6] Partly because of what preceded the report.

After the Ebola epidemic in 2014 and 2015, President Barack Obama created the pandemic preparedness office at the National Security Council. In 2018, Donald Trump disbanded the government's entire pandemic response chain, subsequently shutting down the global health security unit within the National Security Council. For good measure, also pushing out the Department of Homeland Security epidemic team.

Not to mention cutting the budget for the CDC (The Centers for Disease Control and Prevention). It's like Trump ripped out all of the fire extinguishers in the house because Obama put them there. Then he sat by watching a grease fire incinerate everything, thinking he can throw paper towels at the problem. Like he did in Puerto Rico after Hurricane Maria. What kind of imbecile does that? Apparently, the same kind who bankrupts casinos. George Bush ignores a memo and 9/11 happens. Donald Trump goes a step further—not just ignoring a threat, but eliminating the department established to combat it. All while cutting funding to the CDC.

That is GOP incompetence on steroids. As is typical, it gets worse. Rather than direct the problem head-on, Donald Trump goes back to the old playbook. Thinking he could lie his way out of a pandemic, that's what he's done.

He said the virus was "contained" and "under control." It wasn't.

He said, "It's going to disappear." It's everywhere.

He said, "We have very little problem in this country." Just before the country shut down and governors enacted regional lockdowns.

He said the virus was only affecting 15 people in the U.S., and even more unbelievably, that within a couple of days it would be down close to zero before congratulating himself on a job well done. Instead, the U.S. has the highest case count. Mirroring the statistics of our fossil fuel use, we have roughly 4% of the population and 20% of COVID cases. With over a quarter of a million dead Americans, our death toll is projected to surpass 300,000 by year's end (2020).

This is a far cry from what the Liar-in-Chief told us to expect and nowhere close to disappearing. But Dishonest Don did manage to reveal one nugget of truth. It had to do with the availability of test kits. No, they weren't available to everyone when COVID broke out.

We can add that tale to the lie-o-meter. Unless we change the definition of "anyone." Like what happened with this exchange between Donald Trump and a reporter on March 18, 2020.

REPORTER: "How are non-symptomatic professional athletes getting tests while others are waiting in line and can't get them? Do the well-connected go to the front of the line? Should that happen?"

TRUMP: "No, I wouldn't say so... but perhaps that's been the story of life."

Because that has been the story of *his* life. As the coronavirus was becoming a pandemic, what was Donald Trump doing? What he always does. Having a party at Mar-a-Lago. It seems to be what he thinks he was elected to do. That and play golf (300 days and counting). Unfortunately, in attendance were numerous people infected with the coronavirus—mixing, mingling, and turning Mar-a-Lago into a coronavirus petri dish. But don't worry; he's got them covered. They were all point-centers. Winners—and possibly survivors—of Pond Scum. They'll get test kits and ventilators if need be. They're at the front of the line.

It would seem winning Pond Scum may be a life-or-death proposition, perfectly illustrating why Republicans can't keep us safe. Physically and fiscally, they put us at risk. Financially, it goes back to the 2008 financial crisis. Not only did they cause a near global depression, Republicans had little desire to help undo the damage they caused.

Instead, they insisted on austerity, flying in the face of economic fundamentals that insist otherwise. Rather than increasing government spending to help offset plummeting consumer spending, they suddenly wanted to balance the budget. Fighting President Obama at every turn. Unified in their opposition to every attempt he made to help the average taxpayer.

In essence, they prevented a robust economic recovery, which was their intention—in order to run against Obama in four years under the premise the economy they hobbled hadn't recovered. While they failed the win the presidency, they succeeded in preventing the economy from fully recovering. Had it not been for the fiscal stimulus by the Federal Reserve, Republicans may have seen the economic damage from their obstinacy prevail. Instead, low interest rates helped propel the stock market to record highs while the economy limped along. Growing, but proving to be a long and shallow recovery that did not benefit everyone equally.

This has put us at greater financial risk today. Had Republicans helped President Obama in his attempts to right the economic ship President Bush wrecked, a number of things would have occurred. Stimulus would have created jobs, which would have increased consumer demand, which would have increased company investment, which would have led to inflation and higher interest rates. Also, higher tax revenue.

This virtuous economic cycle would have continued to compound, ultimately putting us in a much better position to weather future economic storms. Not only would our balance sheet be stronger, but the Federal Reserve would be operating from a position of more normalized interest rates. Essentially, this would give them much more ammunition to avert future crises.

Instead, the opposite happened and the non-virtuous cycle repeated itself, jeopardizing us today. This has only been compounded by Donald Trump's unnecessary trade war, resulting in a bailout for farmers. Due to his trade wars with China, farmers have received $28 billion (and counting) in government welfare—double that of the auto bailout.[7] Unlike the Great Recession, which was foisted on President Obama, the trade war was a problem of Donald Trump's own making.

One can argue that the Trump pandemic started with the Trump Trade War. Without the latter, we may not have the former. Dominoes fall in unpredictable ways. Minus the trade war, China could have been eating U.S. soybeans instead of infected bats. Wouldn't we all be better off? At the very least, the welfare handed out to farmers would be available now when it's needed most. Instead, things have gone from bad to worse.

Due to the damage Trump's trade war has caused, the Federal Reserve was forced to cut interest rates. Absent the trade war, there would not have been an economic need to do so. By forcing the Fed's hand, he tied them when we needed them most. Being forced to bail out Trump's bad decisions left them ill-equipped to handle a future crisis. Faced with the coronavirus, they have almost no ammunition left to stimulate the economy.

This is a self-made problem further exacerbated by the Republicans' trillion-dollar tax giveaway to the wealthy. Corporations used this not to invest in their companies—and ultimately benefit the country—but rather, their shareholders. Helping push the national debt to over $20 trillion, with escalating trillion-dollar deficits for the foreseeable future. That is the cost of Trump's corporate welfare program. Before the coronavirus hit.

With the virus devastating our economy, we are too weak to respond. But there is no other choice. Trillions of dollars have been spent propping up the economy. Unsurprisingly, companies that used their corporate welfare to enrich shareholders are now short on cash. Despite not helping the economy by investing in expanding their businesses, they feel entitled to a bailout. This proves yet again there is capitalism for the poor and middle class and socialism for the rich.

Fittingly, the airlines are at the front of the line—the same airlines that used the bulk of their free cash flow to buy back their stock. In fact, over the last decade, the biggest U.S. airlines spent 96% of their free cash flow buying back their own stock.[8] This served to enrich shareholders at the expense of their own companies' financial safety. American Airlines Group Inc. took things one step further. They decided buying back stock was more important than having any cash flow, going so far as to generate negative cumulative free cash flow so they could buy back $12.5 billion of its shares.[8]

And $12.5 billion could a long way in cushioning the blow of lost revenue from the coronavirus. It's revenue that would most likely go to buying more stock, but it is revenue nonetheless. At least it wouldn't be a handout from you and me, which is where we're headed. No matter how much you give them, welfare queens will do what welfare queens always do: keep their hand out expecting more free stuff.

Think about that the next time you're sitting in a child-sized seat kissing your knees with someone else's jammed in your back. Fighting for an overhead compartment for your bag. Trying to avoid the onerous baggage fees so you can afford to buy an in-flight snack pack and rent a pillow.

None of this will stop the money from flowing up like it always does. Crisis or not, money doesn't trickle down, but it does siphon up. There's no other way to look at the way Republicans run our collective finances than to say it's fiscal malpractice. Especially considering where this is headed. Part of the Republican stimulus is to give *even greater* tax cuts to corporations. The same ones that did little more than to enrich themselves the last go-around. Most likely with no strings attached.

With a global recession all but guaranteed, this will push us toward a fiscal reckoning. We'll long for the normal negative Republican economic feedback loop because what's coming will feel like Armageddon. With a severe economic retraction coupled with major corporate tax cuts, the already trillion-dollar-plus annual deficits will skyrocket. In fact, they already have. The U.S. government budget deficit will triple this year to $3.3 trillion. Either we continue to spend more or suffer an economic contraction that will cripple tax revenues—spinning our fiscal mess until it's out of control.

All this is setting the stage for massive spending cuts. Republicans have been crippling our finances knowing a crisis would eventually come. It's here. Once the dust settles, they will claim it is no longer possible for the government to provide things like Social Security and Medicare. Dismantling the safety net has been on their agenda since long before Ronald Reagan decried the evils of socialized medicine. Once FDR proved the government could do good, Republicans have been on a mission to prove otherwise.

Life without—or with privatized—Social Security and Medicare would be devastating. Forget about Medicare for all; we'd end up with medical vouchers for the few. Even without the coronavirus, we had a healthcare crisis in this country. Stripping away what little protections we have would be crippling. Another consequence of the coronavirus is how little safeguarding us even matters to the GOP.

Listening to the right-wing echo chamber, it's clear Republicans put party over country even when the stakes are life and death. "Believing what they tell us to believe" imbues new meaning when doing so can be deadly. From February and into early March, Fox hosts lied to their audience about the coronavirus. Rather than warn them about the dangers it posed, they claimed it was a Democratic and media plot against Donald Trump. Never have the consequences of a Foxbotomy been so dire.

Rather than prepare, Fox viewers congregated like nothing was amiss. To them, it was just another media conspiracy. Getting back at the liberals meant ignoring their advice. How much is their propaganda responsible for the failure of a large part of the country to take the coronavirus seriously? Instead of trying to save lives, they chose to weaponize a deadly virus for political purposes. Wouldn't it be nice if something was in place to offset this type of life-or-death propaganda? Like the Fairness Doctrine?

It would be, but it still wouldn't be enough to save the county from Republican politicians. Illustrating just how far down the mammon rabbit hole the GOP has gone is Republican Senator Richard Burr from North Carolina. He may be the poster child for Republican greed and how they view their constituents from one lens—that made of money.

Towing the party line, the Republican Senator from North Carolina wrote an op-ed on February 7. He stated unequivocally: "Thankfully, the United States today is better prepared than ever before to face emerging public health threats, like the coronavirus, in large part due to the work of the Senate Health Committee, Congress, and the Trump Administration."[10]

Nearly three weeks later, on February 27, Burr attended a luncheon at the Capitol Hill Club. It was organized by the Tar Heel Circle, which is a group of North Carolina businesses and organizations. Or should I say a group of well-*heeled* North Carolinians since membership fees range between $500 and $10,000. I know $500 may not sound like a lot, but since half the country couldn't come up with it in an emergency, it's safe to safe the vast majority of us can't afford to join political social clubs. Buying a Republican is expensive.

But maybe we should put the membership fee on a credit card. It might just save your life. Certainly, everyone attending Richard Burr's luncheon felt it was money well spent. That's because public Richard Burr is not the same as private Richard Burr. The version of Richard Burr that shows up depends on who's paying him.

If you lived in North Carolina and your taxes paid him for being a senator, you got one message. Everything is fine. If you paid for it directly, you got another. What Richard Burr told the luncheon attendees, according to a secret recording obtained by NPR, was totally different. Here's what he said.

> "There's one thing that I can tell you about this: It is much more aggressive in its transmission than anything that we have seen in recent history. It is probably more akin to the 1918 pandemic."[9]

Honesty from Republicans is expensive, though. After NPR obtained a copy of the RSVP list, they found out just how expensive it was. According to federal records, those companies or their political committees donated more than $100,000 to Burr's election campaign in 2015 and 2016.[14] But as we all know $100,000 doesn't buy what it used to. Especially after a pandemic decimates the stock market.

Under those circumstances, there's only one thing to do: sell before everyone else knows how serious the pandemic is. Exactly what Richard Burr did. Surprisingly, on Friday, February 13th, he executed somewhere between $628,000 and $1.72 million in stock sales, over 33 separate transactions on a single day, according to public disclosures.[15] Unlucky Friday the 13th turned out to be quite the opposite for old Richard Burr, as he managed to dump stock in industries that would be devastated by the coronavirus before the carnage set it—including in the hotel and travel industries. How lucky is that? Very. Not only that, of those 33 transactions, not one was a buy order.

Luck seems to run with the GOP. *The Daily Beast* reported that another Republican senator, Senator Kelly Loeffler from Georgia, sold off more than $1 million in stock. All during the period leading up to the coronavirus outbreak in the U.S. She also avoided the massive market losses that followed. Was she the lucky recipient of a four-leaf clover or something more insidious—like a briefing on the damage to come? According to the report, Loeffler's sales began on Jan. 24, the day the Senate Health Committee received a closed-door briefing from administration officials on the coronavirus.[10]

Using the government as their own personal piggy bank is what Republicans do. Suffering and financial losses are for the little people. The coronavirus affects the rest of us—not unlike the Republican Party, who's been infecting us for 40 years. There may not yet be a vaccine for the coronavirus, but there is one for the GOP: voting. There's only one thing that can save our country and our planet. Needing a blue tsunami to wash away all the rot we have allowed to infect our government and civic discourse since Ronald Reagan's election, we got a surfable wave. Now our hopes rest on Georgia turning a deeper shade of blue.

Perhaps it's too late. Hindsight will let us know one way or the other. We're either at the tipping point or way past it. The survival of our democracy and our planet depend on it. Both are strapped in an electric chair waiting on the same call from the same governor. The governor is us. Will we accept the call and take back our democracy and middle class? Republicans have their hands on the switch. We're the only thing standing in their way. We have to demand democracy. We have to demand a return of the middle class. In other words, we have to demand an Americans First agenda.

AMERICANS FIRST

i.   End Slavery
ii.   Enact Reparations
iii. End Tyranny
iv.   Ranked Choice Voting
v.   Equal Taxation
vi.   Welfare Wages
vii. Medi-bridge
viii. Gig Gag
ix.   Republican Death Panels & The P.R.T.
x.   The D.R.A.

End Slavery

Remnants of slavery still haunt us today. There is no other remainder from that heinous period more offensive than the Electoral College. It must be abolished along with its racist undertones. Three-fifths of a person is not acceptable. Ending the Electoral College will do what should have been done with the abolishment of slavery: restoring full personhood to all peoples of color and descendants of slavery.

Enact Reparations

Every time an African American is denied their right to vote through racist Jim Crow-style voter suppression, slavery rears its ugly head. Rectifying that is simple. As we are well aware, voter fraud is essentially nonexistent (except for people being caught voting for Donald Trump). That's why voter ID laws are so pernicious and are little more than a thinly veiled poll tax. States that insist on a poll tax must pay it themselves.

Any African American required to have an ID may continue to vote until the state pays to get them one. If a state changes the ID requirement, the state has to pay to get an updated ID. For many poor African Americans, they do not have the financial means or the mode of transportation to obtain IDs. That's why Republican states want them. Since those are slave states or slave state sympathizers, their reparations are having to pay for any ID that could impede a person's right to vote. It'll be the slavery version of "innocent until proven guilty." Either way, it's going to be expensive to be racist.

End Tyranny

The tyranny of the minority must end. The population of the first 13 colonies was approximately 2.5 million people. Our 50 states have a population of roughly 330 million, which is 132 times larger. What worked for 13 colonies and 2.5 million people doesn't work for

50 states with 132 times the population. Our founding fathers may have gotten it right then, but what worked for 2.5 million doesn't work for 330 million.

Unable to predict the future, the founding fathers inadvertently exposed us to the tyranny of the minority—the kind of tyranny we fought the Revolutionary War to extradite ourselves from. It's inconceivable that the founding fathers could have envisioned a senator from a state not even in existence would usurp the powers of the presidency because of their folly.

Their folly was that every state should have two senators. It's well past time to admit their mistake and rectify it. Doing so would prevent an increasing minority of states from terrorizing the majority of voters. Following current trends, the senate will soon have 70% of the voting rights while representing only 30% of the population. Demographic trends continue to reinforce this disparity. Considering how much blue states subsidize these red states financially, it is nothing other than taxation without representation.

That's why the Senate must be reconfigured to represent a future unfathomable to our founding fathers. Each state will get one senator. Based on population, representation will increase from there with a maximum of five senators per state. This five-to-one ratio is very magnanimous given the current population disparity between our most- and least-populated states. Wyoming, with approximately 450,300 people, versus California, with over 36,900,300, is an 82-to-one difference.

Furthermore, to guard against any future Republican malfeasance, there needs to be a 60/40 rule. Anytime enough senators from enough states comprise 60% of the population, they can override the minority. As for the malfeasance in the House of Representatives, gerrymandering must never be allowed in any form. All states must have representation in proportion to the votes cast. For example, if Democrats receive 50% of the vote, they must have half their state's representatives (rounded up or down to the nearest whole number). Anything too out of balance and that state forfeits its delegation until the next round of voting. The minority abused its power for far too long. It's time to balance the scales.

Ranked Choice Voting

One of the travesties of the 2000 elections was Ralph Nader helping to elect George Bush. The same could be said of Jill Stein supporters electing Donald Trump in 2016. Surprisingly, the environmentalists helped elect the environmental Armageddonist. Not surprisingly, there's a fix for that.

Yes, eliminating the Electoral College would have prevented Donald Trump in 2016. But even without the Electoral College, we need to have a voting format that encourages third-party candidates. Without a voter fearing they will help elect someone diametrically opposed to all they stand for, or one that will allow planes to self-regulate. Ranked-choice voting fixes that.

The premise is simple. When you vote, you're not just voting for one candidate, but rather for *all* the candidates. In order of preference. For example, a Jill Stein voter could have voted for her, then Hillary, and down the line. The presumption is that such a system would encourage more third-party candidates.

Once all the votes are tabulated, anyone with 50% or more of the votes wins. Otherwise, the candidate with the lowest vote total is eliminated and their voter's next choice is added to the electoral results. The process continues, eliminating candidates and reallocating their votes based on the ranking until someone wins the majority. Voilà! Democracy. No more holding our noses at our polling station. Now we can vote for Felix the Cat knowing we won't inadvertently help elect Donald the Carnival Barking Clown.

Equal Taxation

Our tax system caters to the wealthy. Any tax code that has something called "carried interest" is all you need to know. It's mostly used by private equity and hedge funds. By classifying their work as a performance fee (regardless of whether they contribute any initial capital), carried interest is considered a capital gain. *Even without contributing any capital?* you might wonder. *Don't you need to put in capital to have a capital gain?*

For mere mortals, you do. But not for masters of the universe. For the winners of Pond Scum, carried interest is just another way for rich guys to change wages into wealth. *Abracadabra,* wages are miraculously turned into capital gains—meaning a lower tax bracket and no need to worry about pesky Social Security taxes.

If this doesn't sound fair, it's because it not. One way to eliminate this contentious classification of what most would consider income is to eliminate capital gains preferences. Why should wealth be taxed at a lower rate than work? Having one set of tax rates, one tax bracket, regardless of the type of income you receive, levels the playing field while eliminating loopholes. All while helping reverse Social Security's Republican-induced liquidity crisis.

Welfare Wages

Speaking of wages, no one should be on welfare working 40 hours a week. The federal minimum wage for 2020 is $7.25 per hour. It has been stagnating since 2009. At 40 hours a week, working 52 weeks without any vacation or sick time, you'd bring in a whopping $15,080 a year. Taking no sick or vacation time off is critical since minimum wage workers may not have paid sick or vacation days. Besides, where could they afford to go?

Minimum wage should be renamed welfare wages. No one can subsist on $15,000 a year. Using that entire amount on housing alone means renting a place for $1,250 a month. Forget about owning a house, or paying utilities, or buying food, or medicine, or clothes, or any of the other things you need to survive. Why should the taxpayer subsidize a corporation that won't pay a living wage?

If a minimum wage worker gets welfare, food stamps, subsidized housing, Medicaid, or any other government handout, the welfare is really corporate. We're paying so they don't have to. If the minimum wage kept pace with productivity growth, it would be over $20 an hour, inflation over $10. Splitting the difference is the fight for $15. While that only equates to $31,200 (before taxes), it's at least feasible to live off of $15 an hour.

Replacing welfare wages with a living wage is the first step toward ending corporate welfare and to stop subsidizing their labor costs. Indexing that number to a combination of productivity gains and inflation will ensure we leave welfare where it belongs: to those truly in need and not the working poor.

Gig Gag

As the Trump pandemic spreads and worsens, it's exposing fissures in our economy and cracks in our safety net. One of these is the gig economy. Companies no longer want employees; they want independent contractors. The problem is that independent contractors aren't really independent. Just ask any rideshare driver.

They're expected to be available like employees and act like employees. Otherwise, they'll be unemployed in short order. In other words, companies want employees they pay as contractors. Because contractors are cheaper. They don't get benefits or have their FICA paid for. Or unemployment benefits.

This will exacerbate what is already a painful recession, if not a second Depression. Clearly, the gig economy is only working for some of us. Since the federal government is expected to bail out everyone, there needs to be an adjustment in the balance of power between gig employee and gig employer.

Balancing the scales will require creating a general economic disaster fund. Individual companies will be required to contribute a specified sum to such a fund quarterly based on the percentage of its workforce that is gig. Contractors who work for larger employers that provide benefits could be excluded. Otherwise, the funds would accrue and offer benefits to a workforce without any.

Medi-bridge

A separate program would be available as a backstop for any American not offered medical insurance or who loses it because they lost their job. This could be funded in part with revenue generated by lifting the income limit on Social Security wages. Under such a plan, all wages and income will be subject to the 15.3% tax, 7.65% paid by employees and 7.65% paid by employers.

Gig workers not offered medical coverage can pay a 2.9% medical premium, which will be matched by their "employer." Self-employed individuals can pay the full 5.8% and receive coverage. Anyone covered under a Medi-bridge program will receive Under 65 Medicare. No American should go bankrupt because of an unforeseen illness. And no one should have to choose between medicine and food. Instead of "Medicare for All," let's try Medicare for those who need it.

Republican Death Panels & The P.R.T.

The death panels Republicans warned us about are here. Crying wolf for over a decade, the boy got tired of being wrong and let the wolf into the henhouse. Contrary to what you were told, the panel is full of Republicans. By hiding the severity of the coronavirus from us, they decided who would live and die.

Also, they decided how that death might unfold. Not only did inaction cause widespread infection and fatalities, it caused a strain on an unprepared medical establishment. Had Republicans warned us in January (when some of them were dumping stock), appropriate action could have been taken to get face masks and other personal protective equipment (PPE) for frontline doctors and nurses. Instead, they're reusing what they have, increasing the chance they'll get infected and pass it on to their patients.

All this is further straining a medical infrastructure on the verge of being overwhelmed. Even worse, since weeks were squandered, it's not just PPE they're short of; it's palliative care equipment for those infected as well. That means doctors may need to decide who gets a ventilator and who doesn't. So Republican death panels aren't just killing Grandma—they're suffocating her to death.

All while suggesting we move toward sacrificing the elderly for the good of the country. Texas lieutenant governor (Republican) Dan Patrick, 69, went so far as to suggest grandparents are willing to die for the U.S. economy. He told Tucker Carlson, "No one reached out to me and said, 'As a senior citizen, are you willing to take a chance on your survival in exchange for keeping the America that all America loves for your children and grandchildren?' And if that's the exchange, I'm all in. And that doesn't make me noble or brave or anything like that,' I just think there are lots of grandparents out there in this country like me... that what we care about and what we love more than anything are those children."

He's not alone. There's a chorus on the right willing to sacrifice Grandma and countless others to protect their own economic interests and hold on to power. This goes beyond the worship of money. Now Republicans want to make *actual* sacrifices at the altar of mammon. No one death panels like the GOP.

By now, it's painfully clear that Republicans can't be trusted and certainly can't keep us safe. The Trump pandemic has laid that bare for all to see. They're not even trying to be evasive about it. With future pandemics all but certain given global warming, something must be done to protect the country. As the planet warms unabated, there's no telling what will be unleashed tomorrow.

Coupled with the rapidly approaching Environmental Armageddon, we'll long for the days of empty shelves. Because they'll all be underwater when it hits. So, we better be prepared. In other words, we need to take it out of the hands of Republicans. We can't count on there being a President Obama to prepare us for the next pandemic when a Trump can undo it all.

That's why we need a permanent threat assessment team. Modeled after the Federal Reserve, its mandate will be to keep the country safe from pandemics and other environmental threats. The Pandemic Response Team (PRT) will be independent, as is the Federal Reserve. Without politicians controlling its message, it will be able to give accurate and unvarnished threat assessments. Donald Trump removed climate change from government websites for political purposes. As an independent agency, the PRT would be able to discuss freely how climate change affects the environment as well as the societal and financial costs associated with such changes and the potential pandemics that may be looming. They would warn us when needed—not when it's politically expedient or as a last resort.

The D.R.A.

Speaking of last resorts, that's where the D.R.A. comes in. It's short for the Democratic Republic of America. If all else fails, blue states can decide to stop subsidizing red states—monetarily and electorally. They're stealing our money and our votes. Not anymore. Wealthy coastal elites can take their money and enjoy it in the Democratic Republic of America. Don't forget, all of our first colonies were coastal, and our founders definitely were elite. Plus, it will be easy to chant if we ever have another Olympics. *D.R.A.-D.R.A.-D.R.A.* It's kind of catchy.

Or we could do nothing and watch as *The Handmaid's Tale* and *The Man in the High Castle* become documentaries. *Contagion* already has. It's not like we haven't been warned. We seem to be living in a real-life version of *When A Stranger Calls*. Unlike the movie, it's not just Jill the babysitter who's in danger. It's all of us.

She was warned, too. Forced to babysit two children in a really large house—punishment for exceeding her cell phone minutes—Jill is haunted by calls from a stranger. She's progressively more terrorized by these intrusions. Initially, a stranger calls and asks, "Have you checked on the children lately?" The calls escalate from there, culminating in a request for "your blood...all over me."

Having contacted the police, the most harrowing call had yet to come. Law enforcement found from where the calls were coming. When the police finally called her, she found out, too. "The call is coming from inside the house. Get out now!"

Needless to say, it didn't end well. At least not for the family for whom she was babysitting. How will it end for us? We answered the phone. We know the threat has been inside our house the whole time. One question remains. What are we going to do about it?

Sources

Chapter 1: Day One

[1] Brady Dennis and Chris Mooney, "Neil Gorsuch's mother once ran the EPA. It didn't go well." *The Washington Post*, February 1, 2017, https://www.washingtonpost.com/news/energy-environment/wp/2017/02/01/neil-gorsuchs-mother-once-ran-the-epa-it-was-a-disaster/?noredirect=on&utm_term=.cb8d40fe868a

[2] David Biello, "Where Did the Carter White House's Solar Panels Go?" *Scientific America*, August 6, 2010, https://www.scientificamerican.com/article/carter-white-house-solar-panel-array/

[3] Philip Shabecoff, "Reagan and Environment: To Many, a Stalemate," *The New York Times*, Jan. 2, 1989, https://www.nytimes.com/1989/01/02/us/reagan-and-environment-to-many-a-stalemate.html.

[4] Suzanne Goldenberg, "The Environment," *The Guardian*, January 16, 2009, https://www.theguardian.com/world/2009/jan/17/environment-george-bush

[5] Dakshayani Shankar, "House Overturns Obama-Era Law to Protect Alaskan Bears and Wolves," ABC News, February 7, 2017, https://www.nbcnews.com/news/us-news/house-

overturns-obama-era-law-protect-alaskan-bears-wolves-n722481

[6] World Population Balance, https://www.worldpopulationbalance.org/population_energy

[7] Jason Stanley, *How Propaganda Works* (Princeton & Oxford, Princeton University Press, 2015), pg. 18.

[8] Coral Davenport, "Major Climate Report Describes a Strong Risk of Crisis as Early as 2040," *The New York Times*, October 7, 2018, https://www.nytimes.com/2018/10/07/climate/ipcc-climate-report-2040.html?emc=edit_dk_20181008&nl=dealbook&nlid=4519898220181008&te=1.

[9] Elizabeth Kolbert, The Control of Nature, *The New Yorker*, April 1, 2019, pg. 45.

[10] Brad Plumer, "Humans Are Speeding Extinction and Altering the Natural World at an 'Unprecedented' Pace," *The New York Times*, May 6, 2019, https://www.nytimes.com/2019/05/06/climate/biodiversity-extinction-united-nations.html

[11] David Wallace-Wells, *The Uninhabitable Earth*, (New York: Tim Duggan Books, 2019), pg. 28.

Chapter 2: Ask ALEC

[1] Steven D, "Remembering Reagan's Sweet Little Lie to the Air Traffic Controllers," *Daily Kos*, July 9, 2012,

https://www.dailykos.com/stories/2012/7/9/1107835/-Remembering-Reagan-s-Sweet-Little-Lie-to-the-Air-Traffic-Controllers

2 Joseph A. McCartin, "The Strike That Busted Unions," *The New York Times*, August 2, 2011, https://www.nytimes.com/2011/08/03/opinion/reagan-vs-patco-the-strike-that-busted-unions.html

3 Brendan Fischer, "Scott Walker: The First ALEC President?" *PR Watch*, June 3, 2015, https://www.prwatch.org/news/2015/06/12851/scott-walker-first-alec-president

4 Scott Keyes, "How Scott Walker Built a Career Sending Wisconsin Inmates to Private Prisons," *The Nation*, February 26, 2015, https://www.thenation.com/article/how-scott-walker-built-career-sending-wisconsin-inmates-private-prisons/

5 Wisconsin Budget Project, "Prison Price Tag: The High Cost of Wisconsin's Corrections Policies," November 19, 2015, http://www.wisconsinbudgetproject.org/prison-price-tag-the-high-cost-of-wisconsins-corrections-policies.

6 Mike Spies, "The Arms Dealer," *The New Yorker*, March 5, 2018, pg. 24, 25, 31.

7 The Florida Senate, CS/SB 128: Self-defense Immunity, March 15, 2017, https://www.flsenate.gov/Session/Bill/2017/0128/?Tab=VoteHistory

Chapter 3: No One's Laughing

[1] Gwynn Guilford, "Almost everything Republicans get wrong about the economy started with a cocktail napkin in 1974," *Quartz*, April 29, 2017, https://qz.com/895785/laffer-curve-everything-trump-and-republicans-get-wrong-about-trickle-down-economics-and-reaganomics/

[2] "Economic Recovery Tax Act of 1981," Wikipedia, https://en.wikipedia.org/wiki/Economic_Recovery_Tax_Act_of_1981

[3] Sheldon L. Richman, "The Sad Legacy of Ronald Reagan," *Mises Institute*, October 1, 1988, https://mises.org/library/sad-legacy-ronald-reagan-0

[4] David Leonhardt, "How the Upper Middle Class Is Really Doing," *The New York Times*, Feb. 24, 2019, https://www.nytimes.com/2019/02/24/opinion/income-inequality-upper-middle-class.html?emc=edit_th_190225&nl=todaysheadlines&nlid=451989820225

[5] Alan B. Krueger, "The Economics of Rihanna's Superstardom," *The New York Times*, June 1, 2019, https://www.nytimes.com/2019/06/01/opinion/sunday/music-economics-alan-krueger.html

[6] Lisa Joyce, "The U.S. President and the Economy," *Advisor Solutions*, Volume 9, Q2 2017, pg. 9–10.

[7] Michael Tomasky, "Why Recent Republican Presidents Have Been Economic Failures," The New York Times, August 20,

2020, https://www.nytimes.com/2020/08/20/opinion/democrats-republicans-economy.html

[8] Jeanna Smialek, "The Business of Equality," *Businessweek*, March 25, 2019, pg. 42.

[9] Jack Nicas, "Apple Says It Will Buy Back $100 Billion in Stock," *The New York Times*, May 1, 2018, https://www.nytimes.com/2018/05/01/technology/apple-stock-buyback-earnings.html

Chapter 4: The Nine

[1] Gretchen Jacobson, "Income and Assets of Medicare Beneficiaries, 2016-2035," Henry J. Kaiser Family Foundation, Apr 21, 2017, https://www.kff.org/medicare/issue-brief/income-and-assets-of-medicare-beneficiaries-2016-2035/

[2] Rachel Garfield, Kendal Orgera & Anthony Damico, "The Coverage Gap: Uninsured Poor Adults in States that Do Not Expand Medicaid," Henry J. Kaiser Family Foundation, Mar 21, 2019, https://www.kff.org/medicaid/issue-brief/the-coverage-gap-uninsured-poor-adults-in-states-that-do-not-expand-medicaid/

[3] Allen W. Smith, Ph.D., "Ronald Reagan and the Great Social Security Heist," Dissident Voice, September 24, 2013, https://dissidentvoice.org/2013/09/ronald-reagan-and-the-great-social-security-heist/

Chapter 5: POC

[1] "The Federal Budget in 2017: An Infographic," The Congressional Budget Office, March 2018, https://www.cbo.gov/publication/53624

[2] Alexander Nazaryan, "Who Broke Congress? Dennis Hastert, Former Speaker, Breaks Two-Year Silence to Deny Role in Gridlock," *Newsweek*, October 12, 2017, https://www.newsweek.com/congress-gingrich-hastert-681653

[3] McKay Coppins, "How Newt Gingrich Broke Politics," *The Atlantic*, November 2018, p. 55.

[4] "How Newt Gingrich Crippled Congress," *The Nation*, January 30, 2012, https://www.thenation.com/article/how-newt-gingrich-crippled-congress/

[5] Johnathan Karl and Gregory Simmons, "Newt Gingrich: Big Spender," ABC News, Dec. 15, 2011, https://abcnews.go.com/Politics/newt-gingrich-big-spender/story?id=15163688

[6] Liam Stack, "Dennis Hastert, Ex-House Speaker Who Admitted Sex Abuse, Leaves Prison," *The New York Times*, July 18, 2017, https://www.nytimes.com/2017/07/18/us/dennis-hastert-released.html

[7] "Pelosi Brings End to 'Hastert Rule," *Rollcall*, May 25, 2017, https://www.rollcall.com/news/-18700-1.html

[8] George Packer, "Ten Years After the Crash," *The New Yorker*, August 27, 2018,

https://www.newyorker.com/magazine/2018/08/27/ten-years-after-the-crash

[9] Dana Milbank, "Mitch McConnell, the man who broke America," *The Washington Post*, April 7, 2017, https://www.washingtonpost.com/opinions/mitch-mcconnell-the-man-who-broke-america/2017/04/07/8e12f1d8-1bbd-11e7-9887-a5314b56a08_story.html?utm_term=.d72a95f2c1ba

[10] Allison Graves, "Fact-checking claims about court filibusters," *Tampa Bay Times*, April 16, 2017, Perspective 6P.

[11] Jason Stanley, *How Propaganda Works* (Princeton & Oxford, Princeton University Press, 2015), pg. 85.

[12] Myths vs. Facts on Filling the Supreme Court Vacancy, Alliance for Justice, https://www.afj.org/myths-vs-facts-on-scotus-vacancy

[13] Paul Krugman, "The Moochers of Middle America," *The New York Times*, July 1, 2019, https://www.nytimes.com/2019/07/01/opinion/2020-democrats-taxes.html

Chapter 6: Monte

[1] Barry Meier, "Cigarette Makers and States Draft a $206 Billion Deal," *The New York Times*, Nov. 14, 1998, https://www.nytimes.com/by/barry-meier?action=click&contentCollection=Archives&module=Byline&region=Header&pgtype=article

[2] "Cosmetology Administrative Rules," tdlr, Administrative Rules of the Texas Department of Licensing and Regulation 16 Texas Administrative Code, Chapter 83 (Effective January 15, 2018), https://www.tdlr.texas.gov/cosmet/cosmetrules.htm

[3] Diane Schanzenbach, Leslie McCall, Brian Melzer, David Figlio & Christine Percheski, "The Great Recession: Over but Not Gone?" 2014, Northwestern Institute for Policy Research, https://www.ipr.northwestern.edu/about/news/2014/IPR-research-Great-Recession-unemployment-foreclosures-safety-net-fertility-public-opinion.html

[4] Kimberly Amadeo, "US Budget Deficit by President by Dollar and Percent," Updated August 30, 2018, https://www.thebalance.com/deficit-by-president-what-budget-deficits-hide-3306151

[5] Jackie Calmes, "Obama Bans Gimmicks, and Deficit Will Rise," *The New York Times*, February 19, 2009, https://www.nytimes.com/2009/02/20/us/politics/20budget.html

[6] Lisa Joyce, "The U.S. President and the Economy," *Advisor Solutions*, Volume 9, Q2 2017, pg. 9–10.

[7] Yoni Blumberg, "Paul Ryan could get a pension of $84,930 a year—here's how that compares to most Americans," CNBC, April 16, 2018, https://www.cnbc.com/2018/04/16/how-paul-ryans-85000-pension-compares-to-the-average-americans.html

[8] "The Budget and Economic Outlook: 2018 to 2028," The Congressional Budget Office, April 9, 2018, https://www.cbo.gov/publication/53651#section5

[9] Max Ehrenfreund, "Analysis: By 2025, 99.6% of Paul Ryan's tax cuts would go to the richest 1% of Americans," *The Washington Post*, September 16, 2016, https://www.washingtonpost.com/news/wonk/wp/2016/09/16/a nalysis-by-2025-99-6-of-paul-ryans-tax-cuts-would-go-to-the-richest-1-of-americans/?utm_term=.e35113fd40db

[10] Jeff Stein, "Ryan says Republicans to target welfare, Medicare, Medicaid spending in 2018," *The Washington Post*, December 6, 2017, https://www.washingtonpost.com/news/wonk/wp/2017/12/01/g op-eyes-post-tax-cut-changes-to-welfare-medicare-and-social-security/?noredirect=on&utm_term=.ed743fa3b674

[11] David Barstow, Susanne Craig, and Russ Buettner, "Trump Engaged in Suspect Tax Schemes as He Reaped Riches from His Father," *The New York Times*, Oct. 2, 2018, https://www.nytimes.com/interactive/2018/10/02/us/politics/do nald-trump-tax-schemes-fred-trump.html

[12] Russ Buettner and Charles V. Bagli, "How Donald Trump Bankrupted His Atlantic City Casinos, but Still Earned Millions," *The New York Times*, June 11, 2016, https://www.nytimes.com/2016/06/12/nyregion/donald-trump-atlantic-city.html

Chapter 7: CINO

[1] "Stephen Prothero, *Religious Literacy* (San Francisco: Harper San Francisco, 2007), pg. 48.

2 Napoleon Hill, *Outwitting the Devil* (New York: Sterling Publishing, 2011), pg. 58.

3 Leslie Salzillo, "Catholic Nun Explains Pro-Life in A Way That Will Stun Many," July 30, 2015, *The Daily Kos*, https://www.dailykos.com/stories/2015/7/30/1407166/-Catholic-Nun-Explains-Pro-Life-In-A-Way-That-May-Stun-The-Masses

4 Randall Balmer, "The Real Origins of the Religious Right," *Politico*, May 27, 2014, https://www.politico.com/magazine/story/2014/05/religious-right-real-origins-107133

5 Liz Calvario, "'Full Frontal with Samantha Bee' Goes Deep Inside The Weirdest Anti-Abortion Art Film Ever Made," Indie Wire, May 24, 2016, https://www.indiewire.com/2016/05/full-frontal-with-samantha-bee-goes-deep-inside-the-weirdest-anti-abortion-art-film-ever-made-288903/

6 Michelle Ye Hee Lee, "Donald Trump's claim he evolved into 'pro-life' views, like Ronald Reagan," *The Washington Post*, March 31, 2016, https://www.washingtonpost.com/news/fact-checker/wp/2016/03/31/donald-trumps-claim-he-evolved-into-pro-life-views-like-ronald-reagan/?utm_term=.eec72333e6d5

7 Clyde Haberman, "Religion and Right-Wing Politics: How Evangelicals Reshaped Elections," *The New York Times*, Oct. 28, 2018, https://www.nytimes.com/2018/10/28/us/religion-politics-evangelicals.html

8 Gabrielle Levy, "Rep. Tim Murphy to Resign After Affair, Abortion Revelations," *U.S. News & World Report*, Oct. 5, 2017, https://www.usnews.com/news/politics/articles/2017-10-

05/anti-abortion-congressman-tim-murphy-announces-retirement-after-pressuring-girlfriend-to-get-abortion

[9] Hollis Johnson, "I ate Trump's absurd, 2,430-calorie McDonald's order — and it was even worse than I imagined," *Business Insider*, Dec. 4, 2017, https://www.businessinsider.com/trumps-mcdonalds-order-review-2017-12

[10] Natalie Schreyer, "The Trump Files: When Donald Took Revenge by Cutting Off Health Coverage for a Sick Infant. Classy." *Mother Jones*, August 25, 2016, https://www.motherjones.com/politics/2016/08/trump-files-donald-sick-infant-medical-care/

[11] Alexi McCammond, "Scoop: Insider leaks Trump's 'Executive Time'-filled private schedules", *Axios*, February 3, 2019, https://www.axios.com/donald-trump-private-schedules-leak-executive-time-34e67fbb-3af6-48df-aefb-52e02c334255.html?te=1&nl=dealbook&emc=edit_dk_20190204

[12] Aldous J. Pennyfarthing, "Another ghost writer says Trump was awful at business. 'He mostly looked at fabric swatches,'" *The Daily Kos*, May 9, 2019, https://www.dailykos.com/stories/2019/5/9/1856618/-Another-Trump-ghostwriter-says-DJT-was-horrible-at-business-He-mostly-looked-at-carpet-swatches?detail=emaildkre

[13] Adam Gabbatt, "The 'exhausting' work of factcheckers who track Trump's barrage of lies," *The Guardian,* January 21, 2019, https://www.theguardian.com/us-news/2019/jan/21/donald-trump-lies-factcheckers

[14] Ernest Becker, *Escape from Evil*, (New York: "The Free Press," 1975), pg. 164.

Chapter 8: Slavery

[1] Thom Hartmann, "The Second Amendment Was Ratified to Preserve Slavery," *Truthout*, January 15, 2013, https://truthout.org/articles/the-second-amendment-was-ratified-to-preserve-slavery/#

[2] Dahlia Lithwick, "The Second Amendment Hoax, How the NRA and conservatives have perverted the meaning of the right to bear arms," *Slate*, June 13, 2016, https://slate.com/news-and-politics/2016/06/how-the-nra-perverted-the-meaning-of-the-2nd-amendment.html

[3] George C. Edwards III, "Five myths about the electoral college," The Washington Post, November 2, 2012, https://www.washingtonpost.com/opinions/five-myths-about-the-electoral-college/2012/11/02/2d45c526-1f85-11e2-afca-58c2f5789c5d_story.html?utm_term=.d6f83c1ac8d2

[4] History.com Editors, "Voting Rights Act of 1965," History.com, Last Updated September 12, 2018, https://www.history.com/topics/black-history/voting-rights-act

[5] "History of Federal Voting Rights Laws," Accessed March 28, 2019, https://www.justice.gov/crt/history-federal-voting-rights-laws

[6] Jens Manuel Krogstad and Mark Hugo Lopez, "Black voter turnout fell in 2016, even as a record number of Americans cast ballots," The Pew Research Center, May 12, 2017, https://www.pewresearch.org/fact-tank/2017/05/12/black-voter-

turnout-fell-in-2016-even-as-a-record-number-of-americans-cast-ballots/

[7] Jelani Cobb, "Comment – House Cleaning," *The New Yorker*, February 18 & 25, pg. 21.

[8] Dexter Filkins, "The Uncounted," *The New Yorker*, September 7, 2020, pg. 39.

[9] David Remnick, "Voter Suppression in the Twenty-First Century," *The New Yorker*, December 3, 2018, https://www.newyorker.com/podcast/political-scene/voter-suppression-in-the-twenty-first-century

[10] Vann R. Newkirk II, "Voter Suppression Is the New Old Normal," *The Atlantic*, October 24, 2018, https://www.theatlantic.com/politics/archive/2018/10/2018-midterms-and-specter-voter-suppression/573826/

[11] Philip Bump, "There have been just four documented cases of voter fraud in the 2016 election," *The Washington Post*, December 1, 2016, https://www.washingtonpost.com/news/the-fix/wp/2016/12/01/0-000002-percent-of-all-the-ballots-cast-in-the-2016-election-were-fraudulent/?utm_term=.bc79a52bf56c

[12] Jason Stanley, *How Propaganda Works*, (Princeton: Princeton University Press© 2015), pg. 18.

Chapter 9: Her Majesty

[1] Jason Stanley, *How Propaganda Works*, (Princeton: Princeton University Press© 2015), pgs. 123, 154.

[2] Gillian Brockell, "She was stereotyped as 'the welfare queen.' The truth was more disturbing, a new book says," *The Washington Post*, May 21, 2019, https://www.washingtonpost.com/history/2019/05/21/she-was-stereotyped-welfare-queen-truth-was-more-disturbing-new-book-says/

[3] Gene Demby, "The Truth Behind the Lies of The Original 'Welfare Queen'," *NPR*, December 20, 2013, https://www.npr.org/sections/codeswitch/2013/12/20/255819681/the-truth-behind-the-lies-of-the-original-welfare-queen

[4] Kathryn J. Edin and H. Luke Shaefer "Ronald Reagan's 'welfare queen' myth: How the Gipper kickstarted the war on the working poor," *Salon*, September 27, 2015, https://www.salon.com/2015/09/27/ronald_reagans_welfare_queen_myth_how_the_gipper_kickstarted_the_war_on_the_working_poor/

[5] Ben Fountain, *Beautiful Country Burn Again* (Harper Collins: New York, 2018), pg. 4.

[6] Matthew Yglesias, "Reagan's Race Record," *The Atlantic*, November 9, 2007, https://www.theatlantic.com/politics/archive/2007/11/reagans-race-record/46875/

[7] Alejandro de la Garza, "Ronald Reagan's Daughter Says Audio of Her Dad Calling African Diplomats 'Monkeys' Made Her Cry," *Time*, August 1, 2019.

[8] Livie Campbell, "Here's what happened when Reagan went after healthcare programs. It's not good," *Timeline*, September

13, 2017, https://timeline.com/reagan-trump-healthcare-cuts-8cf64aa242eb

[9] Alison Kodjak, "States That Declined to Expand Medicaid Face Higher Costs," NPR, October 15, 2015, https://www.npr.org/sections/health-shots/2015/10/15/448729327/states-that-declined-to-expand-medicaid-face-higher-costs

[10] Brendan DeMelle, "Study Confirms Tea Party Was Created by Big Tobacco and Billionaire Koch Brothers", *HuffPost*, February 11, 2013 01:26 pm ET, Updated Dec 06, 2017, https://www.huffpost.com/entry/study-confirms-tea-party-_b_2663125?guccounter=1&guce_referrer=aHR0cHM6Ly9kWNrZHVja2dvLmNvbS8&guce_referrer_sig=AQAAAFNO-0W4Uj5AreFMUAuAylh913MBNlxBKmj1cOAD7vtqjEQgj7dsvIBGPHKF3y1n542SsH6kn-p43SlM-zT3woPtZQHGDUoHAo48SyTHfNU4v1KgOb-FC_dSYHPK2cED4Snp92Z-uV8Qd8mJXdL_U1lZMRWGcAqS329H-FDPgBea

[11] Felkerson, James (December 2011). "$29,000,000,000,000: A Detailed Look at the Fed's Bailout by Funding Facility and Recipient." SSRN Electronic Journal.

[12] "What Is an Average Welfare Check?" Reference.com, accessed November 16, 2019, https://www.reference.com/government-politics/average-welfare-check-86e522b03e9c4606

[13] Dana Nuccitelli, "America spends over $20bn per year on fossil fuel subsidies. Abolish them," *The Guardian*, July 30, 2018 (last modified July 31, 2018 01.51 EDT),

https://www.theguardian.com/environment/climate-consensus-97-per-cent/2018/jul/30/america-spends-over-20bn-per-year-on-fossil-fuel-subsidies-abolish-them

[14] Stephanie Saul and Patricia Cohen, "Profitable Giants Like Amazon Pay $0 in Corporate Taxes. Some Voters Are Sick of It.", *The New York Times*, April 29, 2019, https://www.nytimes.com/2019/04/29/us/politics/democrats-taxes-2020.html

[15] Ben Holland & Liz McCormick, "Borrowing Billions to Buy Stock, Not Invest," *Bloomberg Businessweek*, August 12, 2019, pg. 28–29, 30.

[16] David Leonhardt, "The Rich Really Do Pay Lower Taxes Than You," *The New York Times*, October 6, 2019, https://www.nytimes.com/interactive/2019/10/06/opinion/income-tax-rate-wealthy.html

[17] Margaret O'Mara, "Opinion | A Brief History of the Taxpayer in Chief," *The New York Times*, October 1, 2020, https://www.nytimes.com/2020/10/01/opinion/trump-presidents-taxes-history.html

[18] Daniel Markovitz, *The Meritocracy Trap*, (New York: Penguin Press, 2019), pg. 108.

[19] Lawrence Mishel and Julia Wolfe, "CEO compensation has grown 940% since 1978, Typical worker compensation has risen only 12% during that time," *Economic Policy Institute*, August 14, 2019, https://www.epi.org/publication/ceo-compensation-2018

[20] Anand Giridharadas, *Winners Take All*, (New York: Alfred A. Knopf, 2018), pg. 40.

[21] Caleb Crain, "State of the Unions," *The New Yorker*, August 26, 2019, pg. 76.

[22] Paul Kiel, "IRS: Sorry, but it's just easier and cheaper to audit the poor," *Nation of Change*, October 3, 2019, https://www.nationofchange.org/2019/10/03/irs-sorry-but-its-just-easier-and-cheaper-to-audit-the-poor/

[23] Nicole Goodkind, "Are Republicans Underfunding the IRS to Help Corporations Pay Less?" *Newsweek*, August 15, 2019, https://www.newsweek.com/donald-trump-irs-tax-cuts-budget-republicans-1454619

Chapter 10: Alpha of the Omega

[1] McKay Coppins, "How Newt Gingrich Broke Politics," *The Atlantic*, November 2018, pg. 55.

[2] Lisa Joyce, "The U.S. President and the Economy," *Advisor Solutions*, Volume 9, Q2 2017, pg. 9–10.

[3] Paul Krugman, "Zombie ideas and zombie industries," *The New York Times*, January 28, 2020.

[4] Umair Irfan, "Fossil fuels are underpriced by a whopping $5.2 trillion," *Vox*, May 17, 2019, https://www.vox.com/2019/5/17/18624740/fossil-fuel-subsidies-climate-imf

[5] Jill Lepore, "Annals of Media: Hard News," *The New Yorker*, January 28, 2019, pg. 20.

[6] Jane Mayer, "Trump TV," The *New Yorker*, March 11, 2019, pg. 43–44.

[7] Ben Taub, "The Prisoner of Echo Special," *The New Yorker*, April 22, 2019, pg. 32.

[8] Ferdinand Bada, "10 US States with The Highest Divorce Rates," *World Atlas*, August 21, 2018, https://www.worldatlas.com/articles/10-us-states-with-the-highest-divorce-rates.html

[9] Teen Pregnancy Rates by State Population. (2020-02-06). Retrieved 2020-02-20, from http://worldpopulationreview.com/states/teen-pregnancy-rates-by-state/

[10] Alec MacGillis, "After the Crash," *The New Yorker*, November 18, 2019, pg. 56.

[11] Bill Scher, "Nader Elected Bush: Why We Shouldn't Forget," *Real Clear Politics*, May 31, 2016, https://www.realclearpolitics.com/articles/2016/05/31/nader_elected_bush_why_we_shouldnt_forget_130715.html#

Chapter 11: The Omega

[1] Daily Chart, "Is Congress rigged in favour of the rich?" *The Economist*, July 22, 2019, https://www.economist.com/graphic-detail/2019/07/22/is-congress-rigged-in-favour-of-the-rich

[2] Open Secrets.org,
https://www.opensecrets.org/industries/indus.php?ind=E01

[3] Richard L. Hasen, "The Decade of Citizens United," *Slate*,
December 19, 2019, https://slate.com/news-and-
politics/2019/12/citizens-united-devastating-impact-american-
politics.amp

[4] Philip Weiss, "Adelson has 'more influence' than Pompeo,
'controlling' State Dep't on Israel, says 'NYT' columnist
Egan," *Mondoweiss*, January 18, 2019,
https://mondoweiss.net/2019/01/influence-controlling-
columnist/

[5] Daniel Markovitz, The Meritocracy Trap, (New York:
Penguin Press, 2019), pg. 52.

[6] Hiroko Tabuchi, "How the Koch Brothers Are Killing Public
Transit Projects Around the Country," *The New York Times*,
June 19, 2018,
https://www.nytimes.com/2018/06/19/climate/koch-brothers-
public-transit.html

[7] Jane Mayer, "Back to the Jungle," *The New Yorker*, July 20,
2020, pg. 32.

[8] David Wallace-Wells, The Uninhabitable Earth, (New York:
Tim Duggan Books, 2019), pg. 61.

[9] Sheila Kaplan, "Congress Quashed Research into Gun
Violence. Since Then, 600,000 People Have Been Shot," *The
New York Times*, March 12, 2018,
https://www.nytimes.com/2018/03/12/health/gun-violence-
research-cdc.html

Chapter 12: Tyranny

[1] History.com Editors, "Nazi Party," *History*, Access Date April 10, 2020, Publisher A&E Television Networks, Original Published Date November 9, 2009, Last Updated March 30, 2020, https://www.history.com/topics/world-war-ii/nazi-party

[2] Jennifer Szalai, "A Sobering Look at How Quickly Hitler Transformed Germany," *The New York Times*, March 17, 2020, https://www.nytimes.com/2020/03/17/books/review-hitlers-first-hundred-days-peter-fritzsche.html

[3] History.com Editors, "Apartheid," *History*, Access Date April 10, 2020, Publisher A&E Television Networks, Last Updated March 3, 2020, Original Published Date, October 7, 2010, https://www.history.com/topics/africa/apartheid

[4] Sarah Bufkin, "Jason Chaffetz Admits House GOP Cut Funding for Embassy Security: 'You Have to Prioritize Things'," *HuffPost*, October 10, 2012 01:32 pm ET, Updated October 11, 2012, https://www.huffpost.com/entry/jason-chaffetz-embassy_n_1954912

[5] Jane Meyer, "Russia Won," *The New Yorker*, October 1, 2018, pg. 23.

[6] Jeffrey Toobin, "The Surrender," *The New Yorker*, July 6 & 13, 2020, pg. 54.

[7] Charlie Savage, "Judge Calls Barr's Handling of Mueller Report 'Distorted' and 'Misleading'," *The New York Times*, March 5, 2020, https://www.nytimes.com/2020/03/05/us/politics/mueller-report-barr-judge-

walton.html?emc=edit_na_20200305&ref=cta&nl=breaking-news&campaign_id=60&instance_id=0&segment_id=21917&user_id=5c8851e502fe9b08bcdb92906272f56e&regi_id=45198982

[8] David E. Sanger, Zolan Kanno-Youngs, and Nicholas Kulish, "A Ventilator Stockpile, With One Hitch: Thousands Do Not Work," *The New York Times*, April 1, 2020, https://www.nytimes.com/2020/04/01/us/politics/coronavirus-ventilators.html

[9] Ari Berman, "How the 2000 Election in Florida Led to a New Wave of Voter Disenfranchisement," *The Nation*, July 28, 2015, https://www.thenation.com/article/archive/how-the-2000-election-in-florida-led-to-a-new-wave-of-voter-disenfranchisement/?print=1

[10] Katharine Q. Seelye, "John Pawasarat Dies at 70; Used Data to Address Social Ills," *The New York Times,* January 13, 2020, https://www.nytimes.com/2020/01/13/us/john-pawasarat-dies-at-70-used-data-to-address-social-ills.html

[11] Jason Stanley, *How Propaganda Works*, (Princeton & Oxford: Princeton University Press, 2015), pg. 118.

[12] David Daley, *Rat F**ked* (New York: Liveright Publishing Corporation, 2016), pg. 47.

[13] Ari Berman, "How the GOP Rigs Elections," Rolling Stone, January 24, 2018, https://www.rollingstone.com/politics/politics-news/how-the-gop-rigs-elections-121907/

[14] Steven Levitsky and Daniel Ziblatt, "Why Republicans Play Dirty," *The New York Times,* September 20, 2019, https://www.nytimes.com/2019/09/20/opinion/republicans-democracy-play-dirty.html

[15] Bruce J. Schulman, "Blue states already subsidize red states. Now red states want even more," *The Washington Post*, Oct. 30, 2017 at 6:00 a.m. EDT, https://www.washingtonpost.com/news/made-by-history/wp/2017/10/30/blue-states-already-subsidize-red-states-now-red-states-want-even-more/

[16] Sahil Chinoy, "What Happened to America's Political Center of Gravity?" *The New York Times*, June 26, 2019, https://www.nytimes.com/interactive/2019/06/26/opinion/sunday/republican-platform-far-right.html

[17] Farhad Manjoo, "California's 40 Million People Are Sick of Being Ignored," *The New York Times*, October 14, 2020, https://www.nytimes.com/2020/10/14/opinion/california-voting.html

[18] Philip Bump, "Supreme Court fight highlights the new political reality: America under minority rule," *The Washington Post*, September 21, 2020, https://www.washingtonpost.com/politics/2020/09/21/supreme-court-fight-highlights-new-political-reality-america-under-minority-rule/

[19] Chris Cillizza, "Donald Trump's under-50% presidency," *CNN*, Updated 2:59 PM ET, Mon August 31, 2020, https://www.cnn.com/2020/08/31/politics/donald-trump-polling-2020-election/index.html

[20] Christopher Ingraham, "The United States is backsliding into autocracy under Trump, scholars warn," *The Washington Post*, September 18, 2020, https://www.washingtonpost.com/business/2020/09/18/united-states-is-backsliding-into-autocracy-under-trump-scholars-warn/

Chapter 13: Handmaidens in High Castles

[1] Sarah Jones, "Explosive Tape Catches Paul Ryan And Kevin McCarthy Engaging in Trump/Russia Cover-Up," *Politicus USA*, May 17, 2017, https://www.politicususa.com/2017/05/17/top-house-gop-ryan-mccarthy-caught-tape-discussing-possibility-putin-paying-trump.html

[2] Tina Nguyen, "Donald Trump is Obsessed with the Pee Tape," *Vanity Fair*, April 20, 2018, https://www.vanityfair.com/news/2018/04/comey-memos-pee-tape-trump

[3] Yuval Noah Harari, *Sapiens*, (New York: Harper Collins, 2015), pg. 330.

[4] Jason Le Miere, "Did the Media Help Donald Trump Win? $5 Billion In Free Advertising Given to President-Elect," *International Business Times*, November 9, 2016, https://www.ibtimes.com/did-media-help-donald-trump-win-5-billion-free-advertising-given-president-elect-2444115

[5] Patrick Radden Keefe, "Winning – How Mark Burnett, the king of reality television, helped turn a floundering D-lister into

President Trump," January 7, 2019, *The New Yorker*, pg. 34, 35.

[6] David E. Sanger, Eric Lipton, Eileen Sullivan, and Michael Crowley, "Before Virus Outbreak, a Cascade of Warnings Went Unheeded," *The New York Times*, Published March 19, 2020, Updated March 22, 2020, https://www.nytimes.com/2020/03/19/us/politics/trump-coronavirus-outbreak.html

[7] Chris Walker, "Trump Derided Obama's Auto Bailout, But His Farm Bailout Has Cost More Than Twice as Much," *The Hill Reporter.com*, December 26, 2019, https://hillreporter.com/trump-derided-obamas-auto-bailout-but-his-farm-bailout-has-cost-more-than-twice-as-much-54237

[8] Brandon Kochkodin, "U.S. Airlines Spent 96% of Free Cash Flow on Buybacks," Bloomberg, March 16, 2020, https://www.bloomberg.com/news/articles/2020-03-16/u-s-airlines-spent-96-of-free-cash-flow-on-buybacks-chart?te=1&nl=dealbook&emc=edit_dk_20200317&campaign_id=4&instance_id=16835&segment_id=22304&user_id=5c885 1e502fe9b08bcdb92906272f56e&regi_id=4519898220200317

[9] Tim Mak, "Weeks Before Virus Panic, Intelligence Chairman Privately Raised Alarm, Sold Stocks," *NPR*, Heard on Morning Edition, March 19, 2020, https://www.npr.org/2020/03/19/818192535/burr-recording-sparks-questions-about-private-comments-on-covid-19

[10] Matthew Mosk, "North Carolina Sen. Richard Burr sold off stock ahead of coronavirus spread," *ABC News*, March 20,

2020, 12:53 AM, https://abcnews.go.com/Politics/north-carolina-sen-richard-burr-sold-off-stock/story?id=69699666

About the Author

Steven A. Bové, CFA®, CFP®, MSFS, is a portfolio and wealth manager who has been studying the impact that politics have on the economy and stock market for over twenty-five years. He has used his economic and sociology background to analyze trends, patterns, and impacts on all aspects affecting portfolio management. Early in his career, he developed a proprietary model for automating investment advice that led to two patents, United States Patent 7,552,079 (computer-implemented apparatus for automating and executing investment planning for a client) Bové, et al., as well as United States Patent 7,149,713 (system and method for automating investment planning), Bové, et al.

When democracy dies,
it will be both slow and sudden.

Made in the USA
Middletown, DE
24 December 2020